How God Transfers Wealth to

HIS BUSINESS MINISTERS

DR. NOVA DEAN PACK

Table Of Contents

INTRODUCTION: THE CALL OF GOD'S BUSINESS SERVANTS... *10*

02 THE CALL OF THE BUSINESS SERVANTS INTO MINISTRY... *42*

01 GOD'S MINISTRY FOR BUSINESS SERVANTS IS THE BUSINESS THEY GIVE GOD CONTROL OF... *26*

03 GOD'S PRIMARY PURPOSE FOR THE BUSINESS IS TO BRING MATURITY TO HIS CHILDREN... *68*

04   LEARN GOD'S STRATEGIC METHOD OF THINKING... *82*

05   THE BIBLICAL WORK ETHIC... *102*

06   POVERTY IS USUALLY THE ECONOMIC CONSEQUENCES OF SPIRITUAL DISOBEDIENCE... *122*

07   THERE ARE ECONOMIC CONSEQUENCES TO OUR MORAL CHOICES... *138*

Table Of Contents

08 BUSINESS SERVANTS ARE CALLED TO BE BIBLITARIANS... *155*

09 RISK AND POSSIBLITY OF FAILURE ARE ESSENTIAL FOR GROWTH AND MATURITY... *176*

10 PRIVATE PROPERTY PROMOTES FREEDOM AND MATURITY... *203*

11 GOD'S ORDER OF STEWARDSHIP PROMOTES LASTING WEALTH... *220*

12 HANDLING BEING RIPPED OFF IN BUSINESS AND SPIRITUAL PRINCIPLES OF WISDOM... *236*

14 BIO... *250*

13 CONCLUSION... *249*

INTRODUCTION

The Call of God's Business Servants

There are many Believers operating businesses throughout the world, especially in the United States, who have experienced a direct encounter with God in the marketplace. God has been doing a radical thing in the Christian business community to equip Business Servants for the work of the business as ministry involving finances coming into the Kingdom of God and the maturation of God's children. Who God chooses generally are unlikely candidates in the natural, but God chooses His Business Servants by the condition of their hearts, not their natural stature, education, or financial achievements under the world system. Even though you have a history of failures in business, it does not disqualify you for Ministry as God's Business Servant.

As a Believer, you can be in the world but not be of the world. You can work in the Kingdom of darkness in the world, but your allegiance is as an Ambassador of the Kingdom of heaven. You must become a Biblitarian and apply the wisdom, knowledge, and understanding from the word of God as the principles that guide your life, your family, your investments, your politics, and most of all your faith. You are primarily a citizen of the Kingdom of Heaven, not a citizen of this world system, which is controlled by the evil prince of this world and its government is called the Kingdom of darkness. Most businesspersons never want to be part of a system that has had a history of failure. God can use the fact that you failed in business in the world because then He does not have to convince you to detach your heart from the world's business and financial system. The reason is you already do not trust the world's business and economic principles for your success. God then only has to teach you His Kingdom business and economic principles, and when applied, you will become His mature Business Servant. Therefore, be encouraged as you read this book. The very fact that this topic interests you is a good indication that your ministry calling is in the marketplace, in business. It could be that in managing and conducting God's business that you will fulfill your God ordained purpose in life.

Notwithstanding, as a point of instruction, this book is not an attempt to promulgate and inscribe all the rules based upon scriptures in the Bible that illuminate every ethical dilemma that God's Business Servants encounter in His businesses. The Scribes and Pharisees were bogged down in rules, and they missed God's focus on His children's hearts. 1 Samuel 16:7 says, "...For the LORD seeth not as man seeth; for man looketh on the outward appearance, but the LORD looketh on the heart." Also, this book can be instructive as a manual to transform your mind in your soul from thinking the way the world thinks in business. Business Servants will be used by God to activate the economy of the home, the business, the church, and the government; so God's Business Servants will play a major role in spreading the good news of the Kingdom of Heaven here on earth as the Kingdom of God under the authority of the Lord. In order to transform your mind, God's economic and business principles will be reiterated over and over in this book for different applications. God's laws of economics are the same principles to be applied in the home, in the business, in the church, and in the government. Thus, God's principles of economics will be applied in this book to describe how parents in homes, entrepreneurs in business, leaders in churches, and Politicians in governments are violating these principles. Also will be discussed in different venues the dire consequences for such disobedience of God's economic principles, and the blessings that will come when God's economic principles are obeyed. Finally, God's mature Business Servants are called to teach employees, partners, customers, community leaders, church members, families, and eventually Politicians about God's economic principles. God's mature Business Servants are to teach how people in authority violate God's economic principles and thereby keep Believers from a disciplining Father in heaven Who loves them enough to mature them as God's Kingdom servants.

In praying to the Lord, in listening to the still, small voice of the Holy Spirit, and involving ourselves in the information about these end-time days in which we live, many business men and women know we have been called and chosen to be the Business Servants of God involved in the greatest financial takeover of the world's economic centers of wealth. Pray and see if your heart yearns to grow the seed, which is the word planted in your heart, to activate you as one of God's Business Servants.

This is a special time in man's history. God has chosen this season to pour forth a mighty demonstration of His authority and power in the visitation of His Spirit to facilitate the transfer of wealth from the Kingdom of darkness in this world to and under the control of God's children in the Kingdom of God.

While most Believers seek the comfort of a work-free message of the gospel of heaven, God's true Business Servants after salvation seek the truth of a strong work ethic in the gospel of the Kingdom of God. They know that they are saved by grace through faith, not by works, but after salvation they are chosen by God for good works (Ephesians 2: 8-10; Philippians 2:12-13; James 1:22-25; 2:14-

26). Jesus instructed His disciples that they are to preach the gospel of the Kingdom. Both messages are required, not just one.

Joel 2 has three revivals. The second revival in Joel 2: 23-26 says, "Be glad then, ye children of Zion, and rejoice in the LORD your God: for He hath given you the former rain moderately, and He will cause to come down for you the rain, the former rain, and the latter rain in the first month. And the floors shall be full of wheat, and the vats shall overflow with wine and oil. And I will restore to you the years that the locust hath eaten, the cankerworm, and the caterpillar, and the palmerworm, My great army which I sent among you. And ye shall eat in plenty, and be satisfied, and praise the name of the LORD your God that hath dealt wondrously with you: and My people shall never be ashamed." These scriptures must be fulfilled before Joel 2:28-29 comes to pass, which says, "And it shall come to pass afterward, that I will pour out My Spirit upon all flesh; and your sons and your daughters shall prophesy, your old men shall dream dreams, your young men shall see visions: And also upon the servants and upon the handmaids in those days will I pour out My Spirit." Thus, there is a revival of economic wealth that God will use to finance the end-time harvest of souls. Is it here now? That is the question. I have seen God's hand move with sovereignty in the prospering of His Business Servants to fulfill that purpose. When you have the unction from the Holy Spirit to be used of God for financing the spreading of the Gospel of the Kingdom and repentance and remission of sins, then God will orchestrate circumstances in your life to pour out financial blessings to be used for His end-time purposes.

Similarly, the great wisdom of King Solomon is seen in his prophetic proclamation in Proverbs 13:22: "A good man leaveth an inheritance to his children's children: and the wealth of the sinner is laid up for the just."

Zechariah is an end-time prophet. In Zechariah 1:18-21, business men and women are called to do a mighty work for the enhancement of the Kingdom of God against the forces of darkness who have come to persecute Israel, Judah, and Jerusalem, along with the Church during these end times. God is calling forth business men and women in these end times to make their businesses, professions, or wealth management as their work of ministry, recognizing that it is God who has given them the power to get wealth, so the covenants God has made with Abraham, Isaac, and Jacob may be fulfilled (Deuteronomy 8:18). The Holy Spirit is calling these Business Servants not to just tithe and give their money earned, but also to give the wisdom, knowledge, and understanding they have learned to apply in business, professions, and wealth management as biblical principles of success to activate entire populations of Believers for the work of the ministry in the marketplace (Ephesians 4:12).

Through business as ministry, miracles of finances pour forth income streams which evident the call of the Business Servants as Ephesians 4:11 functioning apostles, prophets, evangelists, pastors, and teachers in the marketplace. These

Business Servants are gifts to the body of Christ. Yet, often, Business Servants of the Lord are considered by spiritual leaders of some established churches to have less than the traditional calling or anointing as those ministers in the institutional church structure. This is religious tradition and religious elitism.

In the Old Testament, all the Patriarchs were business men who served God. Abraham, Isaac, and Jacob were all herdsmen, planted and harvested crops, and had many employees working for them.

While here on earth in His ministry, Jesus saw the value of choosing businessmen as His disciples. Peter, Andrew, James, and John operated fishing businesses which they had their employees continue during their walk with the Lord; and they continued operating these fishing businesses after the Lord's resurrection and ascension. When the Lord called these fishers, He miraculously caused them to catch a bountiful supply of fish, which they sold to support their families while they were ministering with Jesus during His earthly walk. They then left the fishing business to be run by employees and followed Jesus for three and one-half years as His Apostles. After Jesus' death, Peter, Thomas, Nathanael, James, and John went back to the boats and started fishing again and fished all night. Jesus was on the shore and told them to again cast their nets to the right side, and they caught an abundance of fish once again that would support the next phase of their ministry callings (John 21:1-7). There is no record that any of these fishers sold their fishing businesses, but always had them to make money when needed to support their families. At the same time, they fulfilled their ministries as fishers of men for God's Kingdom. Matthew had a tax-collecting business as an independent contractor for the Roman government, but he had been dishonest and gave it up to follow Jesus in ministry. After Jesus' ascension, most of Jesus' Apostles had businesses that they worked periodically for support, especially when the offerings from people were low, but they were supported by offerings when they traveled on missionary trips

Devout women gladly gave into Jesus' ministry. Luke 8:2-3 says, "And certain women who had been healed of evil spirits and infirmities--Mary called Magdalene, out of whom had come seven demons, and Joanna the wife of Chuza, Herod's steward, and Susanna, and many others who provided for Him from their substance." Mary Magdalene was chosen by the Holy Spirit to be the first evangelist and witness of the Resurrected Lord and who was the first one sent by the Lord to declare Jesus' resurrection to His Apostles (John 20:17).

Many of these first century business men and women became Ephesians 4:11 ministers for the Lord, going throughout the world as His witnesses and preaching the gospel of the Kingdom and using their business incomes to help finance the missionary work of the early Apostles.

Paul also recognized and used business men and women as co-ministers. Dr. Luke authored the book of Luke and the book of the Acts of the Apostles. Yet, while traveling and ministering with Apostle Paul, Dr. Luke continued practicing med-

icine, helping finance Paul's work of ministry, along with his own ministry. Similarly, Paul worked with Priscilla and Aquila in their tent-making business, and they were ministers who accompanied Apostle Paul on various missionary journeys. Lydia was a businessperson who made and sold purple fabric, and she received the Gospel of the Kingdom (Matthew 24:14) and repentance and remission of sins (Luke 24:47) from Paul in Philippi (Acts 16:13-15). Lydia was the first European that received the gospel of the Kingdom. Under Jewish law, a synagogue had to be established when there was a population of at least ten Hebrew men in a community. Since there was an absence of a synagogue in Philippi, this small group of mostly women, led by Lydia, set up a home fellowship and established the first Christian church for Europe and the whole western world.

To be sure, there were several other godly women in the New Testament, including Tryphena and Tryphosa who labored with Paul (Romans 16:12); the mother of Rufus, whom Paul claimed to be like a mother to him (Romans 16:13); Apphia (Philemon 2); Claudia (2 Timothy 4:21); "of the chief women not a few," and "honorable women which were Greeks" (Acts 17:4,12); Lois and Eunice, grandmother and mother of Timothy, whose continuous teaching of the Holy Scriptures gave Timothy a solid foundation for ministry (2 Timothy 1:5; 3:15). Some of these women had

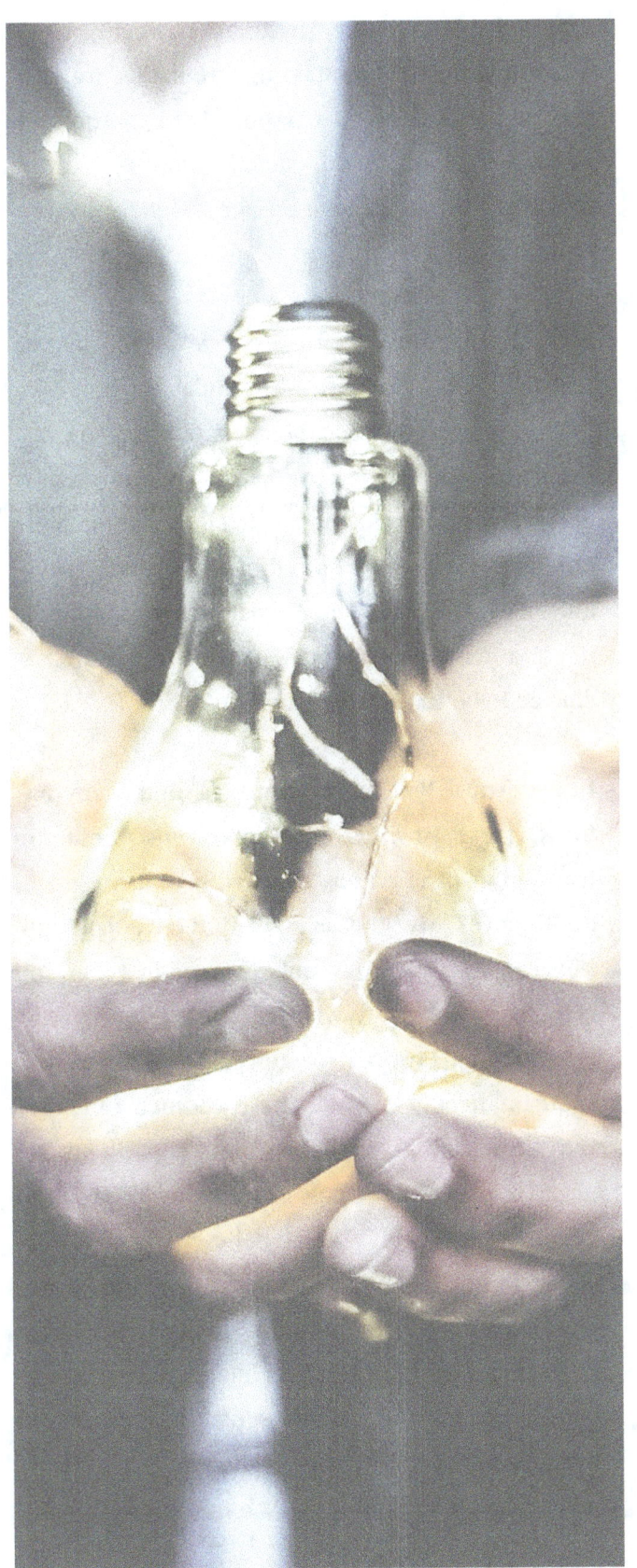

home businesses or managed their family estates. Like the first century business men and women, the Lord, through the Holy Spirit, is again calling business men and women into ministry, bringing with them their skills, wisdom, knowledge, and understanding of business and marketplace interactions with people. The Holy Spirit is showing these business men and women how the world economic system captures the minds, emotions, and wills of lost people, who God wants as His children. The Holy Spirit is influencing them to be transformed into Business Servants of the Lord who follow God's biblical principles. People in the world seek money, riches, and wealth, and these people will listen to business men and women who are successful in their businesses. People will adopt their thoughts, ideas, and lifestyles to try to acquire the same material wealth. However, God's plans are greater than just the acquisition of material wealth. Business men and women who are the chosen servants of the Lord have an awesome responsibility to make their employees mature disciples of Jesus Christ through the daily incremental problem-solving that business offers. God's Business Servants will discover that maturation of the children of God is the greater purpose of God as He has called them to establish their businesses as their ministries

"Tired of the Rat race"

God's Business Servants are tired of a greed-centered, lust obsessed, self-seeking, stress-filled economic world of the so-called "rat race." God's Business Servants want to run a course that is mapped out by the Holy Spirit and put their affection on things from above where the moth cannot eat, the elements cannot rust, and the thief cannot steal.

Like many Christian Business Servants, I once spent most of my time with crisis management, making business decisions through a survival mentality that resulted in responsive hysteria toward a reactionary, money-obsessed culture.

As a lawyer, I had little time for God because my lifestyle demanded most of my time for its maintenance and the seeking to satisfy unfulfilled and unbridled greed and lust in the daily quest for Satan's deceptive promise of the abundant life of the rich and famous. I had to schedule in time for God, as if such time were another social engagement or working appointment. This is what I learned from the world system, and I realized that participation in the world system without God's oversight and direction would cause me an early death. I would have no rest, no peace, and work myself to death following the world's system of economics and business. God offered me His way, and now I have a fulfilling and abundant spiritual life, with rest, peace, and the right focus seeking God's Kingdom.

"Satan's Tyranny of Spiritual Darkness"

There is a tyranny of spiritual darkness ruling over what belongs to God, and this fungus of evil captivates the souls of the people of the world. This prevailing evil is also an all-out act of war by Satan against God's Business Servants who have been attacked by government regulators, license revocation administrators, taxing authorities, workers compensation claims, personal family problems, and shortage of capital, while struggling with the ebb and flow of the market and normal business challenges.

Also, my personal testimony was one of sudden financial disaster, betrayal by Judas' in business, having to pay for other people's wrongdoing just because I was a lawyer overseeing the transaction, and regulations being passed to take away business opportunities. I have found other Business Servants of God with related stories. Financial failure is not an uncommon phenomenon for those God has chosen to be His Business Servants.

I have heard throughout America, and many nations, from Business Servants whose common testimony is "Satan has attacked my business and my finances. My sources of capital have dried up. I have unwarranted lawsuits filed against me. Con men have stolen my whole estate through trickery or fraud. I was financially set for life, but now I am financially ruined. These conmen said they were Christians, and that I should trust them. My negative experiences have affected my faith in an all-protective God." When Believers become involved in these scandals, it hurts others who trusted them, along with the victim themselves. Stories of financial ruin, reversals in business, psychological burnouts, and partnerships being destroyed because of greed, avarice, pride, and demonic attack seem to be epidemic. The harvest of hurting souls in business is plentiful, but the mature laborers in businesses are few.

There is good news. The men that the devil influenced to do evil against you, God has been using for your good, just like He did for Joseph, the son of Israel (Genesis 50:20). It will be Satan's defeat and your victory as you have become wise and not gullible anymore. God has used these demonic spirits, conviction of sins of your flesh, and the temptations common to all humankind in stripping away your excess fat, burning out the briers and brambles in your heart, and flaming the hot furnace of circumstances to extract the fine gold that God wants revealed in you as His Business Servant. God has been purifying your heart through your crucified life as His Business Servant who has allowed Christ to live His life through you while He has been about His Father's business (Galatians 2:20; Luke 2:49). God has been using His living water to soften your heart's hardened clay on His potter's wheel and remolding you as His Business Servant into His chosen vessel. God has been making you more Christ like, so He can prosper you for His name's sake and His gospel's sake. God has been preparing you to be unattached to the hundredfold blessing He will pour out through you to the body of Christ for the work of the ministry. Instead of a lifetime of failures, God sees your experiences as a lifetime of victory through spiritual transformation and deliverance from the world's carnal principles of business. God has been transforming your soul through discipline for a great work to end the Church Age

"It is a Grass Roots Movement"

God is pouring out His Spirit in an unprecedented, explosive way in a mind, emotions, and heart renewal and transformation of His Business Servants. God is choosing those vessels who are listening to what God is saying and responding with boldness as His Business Ministers, even during times of persecution.

Those Business Servants in America and the world are being spiritually transformed and matured. This is a different movement that God the Father has mandated through the visitation of the Holy Spirit manifesting His dunamis power in and through His Business Servants working in the marketplace to do God's will and establishing His Kingdom government in the hearts of humankind.

The devil has made a tactical miscalculation in his battle plan against God's Business Servants. He has been looking for the rise of another one-man business superstar to lead this marketplace ministry movement by the Holy Spirit, so this new Business Servant can be tempted with money, fame, and power and once again bring disillusionment to others in the body of Christ. The devil has been going around seeing whom he may devour, but no one person has been singled out; and the devil is very frustrated. The unknown masses of God's Business Servants have been sitting in the pews of the church buildings of America and the rest of the world waiting for the Spirit of God to shout forth His marching orders. Because these unknown masses of God's Business Servants have been walking through the fire and attacks in the secular world, they now are tough and are the burnt stones, inspired with the living word of God written in their hearts, and energized to build a wall of financial protection, to bring provision to God's people, to manifest God's Kingdom government, and to do God's will here on earth as it is in heaven. God has been preparing these unknown Business Servants to be leaders and to be at the forefront of His great spiritual movement into the marketplace. He has been preparing them with the circumstances

"God is Calling Business Servants with the Heart of David"

and the spiritual warfare which they have encountered in business for a special appointment with destiny.

These Business Servants have been killing the lions and the bears in business. They have been fighting heavy warfare during financial hardship and have been in many spiritual battle skirmishes in resolving daily business problems.

Their hearts have been circumcised, and they have endured the test. Like David's heart, their hearts have been seeking God as their minds have been renewed, their emotions have been stabilized, their hearts have been purified, and their wills have been submitted to do the will of God (Acts 13:22; Romans 12:2; 2 Timothy 2:22). 1 Peter 1:22 says, "Seeing ye have purified your souls in obeying the truth through the Spirit unto unfeigned love of the brethren, see that ye love one another with a pure heart fervently."

With little notice from the leaders in the traditional Churches, God has been preparing these Business Servants to be His anointed giant killers. God has been empowering His Business Servants to fight the biggest Goliath of all, the god of mammon.

These unknown Business Servants are seeing in the spirit the battle lines being drawn between the Kingdom of God and the Kingdom of darkness. Like the Roman Centurion who sought Jesus, after hearing from God, these Business Servants have been endowed with great faith to call in the financial resources to fight against the kingdom of darkness (Luke 7:9; Romans 1:17; 10:17).

God has chosen these unknown Business Servants to have the heart of David, so that He can use them to handle the great wealth that is coming forth from the world, 'so God can build His eternal Kingdom and His children as His house of praise and worship.' Revelation 11:15 says, "The kingdoms of this world are become the Kingdoms of our Lord and of His Christ; and he shall reign forever and ever." "'And I will shake all nations, and the desire of all nations shall come: and I will fill this house with glory,' saith the LORD of hosts" (Haggai 2:7).

God knows that it costs much money for people to wage spiritual warfare. Spiritually sensitive Ministers of the Lord must travel where the war is raging, and the Spirit of God is moving. Business Servants, like the men and women in the first century, can accompany other Ephesians 4:11 ministers to foreign lands, carrying with them the gospel of the Kingdom (Matthew 24:14) and repentance and remission of sins (Luke 24:47) as it is preached and promulgated in the word of God, especially in the gospels. God's

Business Servants can enter those countries where missionaries are being asked to leave. The foreign countries want the money, knowledge, and presence of God's Business Servants, and they will even allow them to preach the gospel of God's Kingdom government privately to business leaders in their country. Business Servants also have control of the income stream in the businesses, so they can pay their own travel expenses and can arrange their schedules to spend time in foreign lands to activate other God's Business Servants in those foreign countries. God's Business Servants have the authority to establish biblical principles as the foundational guide to run the businesses, which will manifest the Kingdom of God in a practical way which will inspire others to duplicate God's Kingdom economic principles of success.

"God's Boot Camp is for Purifying the Hearts of God's Business Servants"

God the Holy Spirit is going to go throughout the Earth looking for circumcised hearts and crucified lives amongst God's business men and women who have hearts to turn their businesses over to God and submit to Him as His Business Servants. God is looking for those who will humble themselves before Him and who will enter intimate relationship with Him as His Business Servants. God wants His Business Servants to be trained as His army for this end-time movement of the Holy Spirit. God has taken much time to send Business Servants through a special "boot camp" in preparing them for spiritual battle, so He can have soldiers of a business army that are holy, blameless, and with purified hearts in their souls. God is mobilizing His Kingdom spiritual economic army led by His Business Servants to seize the wealth and to finance His great end-time harvest of souls, and to deliver possession of the world system and nations to the Son of Man, Christ Jesus, and the Saints of the Most High by the Ancient of Days, Father God (Daniel 7: 14, 22, 27).

One of the hardest things for God to do is to prepare His Business Servants to manage prosperity with pure motives and pure hearts and not fall into greed, avarice, covetousness, lust of the flesh, lust of the eyes, the pride of life, being beguiled by Satan, or bewildered by the pressures of this fallen world system. God calls His Business Servants to be funnels and not just containers of His wealth in this end-time financial revival. Godly purposes, motives, and goals must become the foundational beliefs in the Business Servants' hearts. God the Father requires His Business Servants to be motivated with agape love, discipline, wisdom, biblical principles, and with the heart desire to train to maturity God's children who are working in the business as a ministry.

Father God has anointed His Business Servants with the ministry in Romans 12:8, which is the gift of giving. Yet, Father God conditions wealth acquisition by requiring His Business Servants

to have pure hearts without greed, avarice, or covetousness. When giving God's Business Servants must give liberally and with pure hearts as led by the Holy Spirit, not out of compulsion. 2 Corinthians 9:7-8 says, "Every man according as he purposeth in his heart, so let him give; not grudgingly, or of necessity: for God loveth a cheerful giver. And God is able to make all grace abound toward you; that ye, always having all sufficiency in all things, may abound to every good work." In the same vein, 1 Timothy 6:6-11 says, "But godliness with contentment is great gain. For we brought nothing into this world, and it is certain we can carry nothing out. And having food and raiment let us be therewith content. But they that will be rich fall into temptation and a snare, and into many foolish and hurtful lusts, which drown men in destruction and perdition. For the love of money is the root of all evil: which while some coveted after, they have erred from the faith, and pierced themselves through with many sorrows. But thou, O man of God, flee these things; and follow after righteousness, godliness, faith, love, patience, meekness."

Father God will not allow His Business Servants to prosper who have not had their souls purified from the love of this world, the lust of the flesh, the lusts of the eyes, and the pride of life. 1 John 2:15-16 says, "Love not the world, neither the things that are in the world. If any man loves the world, the love of the Father is not in him. For all that is in the world, the lust of the flesh, and the lust of the eyes, and the pride of life, is not of the Father, but is of the world." James 4:3 says, "Ye ask, and receive not, because ye ask amiss, that ye may consume it upon your lusts."

Acquiring wealth requires warfare to spoil the wealth of the wicked. Proverbs 13:22 says, "A good man leaves an inheritance to his children's children: and the wealth of the wicked is laid up for the righteous." Wealth is the inheritance that is passed on from generation to generation, i.e., houses, lands, gold, silver, precious stones, livestock, food farms, businesses, and family relationships. God's Business Servants must believe in their hearts that the gift of giving comes at the end of a purification process (Hebrews 10:22). The purification process ends in authority and power to seize wealth from the fallen world economic system being governed by the prince of this world and his kingdom of darkness. The authority and empowerment come to capture the spoils of the enemy of God, who is the usurping prince of this world.

Father God wants to place His anointing on purified vessels that cannot be tempted by the evil one or the fallen stimuli in this world. Father God is calling forth an army of His Business Servants to enter His Holy Spirit boot camp as members of the spiritual army of God's Kingdom. God's Business Servants must be spiritually trained to avoid getting entangled with bad business deals that are a set-up by the devil as entrapments. 2 Timothy 2:3-4 says, "Thou therefore endure hardness, as a good soldier of Jesus Christ. No man that warreth entangleth himself with the affairs of this life; that he may please Him who hath chosen Him to be a soldier." God's Business Servants must fight the good fight of faith

(1 Timothy 6:12).

God's Business Servants are called for the purpose of seizing the wealth from the grasp and control of Satan, the very source of strategic temptations. God's Business Servants must stay unattached to the things of the world and must not worship the creation, but the Creator. God's Business Servants must not fall to the wiles of the enemy, nor be tempted by the demonic forces to leave the business as their ministry calling.

"It is Time Father God Decrees the Devil Pays for God's End-Time Harvest."

God's Business Servants must renew their minds, stabilize their emotions, and submit their hearts where their wills reside in their souls by the daily "washing of the water by the word of God" (Ephesians 5:26). God's Business Servants must submit to the disciplinary pruning of Father God (John 15:2) and submit to the mortification of the deeds of the flesh by the Holy Spirit (Romans 8:13).

Mature Believers in business with God's calling and anointing for financing the end-time harvest do not want nice, overly used formulas as to how to obtain wealth or how to be prosperous. Rather, they prefer to learn how to bring the divine, miracle-working, intervening power of God's presence to transform their souls as God's Businesses Servants and to have God's author-

ity and power to gain wealth to pour into God's end-time purposes to build the Kingdom of God here on earth as it is in Heaven. God's Business Servants want to be taught how to pray with the unction and power of the Holy Spirit, with God's divine wisdom, knowledge, and understanding; so, they can request the Lord to dispatch angelic warriors to resist the demonic forces which have come to steal, kill, and thwart the manifesting of God's Kingdom government and God's will from being done here on earth.

God's Business Servants want the anointing of the Holy Spirit to seize the wealth from the world and the authority, power, and permission to command a seven-fold return from the enemy who has stolen God's property.

God's Business Servants do not need their hopes raised, their dreams renewed, and their minds awakened to God's Kingdom dominion mandate without God's authority and power being present to fulfill what is promised prophetically and in God's word. God's Business Servants have willing hearts that want to obey the activated rhema word of the Lord that engenders faith, spirit, and life (John 6:63; Romans 10:17). God's Business Servants want the presence of the divine nature of Jesus Christ, God the Word, with them in the marketplace and want His wisdom, knowledge, and understanding, along with the fruit of the Holy Spirit to be manifested and evident in every business decision they make. God's Business Servants will give their businesses to be used by God as vehicles for prosperity and channels through which rivers of living water may flow to a thirsty world as they hear the gospel of the Kingdom (Matthew 24:14) and repentance and remission of sins (Luke 24:47).

God's Business Servants desire in their hearts to sow finances into ministries that are truly on the frontlines of the battle and the cutting edge of the move of the Holy Spirit to reap the hundredfold return which can be sown again back into ministries that further God's end-time purpose to bring His Kingdom here on earth as it is in Heaven and "pour out His Spirit on all flesh" (Joel 2:28).

God's Business Servants are men and women of action, Gideon's chosen army, trained for battle readiness. God's Business Servants are those who have little fear of man but have the formidable reverent fear of Almighty God.

These are Christian Business Servants who are experienced spiritual soldiers who know how to use God's spiritual weapons of warfare. These are Christian Business Servants who are now standing up and marching forth for God and no longer are satisfied with being just spectators. These are Christian Business Servants who have radically turned all their wealth, riches, businesses, lives, dreams, goals, purposes, and hearts over to God for His good pleasure. These are Christian Business Servants ready to sacrifice, ready to obey, ready to give, ready to serve, and ready to do warfare against the Kingdom of darkness.

God's Business Servants are now marching toward the enemy's city, tearing down the gates of Hell, and taking back possession of the spoils of war for God's Kingdom and His children. God's Business Servants believe it is time they fervently pray that the Holy Spirit make the devil pay for God's end-time harvest of souls. God's Business Servants have the heart cry to be activated into their special business ministry calling. God's Business Servants are ready to have hands laid on them and sent to be about the Father's business of bringing the finances needed to wrap up the Church Age with the outpouring of the Holy Spirit to flow throughout the world as they preach the gospel of the Kingdom (Matthew 24:14) and repentance and remission of sins (Luke 24:47).

ONE

GOD'S MINISTRY FOR BUSINESS SERVANTS IS THE BUSINESS THEY GIVE GOD CONTROL OF

BEING ABOUT THE FATHER'S BUSINESS MEANS USING THE BUSINESS TO MANIFEST THE KINGDOM OF GOD
HERE ON EARTH AS IT IS IN HEAVEN

The original mandate of God to Adam and Eve and their posterity was stated in Genesis 1:28: "And God bless-ed them, and God said unto them, 'Be fruitful, and multiply, and replenish the earth, and subdue it: and have dominion over the fish of the sea, and over the fowl of the air, and over every living thing that moveth upon the earth.'" This is still the foundational dominion mandate that the Believers are commanded to fulfill. The Hebrew word for "dominion" in Genesis 1:26, 28 is *"mamlaka,"* (Strongs H4467), from the primitive root words *"malak"* (Strongs H4427), *"melek"* (Strongs H4428), or *"mashal"* (Strongs H4910), which are the same or similar Hebrew words that elsewhere in the Bible are translated into English as "kingdom" (Exodus 19:6), "reign" (Exodus 15:18), "King" (Genesis 14:8), "rule" (Judges 8:22), and "realm" (2 Chronicles 20:30). Yet, all these Hebrew words are relat-ed to the Kingdom of Heaven becoming the predominate Kingdom of God here on earth.

The point is that Adam and Eve's mission from Father God was to establish the Kingdom of God here on earth as it is in Heaven, and every Business Servant of God is still under that same dominion mandate. To have citizens of Heaven to be citizens of God's Kingdom here on earth as it is in Heaven, Adam and Eve's dominion mandate was to be God's under rulers here on earth as God's servant kings, lords, priests, ambassadors, and soldiers. These functions are every Believer's ministry vocations. With the advent of Christ Jesus, Believers today are not "members" of Jesus' Church or a Christian religion, as Christianity is not a religion. Believers are citizens of Heaven (Philippians 3:20), with citizenship responsibilities and rights that are blessings from God that He manifests here on earth to Believers from His heavenly Kingdom (Ephesians 1:3). Doing God's business of bring-ing back possession of earth to God the Father was Jesus' mission and must be every Business Servant of God.

Like Adam, Believers who are God's Business Servants also are mandated as God's chosen royal priesthood, a holy nation, a peculiar people to take dominion over the earth, the world system, every animal creature, and thus to subdue and take dominion of all things here on earth. God's Business Servants are mandated to use God's Kingdom business principles as Biblitarians to conduct business with God's principles, not worldly princi-ples of economics. Believers' dominion mandate is to take over the world's financial centers, businesses, indus-tries, movie producers, radio programs, newspapers, news media, Internet, schools, secular governments, and every other aspect of the nation in which each Believer lives, while leading their minds, emotions, and heart and Will in their souls in spiritual reality as their souls are transformed, matured, consecrated, and sanctified to make them better Kingdom servants in Christ.

The dominion mandate of Jesus Christ as the Son of Man, along with the saints of the Most High, was clearly written in a vision and prophecy by Daniel. Daniel 7: 13-14, 27 says, "I saw in the night visions, and behold, one like the Son of man came with the clouds of Heaven, and came to the Ancient of days, and they brought him near before him. And there was given him dominion, and glory, and a kingdom, that all people, nations, and languages, should serve him: his dominion is an everlasting dominion, which shall not pass away, and his kingdom that which shall not be destroyed... And the kingdom and dominion, and the greatness of the kingdom under the whole Heaven, shall be given to the people of the saints of the Most High, whose Kingdom is an everlasting Kingdom, and all dominions shall serve and obey Him." Jesus is the Last Adam, and the Second Man (2 Corinthians 15: 45,47). Therefore, Jesus instructed His disciples to preach the gospel of the Kingdom (Matthew 24:14) and repentance and remission of sins (Luke 24:47). God anoints those who are called out from worldly businesses and are anointed to be about God the Father's business (Luke 2:49). God's Kingdom Business Servants have the gift of giving pronounced in Romans 12:8 to be used to bring in the necessary finances for a major outpouring of the Holy Spirit on all flesh, which will be a worldwide end time Church in Revival.

When I go into a business, where there are novice Christian owners, it is often difficult to discern the difference between their business practices than unbelievers' business practices in the world. Why not release the Kingdom of God out of the four walls of a church building and bring it into the world where people work, interact, congregate, and live throughout the week? Why not have employees read one chapter of Proverbs, and five chapters of Psalms per day, with everyone participating in the reading at the workplace during special times in the morning before work begins? God's Business Servants and employees should pray for other employees, help other employees with their work-related tasks, and visit employees who are sick, and bring food for their meals? If you are a true Business Servant, then you will be practicing the commandment to love one another in a practical way at the workplace, not just mere lip service (John 13:34-35).

God's Business Servants and employees could set up a monthly contribution by all employees and owners to give a monetary gift each month to a needy family or a cause that everyone votes to be a donor to those in need? This must be voluntary, though. God's Business Owners should help and teach employees how to establish personal budgets, buy a car, purchase a home, abolish debt, and give with pure hearts to the local Church congregation. So, with the permission of the client or customer, release all the employees to pray for them as the Holy Spirit leads them. This would be evangelism in the workplace. This work will be about God the Father's business.

If there are fellow employees that are unbelievers, it is paramount for Believers to be ready to share the gospel of the Kingdom and repentance and remission of sins with them when they are ready. Believer employees must let unbelievers know that not only will the unbeliever when they convert will receive everlasting life, but they will receive a community of loving Believers in fellowship who will be their support and friends during all seasons and times of their lives. Let new Believers at the business know they will be part of God's Kingdom spiritual government here on earth right now where God's truth and love rules; and let them know they will be a part of God's Kingdom spiritual military that always wins. Let the new Believers know they will have genuine fellowship where they will not be lonely anymore while truth and love will permeate the conversations.

Jesus preached and instructed His disciples to preach the gospel of the Kingdom (Matthew 24:14) and repentance and remission of sins (Luke 24:47), which was His activating message from God's perspective and point of view, which is the will of Father God. Jesus taught His disciples to pray, "Thy Kingdom come. Thy will be done in earth, as it is in Heaven" (Matthew 6:10) and He finished His teaching on prayer by saying, "For thine is the kingdom, and the power, and the glory, for ever. Amen" (Matthew 6:13). Therefore, twice in Jesus' model prayer, He mentioned the Kingdom of God, so why are Church leaders rarely preaching about the Kingdom of God and just preaching about salvation, which is also important, but not the exclusive message.

For God's Kingdom manifesting and God's will to be done here in earth in every Kingdom business, God needs born again Business Servants in the Lord's Kingdom to start thinking Kingdom righteousness, which means thinking what is "right side up" according to the Kingdom of God, not mere religion. All born again Believers are translated from the powers of darkness into the Kingdom of God's dear Son (Colossians 1:13). Therefore, if you are born again, you, as a Business Servant can be in the Kingdom of God where all knowledge, understanding, wisdom, authority, and power is, and the entire Godhead lives inside of you. Thus, you have no excuse not to seek first the Kingdom of God and His righteousness as your place of provision, and you cannot say you will not know what to do as God's Business Servant. Just know that it is always about the King of Heaven and His Kingdom here on earth; and your ministry as a Business Servant is to serve the King of the Kingdom of God. Before making any decisions, seek first the King in His Kingdom as to what to do. Jesus ONLY said and ONLY did what He heard the Father say and do what He saw the Father doing (John 5:19; 14:10). This is your pattern to follow.

Jesus grew up as a Carpenter, in His and His step-father's business. He understood taking dominion over His business. Jesus was trained by His stepfather Joseph by daily being instructed, so He became a mature journeyman, Carpenter. After Josephs death, Jesus trained His younger half-brothers, using the same method to make them qualified as experienced journeyman Carpenters, so when He left for ministry, Mary, His mother, and His sisters were supported by His brothers. In His ministry, Jesus used the same methods to train His disciples how to minister, to preach the gospel of the Kingdom and repentance and remission of sins, how to cast out demons, how to pray with faith for healing of others, and how to take control over the natural world and bring it to subjection to the Kingdom of God. Thus, Jesus mandated His disciples to preach the gospel of the Kingdom, which they did like He did. Jesus told them to cast out demons the way He did, so they did. Jesus told them to heal the sick, so they did. Wherever an employee goes to Church, his Pastor does not have time to be with him every day to disciple him, but you as his employer can. God's Kingdom is also Business Servants place of provision, but also God's Business Servants' place of transformation and maturation of their souls through the daily incremental problem-solving by using biblitarian principles of economics and good management to use the truth and wisdom from above instead of the wisdom of this world. These truths must be taught to the employees, as they need to be promoted to management as they start using biblitarian principles and are dedicated to the Kingdom theology of Christ.

Jesus' whole message was the gospel of the Kingdom and repentance and remission of sins, and that is what leaders need to give to God's Business Servants. Jesus said in Matthew 6:31-33 "Therefore take no thought, saying, 'What shall we eat? or, What shall we drink? or, Wherewithal shall we be clothed?' (For after all these things do the Gentiles seek:) for your heavenly Father knoweth that ye have need of all these things. But seek ye first the Kingdom of God, and His righteousness (born again of spirit and transformation of the soul); and all these things shall be added unto you.'" Jesus always said and did what God the Father said and did, but Jesus did not do things to be popular with people. What is it that is the will of the Lord Jesus Christ and the Godhead? The answer is the primary message of the gospel of the Kingdom (Matthew 24:14) and repentance and remission of sins (Luke 24:47), while living life abundantly here and now with the entire Godhead making disciples of all nations, baptizing them in the name of the Father, Son, and the Holy Spirit, and teaching new disciples all that Jesus commanded (Matthew 28:19).

When the Kingdom Age comes, then God's Business Servants also will live with Jesus' humanity nature Who sits on His Throne in the New Jerusalem after the White Throne Judgment and the Judgment Seat of Christ (Revelations, chapters 20 & 21). Jesus mandated that His disciples preach the gospel of the Kingdom and repentance and remission of sins. Jesus is not Believers' eternal servant. After Jesus' death, resurrection, ascension, and enthronement, Believers are the Lord's bondservants. Jesus, with His dual natures, is the Shepherd; and Believers are the sheep. Jesus' divine nature leads Believers to green pastures and still waters (Psalm 23). Jesus is the Head, and Believers are His body. Believers are not their own. Believers have been redeemed for a price, which is the precious blood of Jesus.

Thus, throughout this book, remember that the primary mandate of God's Business Servants is to seek first the Kingdom of God and His Righteousness as the daily routine of the operation of the business. To a significant extent, this book will speak of the world system and how it has fallen short in this Kingdom dominion mandate, and from that point of view how God's Business Servants can see how they can make a difference for the King and His Kingdom.

God's Business Servants must follow the primary directive of Jesus. Jesus stated His mission for coming to earth after overcoming the temptation of the devil in the wilderness and He started His ministry by declaring in Matthew 4:17, "From that time Jesus began to preach, and to say, Repent: for the kingdom of heaven is at hand." Similarly, in Mark 1:14-15, "Now after that John was put in prison, Jesus came into Galilee, preaching the gospel of the Kingdom of God, and saying, 'The time is fulfilled, and the kingdom of God is at hand: repent ye, and believe the gospel." Towards the end of His ministry, Jesus said in Matthew 24:14, "And this gospel of the Kingdom shall be preached in all the world for a witness unto all nations; and then shall the end come." With Jesus, it was always about establishing the Kingdom of God now and God's will be being done here on earth as it is in heaven every hour of the day, every week, every month, and every year of a Believer's life, not just on the Sabbath or Sunday; and this is what every Believer must follow as an example. Seeking first the Kingdom of God and His righteousness is the mandate for every one of God's Business Servants. Salvation of unbelievers and making them Believers are benefits through preaching the gospel of the Kingdom (Matthew 24:14) and repentance and remission of sins (Luke 24:47). Maturing the Believers souls after initial salvation and being born again with a new spirit are the benefits of accepting Jesus Christ as Savior and Lord and the living in the Kingdom of God but establishing God Kingdom here on earth and bringing possession of the earth and the world system of the Kingdoms of this world back to Father God also is the primary objective and goal.

The understanding must be that Jesus did not come to earth to start a new religion. Jesus came to fulfill God's original purpose of bringing the dominion rule of His heavenly Kingdom here on earth as it is in heaven, and to put redeemed mankind with authority to rule and reign over the world system with Christ (Revelation 5:10). Jesus came to establish redeemed humankind as the dwelling place and Temple of the Godhead (John 14:16-17,23; 2 Corinthians 6:16; Revelation 21:3). To redeem mankind, Believers must have created in them a new born again spirit (John 3:3). How does Jesus do this? A Believer must become Jesus' organic spiritual children of His resurrected humanity nature (Isaiah 9:6; Hebrew 2:13) and become Father God's children by adoption and joint heirs with Christ (Romans 8:15,17). Believer's born again spirit is a perfect new spirit (Hebrews 12:23), born again by the incorruptible Seed of Jesus' resurrected humanity nature through the work of God the Word (1 Peter 1:23). The born again spirit is a new creature in Christ and is part of the Second Man (2 Corinthians 5:17; 1 Corinthians 15:47). The born again spirit does not sin (1 John 3:9). The born again spirit is the New Man in Christ which is created in absolute righteousness and true holiness (Ephesians 4:24), and which is renewed in knowledge after the image of Him that created Him (Colossians 3:10). The new born again spirit is joined with Christ as one spirit (1 Corinthians 6:17), and through Jesus' divine nature, God the Word, who is omnipresent, He "... hath raised us up together, and made us sit together in heavenly places in Christ Jesus" (Ephesians 2:6).

Believers are saved after receiving a new born again spirit, but the problem is the new Believer's Will is in the soul, not in the born again, spiritually perfect, sinless spirit. Thus, spiritually transforming the soul is essential if the soul is going to exercise the Will in the soul's heart to follow the Will of God. God's Kingdom goal is to call certain ones of the redeemed Believers as His Business Servants with the ministry of doing the spiritual work in the natural world in furthering the Lord's mission through the daily incremental experience of problem-solving by applying God's biblical principles of economics while engaging in the business world system to allow the indwelling Godhead to transform and mature each Business Servant's soul into the image and likeness of Christ Jesus (Romans 12:2; 8:29). To this secondary process of making the new Believer into the image of Christ by transforming his soul is a life-long process of continuous intimate relationship with the entire Godhead. The Godhead will make the soul of the Believer spiritually minded, spiritually emotional, and spiritually believing in his heart; so, the Believer decides to exercise his Will in his soul to do God's Will in establishing and in bringing to all relationships encountered in the daily business operations, the righteousness, peace, and joy in the Holy Spirit, which is the Kingdom of God (Romans 14:17).

The transformation of the finite soul from carnality to spirituality is accomplished by the ministry of the entire infinite indwelling Godhead. The Godhead works to remove the influence of the flesh out of the soul. God the

Father removes the spiritually unproductive branches of the flesh through pruning, so spiritual fruit can grow (John 15:2). God the Word sanctifies and cleanses the soul by the washing by the word of God (Ephesians 5:26). God the Holy Spirit mortifies the deeds of the flesh in the soul by an ongoing death process to remove the flesh to bring the blessings of God's everlasting *zoe* life (Romans 8:13).

Again, initial salvation is merely the "benefit" in preparing fallen humans to become redeemed organic born again spiritual children, born again from Jesus' resurrected humanity nature, and adopted children of Father God, who are then joint heirs with Christ. God's Business Servants become the dwelling place of God the Word, God the Father, and God the Holy Spirit as His Temple, live as citizens of Heaven here on earth being about the Father's business, live in the Lord's Kingdom of righteousness, peace, and joy in the Holy Spirit, and are the Lord's Business Servants as submitted kings, lords, priests, brothers, ambassadors, soldiers, church, body, betrothed, and eventually bride and spouse of Christ (Isaiah 9:6; Hebrews 2:13; Mark 3:35; 1 Peter 1:23; 1 John 3:9; John 14:16-17, 23; 2 Corinthians 6:16; Romans 8:15,17; Romans 12:1, Romans 12:5; Romans 14:17; 2 Corinthians 5:17, 20; 1 Peter 2:9; 2 Timothy 2:3-4; 1 Timothy 6:15; Revelation 1:6, 5:10, 21:9).

GOD OWNS THE BUSINESS AND HE HAS GIVEN THE BUSINESS SERVANT THE STEWARDSHIP

God's executive, entrepreneur, and Business Servant must recognize, affirm, and operate the business God has allowed him or her to steward, with the understanding that God is the "true Owner" of the business.

"The earth is the LORD'S, and the fullness thereof; the world, and they that dwell therein" (Psalms 24:1).

God is the supreme business God. God means business. God has a business activity here on earth, and He wants to partnership with you in His Kingdom business. "And He (Jesus) said unto them, 'How is it that ye sought Me? Wist ye not that I must be about My Father's business?'" (Luke 2:49).

GOD OWNS ALL THE MONEY THAT IS EARNED IN BUSINESS

Since God owns the silver and gold, and since silver and gold are mandated under the U.S. Constitution to be the assets that back the U.S. Dollar if printed by the Department of Treasury, then God is uniquely involved in the value of the U.S. currency and how it is to be used and spent. The U.S. Dollar also has printed on it, "In God we trust." Thus, by the permission of the people in the U.S., God has been given the right to be involved in the decision-making policies of the U.S. government as to how the money collected by taxes is to be spent. We are therefore to serve God and not money.

"'The silver is Mine, and the gold is Mine,' saith the LORD of hosts" (Haggai 2:8). "No man can serve two masters: for either he will hate the one and love the other; or else he will hold to the one and despise the other. Ye cannot serve God and mammon" (Matthew 6:24).

GOD GIVES YOU THE POWER TO GET WEALTH TO FULFILL HIS PURPOSES

God's Business Servant cannot take any credit for the profit made in the business activity. God owns the business. It is He that deserves the credit, for it is His power through and by which wealth is obtained. Therefore, it is His children, His purpose, His goal, and His method that the business should operate. Also, it is His decision how money, derived from the business, should be used in line with His principles.

"But thou shalt remember the LORD thy God: for it is He that giveth thee power to get wealth, that He may establish His covenant which He sware unto thy fathers, as it is this day. And it shall be, if thou do at all forget the LORD thy God, and walk after other gods, and serve them, and worship them, I testify against you this day that ye shall surely perish. As the which the LORD destroyeth before your face, so shall ye perish; because ye would not be obedient unto the voice of the LORD your God" (Deuteronomy 8:17-20).

BUSINESS GOALS SHOULD NOT BE BASED ONLY ON FINANCIAL PROFIT

In the world system, businesses are generally operated for financial profit, and most all decisions in business are traditionally determined by the secular world standard as to whether or not the decision will increase net income. Most goals in business have a financial flavor that denote a preoccupation of the goal setters with the mistaken belief that making profit is the primary purpose and function for which the business is established and operating. This is a false principle of the world.

"Go to now, ye that say, 'Today or tomorrow we will go into such a city, and continue there a year, and buy and sell, and get gain:' Whereas ye know not what *shall be* on the morrow. For what is your life? It is even a vapour, that appeareth for a little time, and then vanisheth away. For that ye *ought* to say, 'If the Lord will, we shall live, and do this, or that'" (James 4:13-15).

The point is clear. It is more important to seek God's will in His business than to seek just profit; and it is more important to use God's money earned from God's business for God's purpose, than to use God's money merely to hoard or spend for selfish gain. Jesus said in Matthew 16:26, "For what is a man profited, if he shall gain the whole world, and lose his own soul? Or what shall a man give in exchange for his soul?"

THERE ARE TRULY NO "SELF MADE" BUSINESS MEN OR WOMEN

Our very existence is dependent upon God's steadfast love for us. Contrary to the secular testimonies by so called "successful" people in business, there are truly no self-made businesspeople. The world's definition of success does not conform to God's biblical principles. God's economic principles are based upon His moral laws. God's definition of success is whether a businessperson has followed God's patterns for starting and operating the business to do the will of God and to establish His Kingdom here on earth as it is in heaven.

Paul gave his Sermon on Mars Hill to the Athenians and called them "superstitious" (Acts 17:22). He informed them that the altar which had the inscription "TO AN UNKNOWN GOD," which the Athenians worshipped in ignorance, is truly the Creator of the world and all things in it. He further revealed to them that God is "infinite" and "does not dwell in temples made with hands" and is self-existing and self-sustaining and need not be served by human hands, "seeing He giveth to all life, and breath, and all things" (Acts 17:23-25). "For in Him we live, and move, and have our being; as certain also of your own poets have said, 'For we are also His offspring'" (Acts 17:28).

TO BE A BONDSERVANT OF JESUS, YOUR MIND, EMOTIONS, AND WILL HAVE TO BE TRANSFORMED INTO THE LIKENESS OF CHRIST

God is more concerned with your character in your soul than He is with your charisma. Let your attitude confirm this truth: "Since this is God's business, I must be God's Business Servant. This business is the ministry God has given to me. I must offer my body as a living and holy sacrifice acceptable to God, which is my spiritual service of worship. I should not consider myself 'self-made,' but rather 'God made.' Therefore, I should not conform and run God's business using the world's standards and thinking, but I must be transformed by God through the renewing of my mind to ensure that God's will is being done through His business" (Extrapolated from Romans 12:1-2).

We Believers in business are "bondservants" to Christ Jesus, and we must conduct the business as ministry like Jesus wills us to do daily. We must use God's money to "make disciples of all nations" and go and "preach the Gospel to everyone, everywhere" starting with our partners, employees, customers, and everyone with whom we come into contact.

The attitude God wants His Business Servants to always have in the daily operation of business as ministry is clearly stated in scripture: "Let nothing be done through strife or vainglory; but in lowliness of mind let each esteem others better than themselves. Look not every man on his own things, but every man also on the things of others. Let this mind be in you, which was also in Christ Jesus: Who, being in the form of God, thought it not robbery to be equal with God: But made Himself of no reputation, and took upon Him the form of a servant, and was made in the likeness of men: And being found in fashion as a man, He humbled Himself, and became obedient unto death, even the death of the cross" (Philippians 2:3-8).

YOU SHOULD ACCEPT AND HONOR AND PROMOTE GOD AS YOUR TRUE EMPLOYER AND TRUE OWNER OF THE BUSINESS WHO HAS GIVEN STEWARDSHIP AUTHORITY OVER HIS BUSINESS TO YOU

"With good will doing service, as to the Lord, and not to men" (Ephesians 6:7).

In order to truly have God's favor, we, as Business Servants of God, must be obedient to Him, our "Master," the true "Business Owner."

"Wherefore, my beloved, as ye have always obeyed, not as in my presence only, but now much more in my absence, **work** out your own salvation with fear and trembling. For it is **God which worketh** in you both to will and to do of His good pleasure. Do all things without murmurings and disputings: That ye may be blameless and harmless, the sons of God, without rebuke, in the midst of a crooked and perverse nation, among whom ye shine as lights in the world; holding forth the word of life; that I may rejoice in the day of Christ, that I have not run in vain, neither laboured in vain" (Philippians 2:13-15).

BECOME THE "SALT OF THE EARTH" AND THE "LIGHT OF THE WORLD"

God's Business Servants can have an incredible impact on the world. They can be worth more than their salt as God's bondservants. As a point of contact with the world, God's Business Servants truly can become the "salt of the earth" and the "light of the world" which Jesus, Himself, mandated in Matthew 5:13-16.

To do this, we must become immersed in the active *agape* love of God. Be an imitator of the Owner of the business, who is God Himself. "Be ye therefore followers of God, as dear children; And walk in love, as Christ also hath loved us, and hath given Himself for us an offering and a sacrifice to God for a sweet smelling savour. . . For ye were sometimes darkness, but now are ye light in the Lord: walk as children of light: (For the fruit of the Spirit is in all goodness and righteousness and truth;) Proving what is acceptable unto the Lord. . . See then that ye walk circumspectly, not as fools, but as wise, redeeming the time, because the days are evil" (Ephesians 5:1, 2, 8, 9, 10, 15, 16).

YOU ARE A NEW CREATURE IN CHRIST WORKING GOD'S BUSINESS

You are in Christ; you are a new spiritual creature working God's businesses. The old ways of doing business have passed away; behold new things, new business methods, new business as ministries, have come into present reality (Extrapolated from 2 Corinthians 5:17).

You must set your mind on the things above, while conceiving business plans, and not only on the things below that the secular world teaches as its considerations. "Commit thy works unto the LORD, and thy thoughts shall be established" (Proverbs 16:3).

You must express in God's businesses His perfect unifying *agape* love that draws unbelievers to God unto repentance through your contact with the people in the world. "And though I bestow all my goods to feed the poor, and though I give my body to be burned, and have not charity *(agape love)*, it profiteth me nothing" (1 Corinthians 13:3).

BE SHREWD BUT INNOCENT IN BUSINESS

Business men and women do not usually fail by making business mistakes. They fail because they have bad business habits. These are bad actions done without thinking. Good habits lead to business success. Believers must have a renewed mind, without bad habits before God will open the windows of heaven and pour out His blessings on them as transformed, chosen vessels, who will not squander the wealth given. Maturation is the goal and concern of the Father, and He is using the daily handling of business problems to mature them.

The enemy will come and attack you when you are not looking or not thinking. Bad habits are repetitive actions that turn your mind to automatic. One becomes inattentive at best when operating habitually.

"Behold, I send you forth as sheep in the midst of wolves: be ye therefore wise as serpents, and harmless as doves" (Matthew 10:16).

GOD'S BUSINESS "PURPOSE" IS TO GET PEOPLE INTO HIS KINGDOM
AND SPIRITUALLY MATURE THEM INTO OBEDIENT KINGDOM
BUSINESS SERVANTS, NOT JUST TO MAKE MONEY

The business goals established in business must contain the knowledge, understanding, and wisdom of God in order to be in the Will of God. God's goal in His business is to have His Kingdom and His will manifested here on earth.

"Thy Kingdom come. Thy will be done in earth, as it is in heaven" (Matthew 6:10). God will use His Business Servants to bring unsaved people into His Kingdom and to funnel His money into activities dedicated to establishing the Kingdom of God's government 50% locally and 50% throughout the entire world (Acts 1:8).

If Business Servants in God's business do what God wants them to do, God will provide increased wealth to accomplish the business plan, to expand the business, and share the profits with His good stewards. "He that is faithful in that which is least is faithful also in much: and he that is unjust in the least is unjust also in much. If therefore ye have not been faithful in the unrighteous mammon, who will commit to your trust the true riches? And if ye have not been faithful in that which is another man's, who shall give you that which is your own?"

(Luke 16:10-12). Good stewardship in managing money in God's Kingdom is considered a little thing compared with your management of God's true riches. However, if you cannot handle money properly which is only good for use while you are alive here on earth, God will not entrust you with spiritual matters that are eternal.

USE GOD'S BUSINESS FOR WORLD EVANGELISM

God has clearly mandated that Business Servants are to use the business to bring His Gospel of the Kingdom (Matthew 24:14) and repentance and remission of sins (Luke 24:47) to unsaved people in the world, locally, nationally, and internationally wherever Business Servants travel and do business as ministry.

"And He said unto them, 'Go ye into all the world, and preach the gospel to every creature'" (Mark 16:15). God wants His Business Servants to put their Bibles in their brief cases when they travel. God wants them to have their Bibles in their offices for easy reference throughout each day. God wants His Business Servants praying every day.

In Matthew 28:18-20, the Lord's mandate is clear. As members of His chosen ministers, Business Servants are to make disciples of all nations *(ethnos)*. There are many nations *(ethnos)* within the United States and every other country. Business Servants must see the nations within their local area where they work and live and start thinking nation salvation. "Go ye therefore, and teach all (make disciples of all nations), baptizing them in the name of the Father, and of the Son, and of the Holy Ghost: Teaching them to observe all things whatsoever I have commanded you: and, lo, I am with you always, even unto the end of the world. Amen" (Matthew 28:19-20).

Business Servants must be Jesus' witnesses locally, regionally, to other states, and internationally to all in the world. "But ye shall receive power, after that the Holy Ghost is come upon you: and ye shall be witnesses unto me both in Jerusalem, and in all Judea, and in Samaria, and unto the uttermost part of the earth" (Acts 1:8).

GOD'S BUSINESSES ARE HIS VINEYARDS

The good spiritual fruit God desires to produce in you is for other people which need your caring, cultivating, and watering for proper growth and maturity. Your good spiritual fruit produced by you in God's business will help others to receive the Lord's saving grace and redeeming quality of eternal salvation. God is interested in developing good, godly character in you. God the Father prunes away the non-producing vines of the flesh, so spiritual fruit can grow in the soul (John 15:2); God the Word sanctifies and washes away the influence of the flesh by the water of the word of God (Ephesians 5:26), and God the Holy Spirit mortifies or purges the deeds of the flesh out of the soul to bring to the Believer more *zoe* life (Romans 8:13) in the Business Servant for the transformation of his or her soul. God wants His Business Servant's mind to be renewed, emotions stabilized, heart with godly beliefs, so his will is submitted to become the transformed Business Servant of the Lord.

God wants your stewardship in His business to be a point of contact to the world, so let people see, hear, and feel God's presence in you as you perform the daily tasks in His business. If you are an obedient servant of God, people will come to know God and His love and their need for salvation. His business is His vineyard, and Business Servants are to crush His fruit to make the "new wine."

Business Servants are the caretakers of God's vineyards, which work is an important entrustment. In fact, Business Servants are the branches and Jesus is the Vine. The branches are where the fruit grows (John 15:5). However, like every other Believer, Business Servants' branches need pruning from the Father to grow more fruit (John 15:2). If Business Servants accept the Father's pruning when needed, more fruit will appear. Prosperity becomes more fruit to feed more people with God's spiritual words, the fruit of the Spirit, which is love, joy, peace, longsuffering, gentleness, goodness, faith, meekness, and temperance (Galatians 5:22-23).

As God's business of sharing His gospel of His Kingdom government to increase the number of His disciples becomes the goal and practice of every Business Servant working in the business, then your profit in business will also increase. God desires that Business Servants be mature disciples, themselves, who are good stewards of, and have possession of, His heavenly wealth, both material and spiritual.

Why must the soul prosper by being spiritually transformed? 3 John 2 reveals the reason, "Beloved, I wish above all things that thou mayest prosper and be in health, even as thy soul prospereth."

GIVE THE FIRST FRUITS TO GOD BEFORE
YOU SPEND IT FOR YOUR OWN NEEDS

"Honor the Lord with the substance, and with the first fruits of all thine increase" (Proverbs 3:9).

A Business Servant's tithing and giving cheerfully without compulsion are signs of soul maturity (2 Corinthians 9: 6-7). Your faith is essential in God's Kingdom, as it puts your trust in God. A Believer's tithing and giving show the Believer's transformed heart to have the wealth of the wicked which is laid up for the just to come into the hands of the just. (Malachi 3:8-10; Matthew 23:23; Luke 6:38; Proverbs 13:22)

LET GOD ACTIVATE YOU AS HIS MINISTER IN BUSINESS

In conclusion, before you read the rest of this book, or before you decide to go into business, give the ownership of the business to God. Make the uncompromising decision to be His bondservant in the business. Let the business be the ministry opportunity in which God is using you. I am saying this at the beginning of this book, so that you will have a reason to study the biblical principles contained herein. As a Business Servant, you are a public figure in your community as potential employees and customers and clients look to you to help provide their financial needs and desires, and the Lord will use you to provide them with spiritual leadership and insightful wisdom in these end times.

Uncompromisingly, be God's Business Servant from which God's living water is poured out to those in a thirsty world.

As God's Business Servant, be the salt of the earth that gives proper flavor to the gospel of the Kingdom (Matthew 24:14), repentance and remission of sins (Luke 24:47), the Kingdom government of God, and be the salt that is a preservative of God's truths to people in a deceived world.

Allow God's light to so shine in you that the world is so illuminated that the darkness in your sphere of influence is dispelled. Also, allow God's light to so shine through you that your good works in business illuminates Christ's glory in you and God thereby is glorified.

Share God's perfect love that unifies the Body of Christ, so the world may know Jesus Christ through the love you share with others. Preach the Gospel of the Kingdom (Matthew 24:14) and repentance and remission of sins (Luke 24:47), to everyone, everywhere. Do not be ashamed to preach the gospel of the Kingdom and to preach the repentance and remission of sins. Paul said in Romans 1:16, "For I am not ashamed of the gospel of Christ: for it is the power of God unto salvation to every one that believeth; to the Jew first, and also to the Greek."

For those of you who are called already in business, transfer "ownership" of the business immediately to God and set your mind thenceforth on things from above. Transform everyone who works in the business as God's Business Ministers and God's Business Servants who are Biblitarians. You walk into the opportunity to receive your eternal rewards the moment you enter God's business as your place and focus of ministry if you initiate biblical principles as the guiding operational foundation of the business and submit yourself to be transformed into the image of Christ (Romans 8:29).

Be activated as God's vessel to be used to conduct the perfect will of God to bring His gospel of God's Kingdom government to the entire world.

You should always pursue a business that is compatible with your God given gifts, talents, and abilities. "Neglect not the gift that is in thee..." (1 Timothy 4:14).

Since it is God's business, do God's will and be anxious for nothing (Philippians 4:6-8). Do not be preoccupied or overly concerned with receiving payment for your ministerial services as your primary goal. "But seek ye first the Kingdom of God, and his righteousness; and all these things shall be added unto you" (Matthew 6:33). There will be times in business that you will be directed by the Holy Spirit to give away your services or products as a contribution.

You cannot serve the One and only true God and the god of mammon (Matthew 6:24). Do not let profit be your guiding force that motivates you. Let the Kingdom of God's government be your place of provision and your motivation for being in business as your ministry. Let the rewards waiting for you in heaven be the goal set before you. Let God reward you in His business in the natural realm as you do His work in His business in the spiritual realm.

"Lay not up for yourselves treasures upon earth, where moth and rust doth corrupt, and where thieves break through and steal. But lay up for yourselves treasures in heaven, where neither moth nor rust doth corrupt, and where thieves do not break through nor steal" (Matthew 6:19-21).

LET'S PROCLAIM THIS COMMITMENT TOGETHER

"God's ministry for me is the business I give to God. Since God owns the earth and all it contains, including the gold and silver earned; and since God has given me even the power to get wealth, so He can fulfill the covenant He made to my forefathers; I make this decision today, to be obedient to God and let God be the Owner of the business in which He has placed me. I will be God's Business Servant to use God's business as a point of contact to a hurting world, and to personally use my time, gifts, and talents and whatever money is earned through God's business for God's ultimate purpose of bringing the gospel of the Kingdom (Matthew 24:14) and repentance and remission of sins (Luke 24:47) to the whole world while making disciples of all nations. I will be God's Business Servant to disciple and mature employees by teaching and applying God's biblical principles of business and finances, and all that Christ commanded me to do as the purpose of God's business under my stewardship."

TWO

THE CALL OF THE BUSINESS SERVANT INTO MINISTRY

THE CALL INTO MINISTRY OF THE BUSINESS MEN AND
WOMEN IS AN END TIME CALLING OF GOD

As a Believer, the more wealth you acquire after initial salvation the more likely you are one of God's Business Servants. If you are an employee, then your work and talents are being sold at retail, but you are being paid well below wholesale. As a business owner, you are entitled to the profits. You can never be rich or wealthy being an employee. You can be about the Father's business as a business owner, as you have ownership authority to change your business into God's business (Luke 2:49). Pray about being an owner of a business and one of God's Business Servants.

Zechariah is a Prophet in the Old Testament, prophesying about futuristic vision and words concerning the end of the days. Many leaders in Church believe we are in the end of days. In the first chapter of Zechariah, God gives the prophet an end time vision as to how God will use Business Servants to terrify the worldly authorities, which could be large global corporations, or globalists in governments, which are the authorities that have come up against God's chosen children.

Zechariah 1:17-21 says, "Cry yet, saying, 'Thus saith the LORD of hosts; My cities through prosperity shall yet be spread abroad; and the LORD shall yet comfort Zion, and shall yet choose Jerusalem.' Then I raised my eyes and looked (second vision), and there were four horns [authorities, either global corporations, super rich, or government leaders], and I said to the angel who talked with me, 'What are these?' So he answered me, 'These are the horns that have scattered Judah, Israel, and Jerusalem.' Then the Lord showed me four CRAFTSMEN (Business Servants of God). And I said, 'What are these coming to do?'" So he said, 'These are the horns that scattered Judah (people of Lion of Judah today - See Galatians 3:28-29, 6:15), so that no one could lift up his head; but the CRAFTSMEN are coming to terrify them, to cast out the horns (authorities) that lifted up their horn against the **land of Judah** (perhaps the United States) to scatter it.'"

The Bible records historically how Assyria scattered the Northern Kingdom called Israel, and later Babylon took into bondage the Southern Kingdom called Judah, with its capitol, Jerusalem. However, Zechariah's vision was of the future, not history. This passage of prophetic scripture in Zechariah shows that doing business is recognized by the Lord as a needed and important end-time ministry calling and service. God's Business Servants will be used to wrap up the Church Age as the son of perdition (2 Thessalonians 2:3) and antichrist (1 John 4:3) initiate the end-time economic plan to control the world through most likely global corporations under their evil rule, which will be against Israel, Judah (United States where primarily Christians of the Tribe of Judah live), and Jerusalem. In the new world order promulgated by Satan, the world will be ruled by oligarchies in global corporations as 'one world government', with one world currency, and one world religion (Daniel 2:41-42; 7:16-24; Revelation 13:1-7). Notwithstanding, the United States could be the new Judah, for there are a greater percentage of Believers in Christ Jesus than any other nation, where Christ's humanity nature is of the Tribe of Judah.

Thus, the spiritual weapons of warfare (2 Corinthians 10:3-5) are not carnal but mighty through God to the pulling down of strongholds in the world, while God's Business Servants are hard at work and are about God the Father's business applying God's biblitarian principles to establish His Kingdom and doing His will on earth as it is in heaven (Matthew 6:10), seeking first the Kingdom of God and His righteousness, knowing that all these other things to sustain life for you and your family shall be added to you (Matthew 6:33). With daily prayer, studying the Word, and seeking first the Kingdom of God and His righteousness, God will prosper His Business Servants and make them have more wealth to steward and to rule over cities (Parable of the Talents- Matthew 25: 14-30; and Parable of the Minas- Luke 19:2-26). Those who want to prosper will become Biblitarians as principled Business Servants with the mind and wisdom of Christ.

President Trump is an example of God's Business Servant who stopped the tension and potential warfare between neighboring countries by convincing United Arab Emirates, Kingdom of Bahrain, Sudan, State of Israel, and the United States to sign the "Abraham Accords" to seek peace and economic benefits from each other and enter into financial agreements regarding investment, tourism, direct flights, security, telecommunications, technology, energy, healthcare, culture, the environment, and other areas of mutual benefit, as well as reaching agreement on the reciprocal opening of embassies. Israel's normalization of ties with the United Arab Emirates, Bahrain, and Sudan and soon other countries that will join the Abraham Accords, shatters the status quo in which Arab states withheld recognition of Israel until it allowed creation of an independent Palestinian state in the West Bank and Gaza. Perhaps these primarily Muslim nations joining the Abraham Accords caused Hamas to attack Israel on October 7, 2023 with an unprecedented, multi-faceted and sustained assault from the Gaza strip.

President Trump used his business experience to broker peace between several countries by them agreeing to economic benefits. It was a financial "win win" economic agreement that required peace and the recognition that Israel was a legitimate country in the Middle East. Officials anticipate around $500 million in deals and investments annually through the marriage of Gulf Arab petrodollars and Israel's scientific and technological expertise. This is the kind of work that God's Business Servants can do. They can go to other countries throughout the world carrying their brief cases with a Bible inside.

1 Corinthians 10: 3-6 says, "For though we walk in the flesh, we do not war after the flesh: (For the weapons of our warfare are not carnal, but mighty through God to the pulling down of strong holds;) casting down imaginations, and every high thing that exalteth itself against the knowledge of God, and bringing into captivity every thought to the obedience of Christ; and having in a readiness to revenge all disobedience, when your obedience is fulfilled."

In Matthew 5: 43-45 Jesus taught, "Ye have heard that it hath been said, 'Thou shalt love thy neighbour, and hate thine enemy.' But I say unto you, 'Love your enemies, bless them that curse you, do good to them that hate you, and pray for them which despitefully use you, and persecute you; that ye may be the children of your Father which is in heaven: for He maketh His sun to rise on the evil and on the good, and sendeth rain on the just and on the unjust.'" Whether President Trump knew it or not, he followed this beatitude when he brokered the Abraham Accords between United Arab Emirates, Bahrain and Sudan with Israel and the U.S.

In the meantime, God will use Business Servants as God's economic soldiers, using God's economic principles against those enemies of God who have caused persecution and tribulation to God's children and to stop the attack on God's Kingdom. 2 Thessalonians 1: 4-6 says, "So that we ourselves glory in you in the churches of God for your patience and faith in all your persecutions and tribulations that ye endure: Which is a manifest token of the righteous judgment of God, that ye may be counted worthy of the Kingdom of God, for which ye also suffer: Seeing *it is* a righteous thing with God to recompense tribulation to them that trouble you."

BUSINESS SERVANTS MUST BELIEVE AND OBEY GOD'S WORD AND PROPHETIC CALL

2 Chronicles 20:20 says, "And they rose early in the morning, and went forth into the wilderness of Tekoa: and as they went forth, Jehoshaphat stood and said, 'Hear me, O Judah, and ye inhabitants of Jerusalem; believe in the Lord your God, so shall ye be established; believe His prophets, so shall ye prosper.'"

Amos 3:7 says, "Surely the Lord God does nothing unless He reveals His secret to His servants the prophets." There are God-appointed and ordained prophets in business who have been given a special assignment of knowing the times and seasons of God's visitation. The second revival in Joel 2 is the restoration of wealth into the hands of God's people. God's Business Servants who have the special discipleship training to manage wealth will be used of God to be funnels through which God will pour forth His financial wealth to pay for this end-time harvest of souls (Joel 2:28) and to bless His children.

Business Servants must establish and manage God's business on the solid foundation of God's word and not based on the world's Capitalist, Humanist, and Socialist practices, but based upon a moral foundation of doing business with the principles of God's Kingdom.

Romans 12:2 says, "And be not conformed to this world: but be ye transformed by the renewing of your mind, that ye may prove what is that good, and acceptable, and perfect, will of God."

Luke 6:48-49 says, "He is like a man which built an house, and dug deep, and laid the foundation on a rock: and when the flood arose, the stream beat vehemently upon that house, and could not shake it: for it was founded upon a rock. But he that heareth, and doeth not, is like a man that without a foundation built an house upon the earth; against which the stream did beat vehemently, and immediately it fell; and the ruin of that house was great."

The Lord wants to take His Business Servants beyond what has been revealed and initiated through the evangelistic business outreaches such as CBMC or FGBMFI, and other business "meet and eat" Christian gatherings, although these are godly organizations which I highly respect and recommend for fellowship. However, God's intent is to activate Business Servants as ministers, and then teach them that their business is their focus and place of ministry.

GOD DESIRES THAT BUSINESS SERVANTS ACCEPT THE TRUTH THAT THEIR BUSINESSES ARE MINISTRIES IN THE KINGDOM OF GOD

God's primary purpose is to reveal to the business owners, executives, and entrepreneurs that the business activities constitute a ministry call of God that the business work is a very important ministry in the Kingdom of God.

Discipleship and the training of business leaders to bring spiritual maturity to their employees through the daily interaction with other believers in the business, and through the daily incremental problem-solving work in business, is the primary function of business as ministry. God desires to bring Christ's Church into the marketplace to accomplish better evangelism and discipleship training to be about the Father's business (Luke 2:49).

2 Timothy 2:2 says, "And the things that you have heard from me among many witnesses, commit these to faithful men who will be able to teach others also."

Business as ministry emphasizes godly, trusting relationships, especially with fellow partners, employees, and with customers or clients.

Developing closer, more fulfilling spiritual relationships will require revolutionized mindsets to apply God's Biblitarian principles to operate and make business decisions, along with accepting that profit is not the primary goal of business. Yet, having a loving and caring heart does not mean establishing a business as a welfare center; but, instead, business is a discipleship training center, teaching employees and fellow workers godly principles of managerial skills and excellent work habits through the daily incremental problem-solving routines in business. The workplace becomes God's center to mature His children through work assignments. Business profit is secondary to spiritual transformation and maturation, as prosperity comes with good stewardship of the business entrusted by God.

As will be seen, work is a holy calling, and employees should be trained in this principle of servanthood continuously. Paul admonished in Philippines 2:12-13, "Wherefore, my beloved, as ye have always obeyed, not as in my presence only, but now much more in my absence, work out your own salvation with fear and trembling.

For it is God which worketh in you both to will and to do of His good pleasure." The Business Servant owner should have competently trained managers and work employees to operate successfully in the Business Servant owner's absence.

Paul taught that obedience to employers is required, as employees must be mindful that they are working for a higher purpose as unto the Lord. Colossians 3:22-24, says, "Servants, obey in all things your masters according to the flesh; not with eye service, as men pleasers; but in singleness of heart, fearing God: And whatsoever ye do, do it heartily, as to the Lord, and not unto men; Knowing that of the Lord ye shall receive the reward of the inheritance: for ye serve the Lord Christ."

God's Business Servants must renew their minds into God's way of thinking while conducting business.

GOD'S BUSINESS SERVANT MUST FAITHFULLY FULFILL
THE FOLLOWING RESOLUTIONS

The resolve of God's Business Servant is to change drastically from the world's way of making business decisions, providing goods and services, instituting innovative programs and methods of business management, and setting goals based upon God's principles of economics and teleology (hearing what God wants and being led to make plans and goals to establish His purpose).

The resolve of God's Business Servant is to be about the Father's business, is to lead the unsaved to the Lord, to train the saved as disciples, to preach the gospel of the Kingdom (Matthew 24:14) and repentance and remission of sins (Luke 24:47), to people in the family, city, county, state, nation, and the whole world, and to take back possession for God of the earth, world system, and people that you have a measure of authority and influence.

The resolve of God's Business Servant is to build the business according to God's patterns in His word.

The resolve of God's Business Servant is to expand God's Kingdom and the Body of Christ through business interactions and sharing authority in business to disciple and train employees as God's Business Servants.

The resolve of God's Business Servant is to conduct the business as ministry according to God's word with love as a foundational motivation towards partners, employees, customers, the people in the community, and the Believers in the church.

The resolve of God's Business Servant is to follow and inculcate God's biblical principles regulating business and economics that life promotes life and not bondage.

The resolve of God's Business Servant is to train through biblical instruction and lifestyle witnessing to partners and employees to follow God's biblical principles of business operation, wealth acquisition, entrepreneurship success, and stewardship of assets for their maturation and blessing to their family, church, and community.

BUSINESS SERVANTS ESPECIALLY ARE CALLED BY GOD TO STEWARD HIS PHYSICAL CREATION HERE ON EARTH

BIBLICAL SOCIAL RESPONSIBILITY: In the past, the executives of businesses have neglected their social responsibilities in practicing and applying biblical principles in dealing with their employees, protecting the environment, providing fair compensation for their employees, insuring hope for the future with research and development, setting up and funding savings accounts to pay future expenses, training executives to become Business Ministers, training employees that work is a holy calling, and instilling a sense of loyalty to their Creator. The business sector of society should be performing services now performed by the Civil Government. Unsaved business owner's greed and selfishness have opened the door for big government, big unions, and a false dichotomy of a two-class system of management verses employees. Big government is in unsustainable debt and unions have become big business, and their purpose for organizing has been lost in their struggle for secular and political power. Thus, the truth is that God has mandated Business Servants to be about God's plan of maturing His children who work in the business, practicing biblical principles with love and caring toward their employees, while becoming leaders with a social responsibility toward their fellow man in their community. Business Servants can have a goal of contributing for building a library, contributing to purchase another police vehicle, contributing to purchase computers in schools, contributing to maintain Christian schools, contributing to building new parks, setting up business discipleship training for high school graduates to give them experience, conducting business classes based upon biblical principles of economics, contributing to build facilities and support for unwed mothers to stop abortions, setting up homes for foster children who are 18 years old and who have lost government support, and many other projects too many to list in this limited space.

BIBLICAL ECONOMY: The Free Enterprise System, with a biblical moral base, must be re-instituted through biblical principles, where godly love, godly fruit of the Spirit, godly stewardship, godly compassion, godly leadership training, and godly obedience in seeking first the Kingdom of God and His righteousness become the goals of business over the making of just profit as a revolutionary way to regenerate the economic greatness of a nation's culture and country. The best and only way is to become obedient children of God by becoming disciples of Christ.

BIBLICAL NEGATIVE: Socialist Civil Government's ownership of businesses and real property through imminent domain espoused by the philosophers of Socialism should be avoided, because they promote destruction of the family unit and bring generational bondage to God's people through dependency on 'cradle to grave government support', higher taxes, and bigger government. Socialism is bad because it keeps God's children in bondage and immature; and therefore, must be avoided. God's Kingdom economics is a debt free government, is a loving community, is living and not just existing, is a place where moral and diligent work is a holy calling, is life, liberty, and is the pursuit of God and the Lord Jesus Christ.

The above three biblical foundational principles seriously should be foundational beliefs of God's Business Servants in being about the Father's business of establishing and preaching the Gospel of His Kingdom here on earth (Matthew 24:14) and preaching repentance and the remission of sins (Luke 24:47).

Also, the above three biblical foundational principles will be explored with greater detail, along with why these truths should be instilled in our culture and our economy for the survival of freedom loving individuals, families, and nations.

THE CALL OF THE BUSINESS SERVANTS
IN THESE END TIMES IS FOR THEM TO
USE THE BUSINESSES TO SOLVE COMMUNITY
PROBLEMS USING BIBLICAL SOLUTIONS

Ministers and leaders in the community need to join hands with the Christian Business leaders and professionals in a joint effort to find solutions to people's problems instead of allowing government to grow bigger and bigger. All problems here on earth in the secular world have spiritual solutions in God's Kingdom government. Therefore, God's Business Servant is to be led by the Holy Spirit and is accountable to God to bring His principles into the daily lives of people, especially family members, partners, employees, customers, and other community leaders.

Christian Business Servants should be ordained by God as Ephesians 4:11 Ministers and discover the true meaning and practice of spiritual business servants in God's Kingdom. Christian Business Servants can be an apostle in business, a prophet in business, an evangelist in business, a pastor in business, and/or a teacher in business. God is omnipresent, and He refutes man's attempt to box Him into a church building or home fellowship at times and days each week. God wants His spirit and life to permeate every aspect of people's lives, especially in the marketplace since more people transact business in the marketplace than in the churches each week.

The church leaders need to re-examine their church practices and traditions that separate church leaders from business leaders and should see each other as co-ministers in the same Kingdom of God but in different venues. Psalms 78:41 says, "Yea, they turned back and tempted God, and limited the Holy One of Israel." Both Church and Business Servants have to accept and inculcate the biblical truth that Christ did not come to earth to start a new religion but rather to inaugurate the Kingdom of God and to redeem fallen mankind, so that

God's government is established (Matthew 6:10, 33) and God living in born again Believers as His dwelling place and Temple (John 14:16-17, 23; 1 Corinthians 3:16; 6:19; 2 Corinthians 6:16; Ephesians 2:21-22).

GUIDING PRINCIPLES FOR BUSINESS SERVANTS WHILE MAKING
BUSINESSES THE PLACE OF MINISTRY OF GOD'S KINGDOM PRINCIPLES OF
LOVE, TRUTH, LIBERTY, GRACE, MERCY, FAITH, AND GODLY PURPOSE

The Kingdom of God deals with love, truth, liberty, grace, mercy, faith, and godly purpose; and in the financial realm its commerce operates by "giving and receiving."

The Kingdom of darkness, or the realm of this world system, deals with cause and effect, sin, greed, covetousness, fear, evil, and abuse; and in the financial realm its commerce operates by "buying and selling."

In Genesis 1:28 God told Adam and Eve, "Be fruitful and *multiply*." The Kingdom of God is established based on multiplication. If you plant one seed, the seed can multiply back 1000 times that amount. If you have a cow or sheep, and the cow or sheep has a calf or lamb, then you have received at least 100% return that year. The same creation laws apply to God's Business Servants. "Be fruitful and *multiply*."

The Kingdom of God is a reflection on earth in what we see around about us. God created the heavens and the earth, and His creation testifies of the very existence and the goodness of God and His biblical laws in operation in the natural and spiritual realms.

The world system is established based on percentage of increase. The world system operates outside biblical principles. Therefore, worldly investments have been relegated to a percentage of increase instead of multiplication. Investments in the world give you 8% to 15% per annum at best. If an investment reaches 20% per annum, then most people believe that it is too risky or illegal. However, even at 20% per annum, this is not one time multiplication.

In our hearts, we know that we are supposed to multiply what we steward, so we have such things as the Lotto. A few do win the jackpot. However, they achieve multiplication in the world only at everyone else's expense.

In God's Kingdom you multiply never at another human's expense, but God allows it at His expense; but He can afford it. Business Servants are called to be stewards of God's physical creation and especially the wealth that is biblically defined as: Everything that was created by God is defined as wealth, and it will have the inherent quality of being involved with multiplication.

Psalm 24:1 says, "The earth is the Lords, and the fullness thereof, the world and the people that dwell within." The earth participates in multiplication. You plant a seed, and you get back a harvest multiple times more in seeds, where a portion can be replanted for a greater harvest next year. This is how the wealth grows.

Haggai 2:8 says, "'The silver is mine and the gold is mine,' says the Lord of Hosts."

Thus, silver and gold are part of wealth.

One of the Founding Fathers in the U.S. was Alexander Hamilton, whose financial ideas were accepted and were written into the Constitution, that no money could be printed by the U.S. and State government unless it was backed by gold or silver. Article I, Section 8, Clause 5 says "Congress shall have Power...to coin Money, regulate the Value thereof, and of foreign Coin." Article I, Section 10, Clause 1 says, "No state...shall make any Thing but gold and silver Coin a Tender in Payment of Debts." These 27 words pertain to monetary policy in the founding document of the government of the United States.

These clauses in the U.S. Constitution made the U.S. currency connected with a limited quantity of wealth, so that the government could not go into debt. If the government did not have the gold or silver to back the money, it simply could not spend any more money. The first thing that happened when the U.S. went off the gold standard was that it went into accelerated, runaway government spending, issuing Treasury Bonds as the collateral to have the Federal Reserve to lend the U.S. government more money to spend on social entitlements and extended and continuous wars by each generation.

God is a business God. Jesus said in Luke 2:49, "How is it that ye sought me? Wist ye not that I must be about My Father's business?" That which is from God multiplies. If you had only $1,000 in the business account on January 1st, you could still multiply. Most all small businesses earn gross over $100,000 each year and run this amount through the business bank account. That amounts to a hundredfold return. Again, businesses are wealth assets, and they cause multiplication in your life. Yet, if you do not work the business, you can lose your investment in the business.

Psalms 50:10 says, "For every beast in the forest is Mine, and the cattle upon a thousand hills." Every cow normally has at least one calf each year, which is one-fold return, but still multiplication. Yet, if you do not feed, water, and care for the cattle, they will die, and you lose your wealth.

In the story of the Rich Young Ruler in Mark 10:29-30, Jesus proclaimed the reward of multiplication by those who minister the gospel as His bondservants: "And everyone who has forsaken houses, or brethren, or sisters, or father, or mother or children, or lands for My name sake, and the gospel's, but he shall receive an hundredfold now in this time, houses, and brethren, and sisters, and mothers and children, and lands, with persecutions; and in the world to come eternal life."

In this story, money and riches are not mentioned, but only the things of wealth. There is a distinction in the

Bible between wealth, riches, and money. Jesus says that the principles of multiplication work in the Kingdom of God. A hundredfold return is not the same as one hundred percent return. This is multiplication.

Houses are considered part of a person's wealth, not riches. A house is where people live, and people have children; and the multiplication occurs in the house and home. Wealth is what is handed down generationally as an inheritance of and from family. In this story and discourse, Jesus says that family relationships are part of wealth. An inheritance is when you receive something without having to work for it. Therefore, if you have a loving mother and father who have accumulated wealth assets, you are wealthy because they taught you wisdom with love. A brother or sister is also part of your wealth. They will always be there for you. They will work with you and help you when you are down and out.

Proverbs 13:22 says, "A righteous man leaves an inheritance to his children's children, and the wealth of the wicked is laid up for the just." Wealth is the inheritance that is passed on from generation to generation, i.e., houses, lands, gold, silver, livestock, businesses, and family relationships. In the story of the rich young ruler, wealth is defined by Jesus as lands, houses, and relationships with family. You can be wealthy because of the family you have or because of the friends that you have in the Kingdom of God. Wealth also is God's wisdom, knowledge, understanding, love, and life abundantly. Without these gifts from God, you will lose wealth and will not be able to enjoy life abundantly.

The nature of wealth is that it multiplies when you add your work and talents in stewarding God's creation (Luke 18:29-30), and it is meant to be handed down as an inheritance (Proverbs 13:22). Proverbs 13:22 ends by saying "...and the wealth of the sinner is laid up for the just." Ecclesiastes 2:26 says, "For God gives wisdom and knowledge and joy to a man who is good in His sight; but to the sinner He gives the work of gathering and collecting, that he may give to him who is good before God...."

God's Business Servants with the anointing to spoil the enemy of this world system has to come to the resolve to build the business according to God's patterns for business and economics, the resolve to expand God's Kingdom and the Body of Christ, the resolve to conduct the business by seeking first the Kingdom of God and His righteousness, and the resolve to become God's mature Business Servant who uses godly principles in business and all aspects of his or her life.

The word "wealth" includes the material blessings promised by God through the patriarchs and their descendants, including Christians of today as sons and daughters of true spiritual Israel (Galatians 3:28-29). However, God gives Business Servants the power to get wealth (Deuteronomy 8:18) to establish, verify, and live in the covenant blessings of God for the purpose of financing the end-time Church's mission to lead the worldwide revival when God pours out His Spirit on all flesh (Joel 2:28). The word "wealth" also includes prospering in health (3 John 2), peace, joy, and friendships. It also includes the divine wisdom, knowledge, and understanding to handle God's wealth without it becoming an idol and controlling you. Wealth is given to conduct God's purposes He has called you to fulfill. Therefore, God's wealth is always a means to an end and never an end in itself.

God fellowships with Business Servants by giving them stewardship over His wealth here on earth, and God promotes intimate relationships with His ministers while they are faithful stewards of His business.

God's Business Servant's ministry includes the full time administration of God's physical creation, and the training of people in relationships, by exhibiting the fruit of the spirit and by applying God's biblical principles of prosperity and economics through the daily solving of business problems and the conduction of business transactions.

In fact, everyone who is a Believer in the Lord Jesus Christ is required to steward God's physical creation in one degree or another and is to be about the Father's business (Luke 2:49). Therefore, to this extent, every Believer should be working in the Father's business here on earth and must learn God's business principles of economics. Notwithstanding, there is a special ministry call of those who have engaged commerce with a business enterprise to be God's special Business Servants.

GOD IS THE ONLY TRUE PRIVATE PROPERTY OWNER IN THE UNIVERSE BECAUSE GOD OWNS ALL MATERIAL AND SPIRITUAL REALITY

Regardless of all the large Wall Street mergers, they can never merge enough to be as big of a private property and resource owner as God. God owns it all!

Raw materials are wealth assets that make a nation wealthy. What makes a nation of people have a good economy is when they have wise entrepreneurs and executives of businesses who know how to manage raw materials, such as gold, silver, oil, coal, trees, water supply, cotton, domesticated animals, abundance of agriculture, and the transportation system to get these to the markets. Great management and free enterprise with godly morality are essential to a great economy in furtherance of God's Kingdom. When these raw materials, especially precious metals, lands, and oil are used as assets to back a country's currency, then the standard of living of the people are enhanced as other people in other countries will entrust receiving payment with the asset backed currency of that country. International business today is essential for a healthy economy. When the people of a nation practice biblical economics, stay out of debt, and when authority is given back to the families and local small businesses to handle local problems, then the people have more freedom, less government, less crime, and greater maturity with acceptance of greater individual responsibility.

Newer and better ways are increasing production of products, and more industrious people will boldly step forth and start new businesses.

Some of the best tax advantages today are given to those who start their own home-based businesses. Part of your house rent, or mortgage can be deducted as business expenses, along with business mileage, health insurance, and you can even pay each of your children under 18 years of age a small salary who help you in your home-based business. A home-based business will teach your children the virtues of a good work ethic. There are many other advantages that maximize your income if you just start your own home-based business. The secret is having a business in your home, a fictitious business name, and you will not have all the overhead by having an office outside of your home. I, personally, as a lawyer, could retire today comfortably if I had all the money, I spent for overhead in my law practice since 1974.

TRUTH ABOUT THE EARTH'S CAPACITY TO PRODUCE:

The physical features of the earth can now support all our multiplying humanity at higher standards of living than anyone has ever experienced in the history of man. God has given us a re-supplying earth, which will support and prove His biblical principles of wealth creation through working in the business you are called.

Oftentimes, man creates his own problems.

Ethiopia's food shortage is really a failure to distribute food, not a failure of God to produce food.

The Hindu religion disallows killing of cows. India does not have a hunger problem   they have a religious problem contrary to the word of God. Hindus believe people are reincarnated into animals. Therefore, it is against the law to kill rats, mice, and cows; so, if you kill an animal, you could be killing a reincarnated human being. India has about 200 million "sacred" cows, and each cow eats enough food to feed seven people. Cows are eating the people's grain. India produces enough food to feed one-fourth of the world's population without cows.

DIVINE INTERVENTION IS GOD'S KNOWLEDGE,
POWER, AND WILL TRANSFERRED TO MAN
TO HANDLE MAN'S PROBLEMS HE WANTS TO HANDLE

The ball point pen has millions of dollars of technology in inventiveness.

Divinely revealed inventions show how we have effectively used God's raw materials.

There have been innovations in tire manufacturing as tires use to go only 8,000 miles; now they last over 40,000 miles.

Oil is the raw material used to increase wealth. For example, wealth is increased through oil refinement into gasoline and making of plastic.

Computer technology increases saleable knowledge. In 1975 Bill Gates, then a sophomore at Harvard University, joined his hometown friend Paul G. Allen to develop software for the first microcomputers. They began by adapting BASIC, a popular programming language used on large computers, for use on microcomputers. Gates dropped out of Harvard University during his junior year, and he and Allen formed Microsoft. Microsoft licensed an operating system they had purchased called MS-DOS to International Business Machines Corporation (IBM), who then was the biggest computer supplier in the world; and IBM used the system in IBM's personal computer. MS-DOS became the computer industry standard, and because of Microsoft's success, Gates amassed a huge paper fortune as Microsoft's largest individual shareholder. He became a paper billionaire in 1986, and within a decade his net worth had reached into the tens of billions of dollars. Starting in 1995 and 1996, Gates caused Microsoft to develop consumer and enterprise software solutions adaptable for the Internet; and Microsoft developed the Windows CE operating system for networking noncomputer devices such as home televisions and personal digital assistants. Microsoft also created the Microsoft Network to compete with Internet providers, and, through Gates's company Corbis, acquired the huge Bettmann photo archives and other collections for use in electronic distribution. At that time, Gates became reportedly the world's richest private individual. On October 4, 1957, the then Soviet Union launched Sputnik, the first man-made satellite, which jolted the American public and the government which began the U.S. Space Age. People had been dreaming of space travel for some time before the launch of Sputnik. Satellite technology increases saleable communication. On July 10, 1958, a beach-ball sized satellite was launched into outer space and started electronic communications. That satellite was Telstar 1. The mission was a cooperative effort between AT&T and the space agency to demonstrate, "the feasibility of transmitting information via satellite." As the demand for data grew, existing satellites simply could not keep up. ViaSat in 2011 launched ViaSat-1, which at that time had more communications capacity than all other communication satellites combined over North America. Currently, the two largest players in North America offering satellite internet are Hughesnet and ViaSat. Hughesnet parent company, EchoStar, entered the satellite business by buying Hughes Communications in 2011. Since then, most of Hughesnet has been sold to Dish Network. Wikipedia says, "A communications satellite is an artificial satellite that relays and amplifies radio telecommunication signals via a transponder; it creates a communication channel between a source transmitter and a receiver at different locations on Earth. Communications satellites are used for television, telephone, radio, internet, and military applications. As of 1 January 2021, there are 2,224 communications satellites in Earth orbit. Most communications satellites are in geostationary orbit 22,300 miles (35,900 km) above the equator, so that the satellite appears stationary at the same point in the sky; therefore the satellite dish antennas of ground stations can be aimed permanently at that spot and do not have to move to track the satellite." Satellites are used for Global Positioning Systems (GPS). GPS is used by almost everyone that has a modern smartphone or a navigation system in their automobile. Satellites are also used for radio or television, weather forecasts, ATM Withdrawals, internet, In-Flight convenience, phone and broadband service. How do satellites help NASA? NASA has satellites that face toward space and are used for a variety of missions. Some satellites lookout for dangerous rays coming from the sun. Others study asteroids and comets, the origin of stars, and the whereabouts and condition of planets. In fact, some satellites fly by or orbit other planets for signs of water or life.

Elon Musk has become one of the richest men in the world through investments in new inventions. In 2003, Musk put six million initial investments into Tesla, which had a vision to make electric cars. The company took advantage of new lithium-ion batteries, which were both light and energy-dense, to revolutionize the struggling field. At the time, lithium-ion cells were only being used in small electronic devices, Musk decided that Tesla's central innovations were scaling them up, which caused it to create an electric vehicle with far greater range than other electric cars had been able to invent. Tesla's R&D engineers realized that Tesla's prototype battery packs potentially could catch fire, which almost caused Tesla to go bankrupt during the recession of 2008. Resolving the battery pack problem, Tesla in 2012 began producing its first mass-market car, the Model S. Today. Tesla now controls about two-thirds of the U.S. electric vehicle market, and Elon Musk has become the wealthiest person in the world.

Elon Musk's inventiveness through battery packs for electric cars is now being used to create batteries to back up solar panels in homes. If your home solar system is connected to your utility and you do not have a battery, your home solar system will not work during a grid power outage. Your home solar system is automatically turned off by your utility company during a power outage to prevent solar energy flowing into the utility grid while repair crews perform repairs on electrical lines and electrical equipment. In a power outage, if you do not have batteries to run, then your home will be without electricity. Tesla has invented a revolutionary battery storage solution to allow your home to have electricity during a power outage, which is gaining popularity in the marketplace. Unlike a solar-only system, a homeowner can continue generating and storing solar energy during the day; any excess will be sent to recharge the batteries.

These are only small few examples of how inventiveness can create new wealth.

THE CONCEPT OF PRIVATE PROPERTY

The concept of "privately-owned property" comes from God. He is the private property Owner of His creation.

The moral Free Enterprise System is being challenged through group collective thinking and through governmental Socialist intrusion. Adam Smith was a Scottish economist during the 1700's, and he was a philosopher and author. He is considered the father of modern economics. Smith was a major proponent of *laissez-faire* economic policies and taught that a businessperson's desire to make profit would motivate the businessperson to use good business principles. He taught to leave the businesspersons alone as the desire for profit would regulate them naturally without government intrusion. However, *laissez-faire* economic policies without a moral biblical imperative will still be abusive. The quest for profit alone cannot transform a businessperson's mind, emotions, heart, and will. Only the Godhead can transform the soul; mankind cannot do it themselves. This truth is being revealed in this book.

The rise of eminent domain where government takes ownership of the property for public roads, parks, buildings, libraries, schools is not the only thing that has taken away private stewardship. There also has been abuse against private ownership or stewardship of property by the environmentalists. Yet, Christian Business Servants should be the number one proponent of protecting God's earth. Management in the hands of godly people will cause God's purposes to be fulfilled, the environment to be protected, and the consumer-based society to find godly principles by which to live. True Conservatives should be the best conservationists.

There has been an erosion of property rights through zoning restrictions and occupancy permits along with building restrictions that continue today as the government continues to grow bigger and bigger and more intrusive of rights and freedoms.

There is a false Socialist and Humanist belief that the practice of Capitalism is, at best, a tolerated evil. The Socialists and Humanists believe that Capitalism is ethically inferior to collectivized or Socialist government rulership because they believe the primary goal of Capitalism is only for profit. In the hands of godly Business Servants, profit is not the primary goal, but management of God's physical creation and maturation of God's people through solving business problems, negotiating business transactions, or availing themselves of business opportunities creates servants, not power mongers seeking only riches. Economic moralism based upon biblical principles must be infused into the economy of any nation. Thus, God's Business Servants do business with God's principles in God moral free enterprise, not capitalism per se.

What the Socialists and Humanists government Bureaucrats and Politicians do not tell you is that the primary goal of collectivized government policy is the acquisition and concentration of power to enforce their own Socialist and Humanist elitist philosophy to equalize the wealth of the masses based on "current need" rather than "productivity," or better, based upon giving money to whom they decide are "victims" to justify their Socialist and Humanist agendas and government ruling authority. The truth is that these victims sometimes cause their own problems and will do it again because they often are unprincipled, have addictions, lack maturity, dropped out of school, refuse further education, and often are too lazy to work. These so-called victims need a loving business environment that trains them to be successful, skilled business biblitarians. This is what the goal is trying to teach.

GOD EXPERIENCES FELLOWSHIP WITH BUSINESS SERVANTS
BY GIVING BUSINESS SERVANTS STEWARDSHIP
POSSESSORY RESPONSIBILITY OVER HIS CREATION

The way God chooses His Business Servants to do the work He wants done here on earth in this Church Age, is by giving His Business Servants possession of His natural creation for the purpose of stewardship on His behalf. He looks for those who will be good trustees over His natural resources and shepherds of His children in business.

In Genesis, God said essentially, "Tend my creation, bring order to it, bring it under My rule and My will and I will multiply you as you birth more spiritual beings in My image and likeness." In fact, Genesis 1:26-28 says, "Then God said, 'Let Us make man in Our image, according to Our likeness; let them have dominion over the fish of the sea, over the birds of the air, and over the cattle, over all the earth and over every creeping thing that creeps on the earth.' So God created man in His own image; in the image of God He created him; male and female He created them. Then God blessed them, and God said to them, 'Be fruitful and multiply; fill the earth and subdue it; have dominion over the fish of the sea, over the birds of the air, and over every living thing that moves on the earth.'"

Further, in Genesis 2:15, it says, "And the LORD God took the man, and put him into the Garden of Eden to dress it and to keep it." To replace the words "dress" and "keep," today we might say "embellish" and "guard" or "add to" and "keep from deterioration." Anybody who has taken care of a farm, garden, or even a house, car, business, or a church building, knows that one can dress it and embellish it to make it more attractive. It also takes daily work to maintain it and to guard it from falling into a state of disrepair.

In Genesis 2:15, God also was considering something much greater than the physical part of "dressing" and "tending" the Garden of Eden; He was referring to a maleficent spirit connected with the Serpent. This Serpent in the garden was also what Adam was to guard against. In a practical way in your own life, God is indicating that spiritual demonic presences must be subdued to stop them from deteriorating your life and business, and the lives of your employees and family must be guarded through prayer. Likewise, there is continuous work in keeping your own heart pure and desirous of serving the Lord. This requires mature management and the taking of dominion over assigned areas in the world with God's business, along with maintaining and guarding your spiritual life at the same time. One is not to be neglected over the other. Being a good steward of the physical assets, you are assigned to manage, and your spiritual engiftment and calling is equally important in God's eyes. Neither can be neglected.

In the King James Version, the word "dress" means "tend" or "cultivate." The Hebrew for "dress" is *"abad,"* which means "to work at" but in context to farming, the Hebrew word means to "cultivate." In 1611, when the King James was translated from Greek into English, the word "dress" meant "to set in order," but gradually it came to mean to apply decorative details, to "embellish" or "make attractive." Today, when we speak that we are going to "get dressed," we mean we are going to "put ourselves in order" and "embellish" ourselves to look "attractive."

The Garden of Eden was a beautiful, serene place where Adam and Eve met God every day in the cool of the evening (Genesis 3:8). Yet, as beautiful as the Garden of Eden was, it would not stay that way without good stewardship by Adam and Eve. The Garden of Eden needed to be dressed and kept. That required a great deal of work by Adam and Eve. Adam was assigned to name all the living creatures, and that was a full-time job by itself (Genesis 2:19).

As a Business Servant, you must put what God puts into your hands to go through a finishing process, watch over it, guard it, protect it, and preserve its beauty for a good testimony as a servant of God. It becomes clear also that God intends for His Business Servants to see the spiritual side of the business in God's Kingdom. The way Business Servants "dress" and "keep" God's "garden" business will have a greater importance in their spiritual development. Godly work in business requires development of a Business Servant's spiritual life in Christ.

When God established as part of the foundations of His Kingdom the creation of man in God's image and likeness, God chose to delegate dominion on the earth to man. God chose to fellowship with man through the stewardship of His creation. However, the mandate for dominion followed image and likeness, and this is God's pattern. God entrusts you with His business and resources as you mature and become more like Him in character development and mature in your experience in being led by the Spirit in managing your daily business responsibility.

God gave mankind *dunamis* power, *exousia* authority, and *kratos* territorial assignment for exercising this under-rulership, which originated in God's mind where He had the intent to make mankind in His own image and likeness. Mankind was created or made to rule as under rulers of God, which means in obedience to God's rules, directions, principles, and authority. Mankind's ability to sustain their role as delegated under-rulers of the earth rests in mankind's obedience to God's rules or principles of rulership. In other words, as mankind is faithful to obey God's Word, and has developed good character in the image and likeness of God, then God will give workforce and authority to reign in this life and the age to come over God's creation. When mankind is disobedient, then God takes away His power and authority to rule.

The key is faith in God and obedience to His biblical principles, while maintaining a love relationship between believers and God. Believer's very lives must be focused on the hearing and obeying of God's voice, while loving God and other Believers. Matthew 4:4 says, "Man does not live by bread alone, but by every word that proceeds out of the mouth of God." Matthew 13:34-35 says, "A new commandment I give unto you, 'That ye love one another; as I have loved you, that ye also love one another. By this shall all men know that ye are My disciples, if ye have love one to another.'"

THE FALSEHOODS THAT INTERFERE OR ARE OBSTACLES TO GOD'S
TRUTH THAT GOD FELLOWSHIPS WITH MANKIND BY GIVING MANKIND

STEWARDSHIP POSSESSION OVER GOD'S CREATION

RELIGIOUS DECEPTION: Jesus talked about the deception in religious practices. Matthew 15:6 says, "Thus you have made the commandments of God of no effect by your traditions." Often, religious traditions do not conform to biblical truths or principles. Similarly, teachers and preachers frequently mix Humanist ideas of self-aggrandizement with biblical truths in their sermons. God has certain commandments in His word that must be followed, and those who try to skirt around them violate them. Ninety percent obedience to God's New Testament commandments means you are not obedient. It is all or nothing with God. You must be either hot or cold; God does not like lukewarm (Revelation 3:15-16). The devil cannot nullify God's Word. Yet, religious traditions can make God's word to not have the effect it should have in believers lives.

FALSE SPIRITUALITY: It is a false religious belief that God does not care about the material world, but that Believers should function only in God's ethereal spiritual realm. God gave people their five senses to interact with the physical world. God made humans to have emotions, thoughts, and beliefs about the material world. The opposite is Hinduism, which tries to annihilate the thoughts and emotions of the soul and considers the natural realm of little importance. After the creative act of the earth and the earth's plants, trees, fish, birds, cattle, insects and the man and woman, God pronounced, "It is good...." The earth was brought under a curse as Adam and Eve fell in the Garden of Eden. God came not just to redeem fallen humankind but to regain the possession of the earth and bring the rule of His Kingdom through His Son, Christ Jesus, and the Church as under rulers (Daniel 7:9-14). The truth is that the Kingdom of God includes all of God's creation, even though in the Church Age the Kingdom of God is primarily manifested inside the born again Believer. In the ages to come, God's Kingdom rule will be manifested here on earth for all to experience and see.

FALSE CONCEPT: It is a false concept that God's Business Servant somehow has a carnal, inferior, secondary call to someone who is ordained, working full time in the ministry as an Ephesians 4:11 minister. This paradigm separates clerical life from business life. This is a false dichotomy which does not exist in the Bible. Most leaders in the Bible, including Jesus, Himself, received their journeyman training first in the natural business field. In the Old Testament, Abraham, Isaac, and Jacob, and David were Business Servants. They were sheep and livestock herders. Peter, Andrew, James, and John were fishermen. Matthew was a tax collector. Luke was a medical doctor. Priscilla and Aquilla, with Paul, were tent makers. Lydia was a purple die fabric manufacturer. Jesus was a journeyman carpenter. A journeyman trains his apprentices using on the job training. Jesus used journeyman training toward His disciples. Even today, Jesus' divine nature sees Business Servants as a pool from which He can choose His ministers here on earth.

FALSE BELIEF: The beliefs that business is not a ministry, and that God's Business Servants are not Ministers, have caused enormous damage to the Church and thwarted the expansion of the Kingdom of God because this has set up a false distinction of business versus church. There exists in Church tradition the false belief that Business Servants are engaged in worldly practices while Church men and women are engaged in spiritual matters as the true Ministers of the Lord. The Greek philosophers had the false viewpoint that business work was inferior to philosophical thought; and therefore, business ventures should not be sought as a lifestyle for the philosophical elite. This is contrary to biblical teaching. Every leader in the Bible was engaged in livestock or business and yet was chosen by God to fulfill God's historical purposes.

FALSE EXPERIENCE: The false experience of Adam and Eve through their disobedience by gaining self-aggrandisement knowledge from the Tree of Knowledge of Good and Evil impoverished them and did not give them dominion, wealth, or power. When God takes away your authority, you lose your power. Accepting Socialism, Humanism, or demonic wisdom of the world as the foundation of your belief system in your heart of your soul will cause poverty in the long run. The Socialist and Humanist philosophers champion knowledge of this natural world, but do not seek the wisdom, knowledge, and understanding from God, which is of higher dimensions that correspond to the moral principles that God put in the world for it to operate best and to operate His Kingdom and His will to be done on earth as it is in heaven (Isaiah 55:8-9; Matthew 6:10).

FALSE TEACHING: Another false teaching is that believers are not empowered until they die. This religious falsehood goes like this: "When we die through the experience of death, we will somehow automatically acquire power." This is a similar deception Satan enticed Eve in the Garden of Eden. Genesis 3:5 says, "For God knows that in the day you eat of it your eyes will be opened and you will be like God, knowing good and evil." In other words, the Serpent told Eve that she would receive power through her experience of eating the fruit of the Tree of the Knowledge of Good and Evil. In truth, power is received through God's intimate relationship with you, your obedience, and God's sovereign rule and protection, not through a particular experience. There will be more power and knowledge in the age to come, although we are privileged to have a "taste" of the knowledge and power in this life as well (Hebrews 6:5). It is a false teaching that death empowers the Believer. Death moves Believers into another phase of their work and continuous training in the Kingdom Age to come. "Impotency" or lack of power occurs in this life when Believers do not think they can be empowered until the day they die. Hebrews 11: 1, 6 says "Now faith is the substance of things hoped for, the evidence of things not seen... But without faith it is impossible to please Him: for he that cometh to God must believe that He is, and that He is a rewarder of them that diligently seek Him." If you have no hope, then your faith is a substance of nothing. Yet, if your hope is only your rewards when you get to heaven, then your faith is merely to get you to heaven. If your hope is for the establishment of God's Kingdom and to do His will on earth while you are living here on earth, then your faith will be the substance of your hope while you are alive here on earth seeking God and His Kingdom and doing His will.

FALSE PREACHING OF ONLY INITIAL SALVATION: Here is a modern-day Church Leader's anemic teaching. "Get saved and wait and do nothing in this life until the Lord returns for His Bride." This mindset is an impotent teaching and causes apathy in the Church and is not making leaders in God's Kingdom but mere followers of a particular leader or denomination. The spiritual life experience of Believers after initial salvation is not to go a couple of times a week to a building and listen to a sermon, although sermons are good, but listening to sermons is not what God wants as Believer's sole experience as members of the Body of Christ.

The life of the Believer is to be a lifestyle of living by being needed. When you hear a good teaching, go out immediately and share the teaching with someone else.

If you experience a miracle of healing, go out and share that healing with others. Your life in the Kingdom of God is a dynamic time of witnessing to others of the goodness of the God, which leads a person to repentance (Romans 2:4), being about the Father's business in the marketplace (Luke 2:49). Your life in the Kingdom of God is a continuous, ongoing spiritual growth unto maturity in the Believer's soul yielding the fruit of the spirit for others to be spiritually nourished. Ecclesiastes 3:11 says, "He hath made everything beautiful in his time...." A beautiful time in God's Kingdom is when you are mature, just like a blueberry is most delicious and nourishable when it is ripe. The gospel of the Kingdom (Matthew 24:14) and repentance and remission of sins (Luke 24:47) transforms your soul from carnality to spirituality, is the truth of all of God's blessings for you and your family and is for the activation of you to your holy calling and good works for which you were saved to do.

Believers falsely are taught they are rewarded, promoted, and empowered only when they arrive in heaven after they die. Every Believer is a King, Lord, Priest, Ambassador, and Soldier (1 Timothy 6:15; Revelation 1:6; 5:10; 17:14; 2 Corinthians 5:20; 2 Timothy 2:3-4). These titles and authorities are every Believer's vocation. Not every Believer has the same gifts. Spiritual gifts are different than vocation.

FALSE ELITISM: This false dichotomy of Priesthood and laity, Jesus hated, and is called elitism. In Revelation 2:6, Jesus said, "But this thou hast, that thou hatest the deeds of the Nicolaitans, which I also hate." Nicolaitans means the hatred of the laity, which is setting up an ecclesiastical structure that separates the Priests, Teachers, or Pastors as better than the rank-and-file Believers of the congregation. In John 13:5-14 Jesus demonstrated a lesson of humility by washing His disciples' feet. Jesus said in Mark 10:42-45, "But Jesus called them to Him, and saith unto them, 'Ye know that they which are accounted to rule over the Gentiles exercise lordship over them; and their great ones exercise authority upon them. (43) But so shall it not be among you: but whosoever will be great among you, shall be your minister: (44) And whosoever of you will be the chiefest, shall be servant of all. (45) For even the Son of Man came not to be ministered unto, but to minister, and to give His life a ransom for many.'"

FALSE THINKING: Work in the world is a curse. In God's Kingdom, work is a holy calling, not a curse, as God uses work to mature His children through problem-solving on a daily basis. Believers are created for and are mandated to do work as servants for their own maturation and support of their families (Ephesians 2:10; Philippians 2:12-13).

These false thoughts, teachings, and beliefs will be explored with greater depth and with historical perspective in later chapters.

MORE OF GOD'S TRUTHS ABOUT THESE ISSUES:

BIBLICAL CALLING: What business men and women in the world want is loyal employees that do their work well but that will not go out and start their own competitive business. The truth is that upon being born again, every Believer is an appointed king, lord, and priest under the headship of Christ (1 Timothy 6:15; Revelation 1:6), whose authority is granted in those vocations in order to preach the gospel of the Kingdom of God and preach repentance and remission of sins. God is in the process of transferring a Believer's soul to make him or her a mature king, lord, and priest under the Headship of Christ Jesus. The purpose and function of the Ephesian 4:11 Ministers is stated immediately following in Ephesians 4:12-13, "For the perfecting of the saints, for the work of the ministry, for the edifying of the body of Christ: (13) Till we all come in the unity of the faith, and of the knowledge of the Son of God, unto a perfect man, unto the measure of the stature of the fullness of Christ." The duty of the Ephesians 4:11 Ministers is to make leaders in the Kingdom of God as kings, lord, and priests, not as followers of a particular Church or denomination or a particular Ephesians 4:11 Minister. Also, all Believes are called to be Ambassadors of Christ (2 Corinthians 5:20) and soldiers in God's Kingdom army (2 Timothy 2:3-4).

BIBLICAL HUMILITY: All Believers are not here on earth for God to serve them but for them to serve God and the Lord Jesus Christ as Head of the Church. Jesus' Apostles were leaders, and many were businessmen; and they had business experience of being a boss who told other people in the business what to do. Jesus' Apostles were men who were used to exercising authority as business owners. The Apostles had to change to be men of humility. Jesus said in John 13:14, "If I then, your Lord and Master, have washed your feet; ye also ought to wash one another's feet." Washing someone's feet was one of the lowest jobs in Israel, and that is how far the Lord beckons Believers into a life of humility. Thus, Jesus taught that leaders need to be humble and rank and file members of the Church who are being trained as spiritual leaders need to be humble. Humility is a prerequisite to promotion in the Kingdom of God. Jesus said in Luke 14:11, "For whosoever exalteth himself shall be abased; and he that humbleth himself shall be exalted."

BIBLICAL PROMOTION THROUGH HUMILITY : Paul said in Philippians 2:3-9: "Let nothing be done through strife or vainglory; but in lowliness of mind let each esteem other better than themselves. (4) Look not every man on his own things, but every man also on the things of others. (5) Let this mind be in you, which was also in Christ Jesus: (6) Who, being in the form of God, thought it not robbery to be equal with God: (7) But made himself of no reputation, and took upon Him the form of a servant, and was made in the likeness of men (8) And being found in fashion as a man, he humbled himself, and became obedient unto death, even the death of the cross. (9) **Wherefore God also hath highly exalted Him and given Him a name which is above every name.**"

BIBLICAL EMPOWERMENT: What empowers Business Servants, and the entire Church in this life, is covenantal obedience to our Creator over a long period of time that changes our character, matures our souls, and makes us fruit bearing trees of righteousness that the Lord may be glorified (Isaiah 61:3). The Lord will say, "Blessed is the man that walketh not in the counsel of the ungodly, nor standeth in the way of sinners, nor sitteth in the seat of the scornful. But his delight is in the law of the LORD; and in His law doth he meditates day and night. And he shall be like a tree planted by the rivers of water, that bringeth forth his fruit in his season; his leaf also shall not wither; and whatsoever he doeth shall prosper" (Psalms 1: 1-3).

BIBLICAL TRUTH: It is a biblical truth that authority and power from God do not come from a single experience but from an ongoing intimate relationship with God where you have proven your faithfulness and have developed good character and maturity in your soul. Authority and power are designed by God to come through the covenantal process of working in obedience with God in the stewardship of God's creation and the responsibility to develop relationships based upon the leading of the Holy Spirit, Who plants in your heart the seeds that germinate, grow, mature, and bear the fruit of the Spirit. Galatians 5:22-25 says, "But the fruit of the Spirit is love, joy, peace, longsuffering, gentleness, goodness, faith, meekness, temperance: against such there is no law. And they that are Christ's have crucified the flesh with the affections and lusts. If we live in the spirit, let us also walk in the spirit."

BIBLICAL WITNESSING: Christ has already commissioned Believers with enough authority (Matthew 28:18) and power (Acts 1:8) to go out and be His witnesses to make disciples of all nations starting at Jerusalem, then to Judea, Samaria and to the ends of the earth. Witnessing occurs in the school place, home place, marketplace, workplace, and every place as God is omnipresent, while the Holy Spirit leads Believers to the persons in need of salvation and the Kingdom of God. Wherever people live and engage in life here on earth, Believers are to be witnesses bringing the gospel of the Kingdom (Matthew 24:14) and repentance and remission of sins (Luke 24:47), locally, regionally, nationally, and globally.

BIBLICAL SUBMISSION: God requires soul transformation that leads to willful submission. There is no such thing as a Christian business. Only a human can be God's Business Servant, not things or businesses. However, God's Business Servant must have his or her soul transformed by the entire Godhead where he or she becomes spiritually minded, emotionally stabilized, heartfelt believing, and then willfully submitted to the Lord. God's mature Business Servant's character will be an extension of his or her life as a business minister as he or she grows in intimate relationship with the Lord. God's Business Servant must build the business according to God's pattern of bringing God's Kingdom and will to be done here on earth as it is in heaven. God's Business Servant must reject the world's pattern of everything being focused on the god of mammon supplying money for the fulfillment of individual lust of the flesh, lust of the eyes, and pride of life.

BIBLICAL PATTERN: God's Business Servants must build God's businesses according to the pattern He presented in His word, so they must seek and submit to the leading of the Holy Spirit. This is an especially important principle to learn and apply. Moses was told that the work of building the Tabernacle had to be done according to God's revealed pattern. God's pattern for business and economics is delineated in scripture and can be found when you diligently search for His principles in His word.

BIBLICAL FOCUS: God's business pattern is not to be just profit focused; rather, God's Business Servants must be Kingdom seeking (Matthew 6:33), faith believing (Hebrews 11:6), and covenant keeping with God for the wealth He brings to fulfill the covenants He has given to the forefathers (Deuteronomy 8:18).

BIBLICAL MOTIVATION: Making money should not be the primary goal and motivation of God's Business Servant, as making profit is a secondary function. If being God's Business Servant to minister to others seeking help, maturing employees through daily problem-solving, and preaching the gospel of the Kingdom (Matthew 24:14) and preaching repentance and remission of sins (Luke 24:47), then you will prosper in business. Matthew 6:33 mandates, "Seek first the Kingdom of God and His righteousness, and all these other things will be added." You must not work for money but have money work for you to support your family, your employees, church community and your physical community. Do not allow the god of mammon to be your master but subjugate money to be a means to further God's purposes. If money is your servant, then you must know what it is always doing. This is being accountable as a good steward with what God has given you. Then, God will show you how the money is to be used for God's purpose and not to fulfill your greed, avarice, or covetousness. James 4:3 says, "Ye ask, and receive not, because ye ask amiss, that ye may consume it upon your lusts."

BIBLICAL GOAL: God's goal for those chosen as God's Business Servants in business is not to just to make more money. God's goal is to help His Business Servants build the businesses according to the pattern that God is building His businesses as a ministry outreach and as a Kingdom training center for employees and partners in business to mature and develop their work skills to be better stewards of God's creation and to have open ears to hear God's ministry commands and call unto servanthood.

BIBLICAL RESULTS: Making money will only be a derivative of a Business Servant's moral and faithful work because he or she built the business according to God's pattern. God rewards those who diligently seek Him (Hebrews 11:6) and are obedient to His Word. God rewards those that seek Him, not only spiritually but also for the purpose of stewardship of God's natural creation. Hebrews 4:12 says, "For the word of God is quick, and powerful, and sharper than any two-edged sword, piercing even to the dividing asunder of soul and spirit, and of the joints and marrow, and is a discerner of the thoughts and intents of the heart."

BIBLICAL POWER AND AUTHORITY: Power and authority given to a Business Servant by God during the Church Age, and the Kingdom Age to come, continues as the Business Servant's diligence in the incremental problem-solving done to mature the business owners, partners, and employees. God balances power and authority with responsibility. The more responsible a Business Servant maturely manages, the more additional power and authority God gives to the Business Servant. God is a good, wise Father; and He will not give to His children more than they have maturity to manage.

BIBLICAL WORK: The Bible teaches that work is a holy ministry calling that lasts forever. In the Kingdom Age to come, the business and commerce of God will be not based upon buying and selling, but upon giving and receiving, because He is the same yesterday, today, and forever. His Kingdom never changes. There is no buying and selling in heaven, and this will be the pattern when the Kingdom Age begins when the New Jerusalem comes down from heaven. Everything we have from and in the Kingdom of God come to us by way of love, gift, good stewardship, and humility. God the Father gave us His only begotten Son (John 3:16) to bring the Kingdom of God here on earth and to provide through His only begotten Son's death, our salvation.

SPIRITUAL GIFTS: Also, God the Father gave Believers operational spiritual gifts (1 Corinthians 12:6; Romans 12:6-8). God the Word gave Believers the office administrative gifts of the Apostle, Prophet, Evangelist, Pastor and Teacher (1 Corinthians 12:6; Ephesians 4:11). God the Holy Spirit gave Believers nine manifestation spiritual gifts (1 Corinthians 12:7-10). In the Kingdom age to come, God will still need people who are good stewards as Business Servants to conduct His new commerce based upon principles of giving and receiving.

THREE

GOD'S PRIMARY PURPOSE FOR THE BUSINESS IS TO BRING MATURITY TO HIS CHILDREN

GOD'S BIBLICAL WORK PATTERN: GOD BRINGS PEOPLE TO MATURITY
BY MAKING THEM WORKING PARTNERS WITH HIM, SO THEY WILL HAVE
GOD'S SERVANT MENTALITY, INSTEAD OF A HIRELING MENTALITY

Again, Genesis 1:26-28 says, "Then God said, "Let Us make man in Our image, according to Our likeness; let them have dominion over the fish of the sea, over the birds of the air, and over the cattle, over all the earth and over every creeping thing that creeps on the earth.' So, God created man in His own image; in the image of God He created him; male and female He created them. Then God blessed them, and God said to them, 'Be fruitful and multiply; fill the earth and subdue it; have dominion over the fish of the sea, over the birds of the air, and over every living thing that moves on the earth.'"

The making of man in God's image and likeness preceded the giving of man authority and dominion over the rest of creation. God has a divine order. The more of His image and likeness in your soul that He can instill as you manage God's creation and business, along with managing relationships with those He sends to you, the more power and authority to take dominion of your assigned territory and society He is going to give to you. Dominion is allowing Christ to live His life in you and through you to establish God's Kingdom, obey God, and do His will here on earth as it is in heaven (Galatians 2:20; Matthew 6: 10, 33).

Also, after God made Adam and Eve in His image and likeness and gave them dominion over the things and creatures of the earth, "And God blessed them" (Genesis 1:28). There is nothing in business like being blessed of the Lord. God's young people who obtain education, work hard, and live with deferred gratification while in their twenties, especially are blessed and protected through God's sovereign grace.

When I was in my late twenties after becoming a lawyer at age twenty-five, I seemed to have God's grace upon me and was prosperous. I was blessed with God's protection, even though I really had little life experience and certainly little of God's wisdom from above. I did not lose any money in my twenties. Every year during the first five years that I was an attorney (from ages 25 to 30), I made more money the current year than the previous year. When I became thirty years of age, I thought each year I would continue making more money than the previous year. I did not study the word of God in my twenties to learn the principles of business, relationships, investments, and wise economics. I started making business mistakes, investment mistakes, trusting the wrong people, and was taken by con men as I started doing things outside of the practice of law. I took risks and trusted in people's representations without vetting them fully. Almost everything I did outside the practice of law I was unprofitable because I had no experience in those other areas; and I did not pray for discernment. I did not learn enough of life to make practical decisions.

Until I was 25 years old, when I graduated from Law School, I lived in the institution called "education," eating fruit from the Tree of the Knowledge of Good and Evil. My relationship with God was not intimate. I did not seek God with my whole heart. Oh, I was a decent and good person, but my definition of good was as the world defines "good," not as God established as His good. I was full of covetousness and greed which I thought were just my attempt to live the American Dream. I sought more after money than I did God, even after I rededicated myself again to the Lord at age 28. I was saved, but I was not serving. My entire life changed when I discovered the biblical words were "living" in Hebrew 4:12 when I was 38 years old. I discovered the truth that if I caused the word of God to enter the heart in my soul, that the living word would start growing there as a seed and the spiritual fruit would be my nourishment and a better and fulfilled life. As the spiritual fruit ripened in my heart, it became nourishment for my mind and emotions. Worldly thoughts were replaced with Kingdom truths. Worldly run-a-way feelings became Kingdom emotional stability. I no longer was just existing but was living life with Kingdom purpose. My time on earth then had a spiritual destiny. I was no longer chasing rainbows looking for the pot of gold; I found the Creator of the rainbow and submitted to Him to receive His eternal spiritual blessings.

As I was growing up as a young man, I never learned that God had a biblical pattern that as a Believer I was supposed to follow in every area of my professional career as a lawyer, husband, father, and man of God. The Holy Spirit revealed my failure was based upon wrong thinking, wrong emoting, and wrong believing. The problem was there were lessons in my twenties that I did not learn, partly because I had no natural father to guide me; so, I did not have the wisdom from experience or guidance that I needed in managing the problems with which I was confronted in my thirties. Additionally, I did not know that I was to seek the wisdom from above instead of making decisions based upon the wisdom of this fallen world.

Here is a fact that I discovered to be true. **"People tend to stop learning new things when things are going well for them."** Only when things start going wrong or tough do people tend to look for correct answers. Sometimes, the problems are caused by an all-out attack by the Kingdom of darkness, but other times the problems are created by a person's own immaturity, or a person's own carnal nature being manifested as sin which opposes the spirit. People mistakenly think they should be promoted with more responsibility because they have some success based upon the world's standards of accomplishment. However, God's purpose is to make you grow with spiritual mature character and with more obedience to God's word and the leading of the Holy Spirit. God wants to ensure His will is being done here on earth as it is in heaven. God does not want you to exercise your disobedient self-centered will, influenced by the flesh, the fallen world, or the Kingdom of darkness when making your decisions in business, in family, in relationships, in voting, in entertainment, in making investments, in seeking truth, and in every other encounter in life.

GOD'S BIBLICAL "PATTERN" IS TO BE MANIFESTED
BY ESTABLISHING A WORKING PARTNERSHIP
BETWEEN EMPLOYERS AND EMPLOYEES

As God's Business Servant, you should encourage your employees to be more industrious and take on more work and decision-making tasks to lessen your own workload to free up your time for spiritual, godly pursuits. God's biblical pattern is to build the business to encourage employees to work by the principle of being "working managers" with you as their employer. You can have your employees on commission if allowed under government regulation (which is becoming less allowed) or give them a partnership in the income stream only, not the assets, which does not include the accounts receivables or equity. This way, if the employee leaves, you do not have to buy him or her out of the business as the accounts receivables are being paid by customers or clients. If you let your employees know they are working managers with you, then they will develop a stewardship mentality working for God's business instead of an employee mentality. This is God's pattern and principle for success. As many employees as you can train to have this management mentality or outlook, the more successful you will become, and the more possessions and business opportunities God will give you to possess and manage for Him. Those who develop the management mentality you can give them special bonuses. Although this biblical principle seems simple, it takes planning and forethought to implement this pattern in the business. It also requires retraining and rethinking about what is the business purpose. Additionally, profit sharing should conform to the laws and regulations in your state or province, or according to the dictates of your professional license. Lawyers, for example, cannot have non-lawyers as partners, but can have managers.

BUSINESS SERVANTS AND EMPLOYEES MUST
UNITE IN A COMMON VISION FOR THE BUSINESS

In John 5:19 Jesus said, "... Most assuredly, I say to you, what He sees the Father do; for whatever He does, the Son also does in like manner." You must build the business on the same principles the Father is using as a pattern to build His spiritual business here on earth. Unity between the employer and employees comes by sharing goals and vision, while the employer encourages employees to take on managerial responsibility of contributing to the achievement of those goals. What employees see the employer do, instruct them to do likewise. If you do this, you will be blessed with obedient, godly employees who have become working managers in their thinking.

Working managers start thinking what is best for the business instead of what is in their own best interest. This includes developing in your employees 1). long run thinking, 2). to capture a market share, 3). establishing research and development (R&D) that maintains a market share with new products, 4). setting aside a saving account for future expenditures to avoid debt, 5). paying for continued education of employees to maintain competence, 6). considerate to help employees with their personal lives, 7). Meeting the needs of the community, such as setting up an internship program for high school and college students to gain practical experience in industry, giving money for missions, providing ongoing support for the cost of operating the local church, teaching godly business principles to church members, and going on part-time mission field excursions to various countries to support orphanages, build houses, and minister the gospel of the Kingdom (Matthew 24:14) and repentance and remission of sins (Luke 24:47). To fulfill my purpose, I minister the word of God, and I write books and teachings and send them to people in over 65 countries at time of this writing. I also have podcasts on youtube, facebook and other media under 'Biblitarian Ministries'.

Practically, how do you as an employer receive "common unity" or "spiritual community" with employees?

Share your spiritual vision with your employees, but let your employees choose to participate of their own free will.

Share, through delegation, your responsibilities with your employees, but always have proper follow-up to ensure each employee is doing an excellent job and completing the tasks for the benefit of customers and to further the good reputation of the business.

Share your time with your employees, avoid being close friends, but do be friendly. As an employer, you are in the "parent" role. Parents should not be just friends with their children, but parents should be friendly.

Lead your partners and employees in daily prayer when you start your workday, and if it is possible, when you have several Believers in the business, read one book of proverbs and five books of Psalms before work starts. This must be a voluntary time before work, and it is not the time they are paid. Thus, those who do not attend cannot cry discrimination or underpayment.

Show your care and compassion with your partners and employees and their families but offer your employee over-time instead of giving a continuous hand out to meet their needs. Do not let anyone think that your office is the "Department of Welfare." Teach them through application that work earns money, and this is a biblical principle.

Celebrate and reward employees who become mature in moral self-government, who solve problems by joint efforts which encourages teamwork, who continuously satisfy customers or clients, who have contributed to increase the bottom-line profits of the business, and who show good stewardship by following biblical principles of economics and biblical agape love.

GOD'S ORIGINAL PURPOSE FOR MANKIND HAS NOT
CHANGED. HIS WORK IS THE PATTERN FOR HIS BUSINESS SERVANTS.

God has always wanted to share vision, responsibility, and time with His Business Servants by building together as partners in His business that He has here on earth.

For example, man's original sin did not catch God off guard, nor did it destroy God's business plan for humanity. **God is a strategic thinker, an analytical thinker, and a methodical thinker**. He foresaw the consequences of sin before the natural world was created (Acts 2:23). **Father God** had foreknowledge of the crucified death of His only begotten Son for the sins of humanity because He practices **teleology** (Revelation 13:8).

"Teleology" is looking at the result desired and deciding how to accomplish what is necessary to obtain the desired outcome. God considers the result He wants and makes plans to ensure he reaches that result!

Although God foreknew the fall of man, He wanted someone His only begotten Son could love as His bride, so He still created man. Believers know that their children are born in a fallen state, but they still have children because they want someone to love. God provided Believers with a Redeemer before He created Adam. In fact, the Lamb of God was slain before the foundation of the world (Revelation 13:8). God chose us and wrote our names in the Lamb's Book of Life before the foundation of the world. Ephesians 1:4 says, "According as He (God) hath chosen us in Him (Christ) before the foundation of the world, that we should be holy and without blame before Him in love." This is how God plans things.

You can see God's confirmation of teleology in these verses. Revelations 13:8 says, "All who dwell on the earth will worship him, whose names have not been written in the Book of Life of the Lamb slain from the foundation of the world." Revelations 17:8 says, "The beast that you saw was, and is not, and will ascend out of the bottomless pit and go to perdition. And those who dwell on the earth will marvel, whose names are not written in the Book of Life from the foundation of the world, when they see the beast that was, and is not, and yet is."

God's Business Servants should practice teleology in business, and by doing so, they will find greater success. God's Business Servants' business plans should be in line and supportive of God's spiritual business plans, not the business plans for self-gratification. Self-gratification plans resemble that of the world or are just plans you make up without first seeking the counsel of God and mature men and women in the Lord.

As God's Business Servant, you can make godly relationships with your employees while maintaining your authority as a good pastor and teacher of your employees. A pastor is a shepherd, and as a sheep herder, the shepherd must show tough love at times. He wants to lead the sheep to green pastures and still waters, not out to the desert. You cannot, though, treat employees as if they are your children. You must be a tough disciplinarian, so if you are absent for a season, the employees will be diligent and competent in their work. As a business shepherd, you should know your sheep employees.

"He who pampers his servant from childhood will have him as a son in the end" (Proverbs 29:21).

"Know them which labor among you..." (1 Thessalonians 5:12).

"And be not unequally yoked together with unbelievers. For what fellowship has righteousness with unrighteousness? And what communion does light have with darkness?" (2 Corinthians 6:14). It is imperative that you follow this principle in the business dealings. Every time I have lost money in business or investment it has been because I was unequally yoked, and almost every time the person said he was a Christian. Yet, what he said did not match his actions.

"Withdraw yourself from every brother that walks disorderly" (2 Thessalonians 3:6). Even though the employee or partner says he is a Believer, you should look and determine if he or she is living an orderly life based upon God's biblical principles. If his personal life is out of order, his business life will be out of order. If a partner cheats on his or her spouse, he or she will cheat on the business partner.

"He who is partner with a thief hates his own life, He swears to tell the truth but reveals nothing" (Proverbs 20:24). The first time you catch your partner or employee in a lie or even a small theft, then you should start thinking about replacing the person with someone else. People lie because they have done something wrong. It is as simple as that. What they did wrong may be that they have a habit of procrastination. Sometimes, they lie to cover up their sin.

Jesus allowed the betrayal of Judas, who was lying about the money collected and stealing money out of the money purse, to teach us by example how to deal with the problems with the dishonesty of employees and partners. Jesus knew Judas was stealing the offerings. Jesus had a reason not to confront him. What would the Church leaders say today if Jesus was here on earth in ministry, knowing and letting slide a man stealing from His ministry? Yet, Jesus had a higher purpose. He had to be betrayed and defeat on the Cross of Calvary the idol of mammon and employee and partner theft.

Again, you can forgive a person caught stealing and not fire them, but you must completely take them out of any task where the person should manage money. Sometimes, you are required to get rid of him or her. Judas was replaced with another apostle just before the Day of Pentecost. Judas lost his job. The truth is, if an employee lies to you as his Employer, then you have a liar in the business. If you discover an employee or partner has stolen from you, no matter how small, then you have a thief in the business. Why would you do business with, or subject your customers to, liars and thieves in the business? You can put them on restriction with severe conditions to see if their character changes. You can make them read the book of Proverbs every day; you can read Proverbs with them every morning. You can do this privately at first, then rebuke them publicly, and eventually fire the employee or dissolve the partnership.

IF WE WANT THE FATHER'S BLESSING ON WHAT WE ARE
BUILDING, WHETHER CHURCH, GOVERNMENT, FAMILY, OR
BUSINESS, WE HAVE TO BUILD ACCORDING TO GOD'S PATTERNS

As Business Servants, we should encourage and teach partners and employees the blessings involved in tithing and giving offerings, but most pastors have taught on this; and it is not necessary to repeat teachings that are important, but already known.

God's Business Servants are mandated to make the following top order of priority in business.

God's Business Employers must discover God's inspired motivations, talents, engiftments, and ministries of those people with whom they work, whether saved or unsaved.

God's Business Employers must hire employees with the goal of drawing them into what God created them to be and do.

God's Business Employers must have the motivation to make obedient, mature executive leaders in business, not just followers. Leaders may be motivated to enhance the Kingdom of God. The more leaders in the business who are submitted to Christ as His servant will be motivated by servanthood, and servanthood is a principle that brings prosperity and the more freedom the owner will have because he has the time to pursue a greater spiritual life and is no longer just existing from day to day.

God's Business Employers must discover that the healthiest businesses are those where each employee is developed into a mature leader who makes it a priority to mature others into thinking and operating the business with biblical principles of economics and servitude. With this purposeful priority firmly planted as a motivating goal, employers and employees will truly be about the Father's business (Luke 2:49).

God's Business Employers should reach into the lives of the unsaved employees and saved employees and discern by the leading of the Holy Spirit what their engiftments from God really are, and then begin to draw them into what their potentials are in Christ Jesus. With this purposeful motive and goal, the unsaved employees will see the love and benefit of being saved and living in God's Kingdom, and they will no longer be satisfied with what the world offers. They will seek after what you have with Jesus. This is economic evangelism and economic discipleship in the marketplace.

Why will economic evangelism have a great impact in the world system?

It is because God's Business Servants will have begun the redemptive process of bringing employees and business associates into what they were created by God to be and do. They will find and experience spiritual meaning in life that brings to them God's Kingdom life instead of just daily worldly existence; they will be working with purpose and find and experience a real sense of worth purpose in their lives.

Economic evangelism and economic discipleship are the most important priorities of business as your ministry. All Business Servants must encourage economic evangelism and economic discipleship in the businesses. As God's Business Servants, by following the priority of releasing people into their God-ordained potential,

Business Servants will be building a business as ministry according to God's pattern.

Thus, God's Business Servants as Ephesians 4:11 ministers are to bring unsaved people into the family of God by employing them, leading them into salvation, discerning their engiftments, training them in the ways of God's Kingdom, maturing them through the handling of daily work assignments using biblitarian principles from the Bible, and in drawing them into their God-appointed authority where they will be best for the business and their own spiritual advancement. This is equipping the saints for the work of the business as ministry until they come in the unity of the faith, unto the knowledge of the Son of God, unto a perfect man, unto the measure of the stature of the fullness of Christ (Ephesians 4:11-13). 1 Corinthians 15:58 says, "Therefore, my beloved brethren, be ye steadfast, unmoveable, always abounding in the work of the Lord, forasmuch as ye know that your labour is not in vain in the Lord." For most believers today, the church tradition is not a place for "abounding in the work of the Lord." Jesus trained His disciples by living with them 24/7, and the Pastors today cannot do that. This is why God is training business owners to be Pastors who will train disciples who are employees five days a week with biblical economics to be about the Father's business. Christ is moving His Church into the marketplace for deeper spiritual training through kinesthetic learning all people in trades learn through doing the tasks required. Dentists have to learn dentistry through kinesthetic training.

Following God's pattern of continuous economic evangelism and economic discipleship will make the business a place of ministry and a prosperous business to hand down to God's Business Servant's children and children's children. God's Business Servant will find his or her spiritual purpose of being about the Father's business (Luke 2:49). Employees will learn not to work just for the privilege of being paid money, but "with good will doing service, as to the Lord, and not to men" (Ephesians 6:7). There will develop a culture of God's Kingdom. Employees will praise the Lord when a new sale has come into the business. They will pray over their meals in the lunch room. They will develop the fruit of the Spirit, which will become the new norm. They will share the gospel of the Kingdom of God with others and the virtue of repentance and the remission of sin. They will become honest, respectful, and through time will adopt as their own the mores, ethics, principles, morals, and love that is in the Kingdom of God. They will come to work with righteousness, peace, and joy in the Holy Spirit because they are touching and experiencing the invisible, spiritual Kingdom of God. They will experience a little of heaven here on earth. Strangely enough, the Kingdom of God will be found in the workplace.

YOU NEVER KNOW WHAT GOD HAS PLACED IN AN EMPLOYEE WHEN HIS OR HER POTENTIAL HAS NOT BECOME REALITY

It stands to reason that the mother of the number one employee of the U.S. Federal government, the President, did not know that she was feeding, changing the diapers, and disciplining a future President of the United States when he or she was just a small baby and young boy or girl.

Every Believer and non-Believer who comes into the business as a customer, client, or employee must be treated with respect. You never know who he or she really is in God's higher thoughts, calling, and purpose. God may lead someone to you who He wants you to evangelize through economic evangelism. Also, you really do not know who your employee is either, for you see him or her in the natural in only potential form. Speak to your employee his or her potential in Christ Jesus rather than your assessment based upon his or her immature misconduct.

What if the Virgin Mary had an abortion, then she would have killed the Messiah? If you are pregnant, you never know whom you are carrying in your womb. The baby could hold the cure to A.I.D.S. or the cure for cancer. The baby could be the one who takes care of you in your old age.

Abraham Lincoln was brought up in a log cabin. He borrowed books and went and read them in the forest finding shelter for hours in a barrel. Yet, in that barrel reading borrowed books was more than a small boy desiring to acquire more knowledge; he became one of the greatest Presidents this country has ever known. Abraham Lincoln ran and lost in many elections before he was elected President of the United States. By secular standards, as a child, Abraham Lincoln could have been labeled wrongfully as "poor white trash." This country needed a President who knew how to keep going during times of failure. The Civil War meant Americans had failed to maintain our unity as a nation, and we saw cousins fighting each other, friends fighting friends, and a whole country divided against itself. President Lincoln fulfilled his destiny! During this country's most dismal hour, President Lincoln had his greatest moment in history. He realized his greatest potential and fulfilled his God ordained purpose in life as President of this great country.

You never know with your natural eyes God's potential inside of a born again Believer who is sharing his or her precious time and labor with you in the business.

Your employee could create an invention that could change the direction mankind is heading in your nation and prosper the business beyond measure. You rarely know! Even though all the disciples lived with Jesus for three and one-half years, the only one that knew Jesus was the Messiah, the Christ, was Peter; and he was revealed that by God the Father (Matthew 16:16-17). God's Business Servants' duty is to go deep in God and encourage the employees to go deep in their relationship with the Lord and live their potential. With this purpose at the forefront in your mind, God will cause you and your employees to go wide and bless the world with knowledge, wisdom, and understanding, along with unique and anointed ministry callings.

Therefore, you really do not know the potential of the employees who are working with you, so treat them with respect. God did not make any of us to be slaves of someone else. We are truly and only the bondservants of the Lord. Once saved, God adopts every Believer as His royal children. Even be careful how you treat those whom you meet as strangers in the business. You do not know if they will be saved and what part of Christ's image, likeness, and steward and their work in the advancement of God's Kingdom they accomplish and fulfill in their lives.

GOD WILL NOT DEMAND ANY TASKS FROM HIS BUSINESS
SERVANTS THAT HE HAS NOT ALREADY PLACED THE
AUTHORITY AND POWER TO PERFORM THE TASKS

As employers, God's Business Servants should delegate authority and power to mature their employees by them successfully handling the daily incremental problems encountered in the business. Every employee was born with certain talents given by God. The focus of God's Business Servants is to discover those often-hidden talents in each employee and help activate those talents for the benefit of customers, clients, and the successful operation of the business. Some employees may have a gift of encouragement. We hired a receptionist in my law office, named Bunnie, and we had five secretaries and clerks and the coffee room was always disarranged, with coffee stained cups. Bunnie would come in early, have the break room totally clean, with every cup washed, and when I and the other partners came in, she would immediately bring us a cup of coffee. We all praised her, thanked her, loved her, and were all there for her when her husband died. Following her lead, employees started cleaning their own cups and cleaning up their own messes, and Bunnie would just smile and say, "thank you."

When a manufacturer creates a product, it designs the product with the capacity to perform the purpose for which the manufacturer wanted it to accomplish. Every product has a manufacturer's manual which describes what services or tasks the product can accomplish if the product is used according to the manufacturer's specifications. How can the manufacturer know what the product will do before you use it? Because the manufacturer always builds into the product what he is going to demand from it.

God used the same principle when He created you as His Business Servant that He wants you to apply to your soon to be, or already have, Christian employees. God built in your employees in seed form what He is going to call them to accomplish the business purpose in the vapor time they have on earth. The Bible is our Creator's design specifications and operating manual, and every employee needs to know that the principles in the Bible are to be followed in the business for the betterment of all other employees, customers, and the Business Owners.

Ephesians 1:3-5 says, "Blessed be the God and Father of our Lord Jesus Christ, who has blessed us with every spiritual blessing in the heavenly places in Christ, just as He chose us in Him Before the foundation of the world, that we should be holy and blameless before Him. In love He predestined us to adoption as sons through Jesus Christ to Himself, according to the kind intention of His Will."

Therefore, what God has told your employees to do, there is no room for denial or questioning because He has given them the authority, power, skills, and provision they need to accomplish what He has called them to do in the business. If your employees cannot support the vision of the business with enthusiastic effort and motivation, then tell them they should seek other interested employment where their talents can be fully utilized and where they can support that employee's vision that matches the employer's vision.

If your employees have been given a vision from God which can be accomplished within the vision of the Business Servant owner, then God has already given them the provision to accomplish it. Train your employees that "provision" is a "vision" with a "pro" connected with it. God makes each person in the business a "pro" around their assignment to fulfill the overall business vision given by God. God makes each employee a "pro" by developing and maturing his soul. 3 John 2 says, "Beloved, I pray that you may prosper in all things and be in health, just as your soul prospers." God is in the business of saving the lost, giving them a born again spirit, maturing their souls, developing their skills, and chiseling good character in them through incremental problem-solving in the daily business activity of overcoming business problems and challenges.

No word spoken or illuminated to the Business Servant by God is devoid of God's authority and power because God's word shall accomplish the purpose for which it was sent to the Business Servant (Isaiah 55:11; Luke 1:37; Psalms 33:9).

While they were growing up, some of your employees may have heard others say they were "slow" or "dumb" or "just an average person," and they may have accepted these opinions from others as fact, but it was not truth. Now, as an adult, they may have agreed with these negative opinions and have become an average employee, an average spouse, an average parent, and an average Believer. When your employees submit and humble themselves to the Lord, the Lord will put His image and likeness in their souls. When they are transformed in Christ's image and likeness, then they will exhibit the character of Christ to other employees and customers. Any negative people disparaging these employees were not from their Creator. Therefore, these negative people did not know the seed potential that God had placed in these employees. These negative people did not know how God designed your employees to be part of your business. As God's Business Servant, your duty in Christ is to help each employee find his or her God-ordained potential and encourage them to start moving in that calling. Most Believers will find their ministry potential in the marketplace. Instead of simply going to a building called "the church" and sitting in a chair or pew watching "professional ministers" work but not equipping them for the work or the ministry (Ephesians 4:11-12).

I told Believers when I was a Pastor that the missionary field started the moment they walked out the front door of the church building. I instructed them that everyone must lead the unsaved to the Lord, teach the Believers to become spiritually mature, and be an example to others in their own spiritual walk. This is real lifestyle evangelism. Believers can find more people that attend work during the week than attend Sunday morning Church services. Do not think first to invite them to Church. First, invite them to lunch, shopping on the weekend, to the movies, or to a barbecue at your home. Become their friend, and then they will want to be with you in Church. You are not just trying to find a convert, but a trusting, caring, and loving friend, who you want to lead to a loving Savior.

Whatever God has given an employee a dream determines their spiritual calling, ability, and potential in Christ. The reason is God would never give your employee a dream or desire without also giving the employee the ability to fulfill it. Your obligation as a business minister is to instill into each employee the desire to be obedient to their individualistic call of God that motivates them to run the race only He has called them to run. Yet, you should instill in each employee that it counts for little with God that the employee ran and won in a race where the employee was not registered in the tournament. Employee winning in an unauthorized race will result in little rewards even though by religious standards it seemed like an excellent work here on earth. Just because something seems good in a Humanist perspective does not mean it was ordered and directed by the Holy Spirit for the employee's ministry assignment.

If God called an employee outside of work to a street ministry, the employee would get very little rewards for trying to have a pulpit-type ministry. It may be a good work in the natural but not God's perfect ministry service for the employee. If God called the employee to be a law enforcement officer and the employee instead disobeyed and became an employee in your business, then the employee would never have satisfaction in your business and would be a less effective employee. Every employee must discover God's mission for himself or herself to build and minister God's Kingdom in a particular area or industry of society. Thus, as your employees mature in their ministry calling, do not be surprised if they leave your business when they find their true ministry calling in seeking first God's Kingdom and His righteousness (Matthew 6:33). Likewise, if God called you as His Business Servant and Minister and instead you were a pastor of a church full time, then you would be unsuccessful and disobedient to your Creator's call.

FOUR

LEARN GOD'S STRATEGIC METHOD OF THINKING

GODLY STRATEGIC THINKING COMES WITH SPIRITUAL MATURITY

Again, let us look at a word that has already been mentioned, but needs further clarity. Maturity and strategic thinking are functions of **"teleology,"** which mean "the study of where somebody is going, how they are getting there, and the motivation that has led them to go in that direction." *"Télos"* means "the mature end of the matter." The suffix *"logy"* means the "study of a particular subject."

"Spiritual maturity" means the Business Servant has gone beyond "What's in it for me in Christ mode," as self-interest Business Servants seem to be pursuing.

Business Servants must ask, "Where is God going in building His family business? What is God's teleology for me in this business as ministry?"

God's business purpose is populating the earth with Christ's redeemed, mature Believers obediently living victorious lives as Business Servants with the mind of Christ in building God's family businesses, establishing God's Kingdom, and doing God's will.

God's Business Servants must ask, "Does this business decision and activity line up with the pattern on which God's business is built?" God's Business Servants must have a Kingdom focus on what they are doing, and not adopt the world's standards of having profit as the underlying motivation for the business.

As God's Business Servant, the closer in relationship you are with God in Christ Jesus, the more "long run" in your strategic thinking you become, and the more concerned you will be in asking the right questions, such as:

The Business Servant must ask, "Where is this business as ministry going, spiritually and naturally?"

Is the purpose of this business as ministry simply to provide income for my family, or income to tithe and give offerings to my church? If so, would this be a stunted, anemic purpose?

How does the business as ministry fit into the larger purpose of God in expanding His invisible Kingdom in the hearts of men and women throughout the world, and for Jesus to have a bride without spot, wrinkle, so that she will be holy?

In this context, the Business Servant's "strategic thinking" means thinking back from the end to the beginning and establishing business plans and practices to reach God's intended purpose, not just doing business to make a profit. The Business Servant must have the mind of Christ in the operation of business and a heart that seeks the heart of God.

The Business Servant must learn to think with God's higher thoughts and act with God's higher ways. Isaiah 55:8-9 says, "'For My thoughts are not your thoughts, nor are your ways, My ways' says the Lord. 'For as the heavens are higher than the earth, so are My ways higher than your ways, and My thoughts than your thoughts.'"

Strategic thinking involves **"cash flow management"** which means managing the costs or accounts payable where possible and establishing the real cost of each project. Jesus said in Luke 14:28, "For which of you, intending to build a tower, sitteth not down first, and counteth the cost, whether he have sufficient to finish it?" Many business owners in the world take the money from a current job to finish a prior job. Eventually, it will catch up with the business and can cause God's Business Servant to breach the terms of contract with a customer or client. This is often the case in the construction business. Cash flow management also means making sure there are personnel assigned to bring in new customers or clients on a continuous basis, which would include the continuous advertisement or solicitations. Without the influx of new business, the income will stop. Cash flow management also means making sure customers and clients pay on time what they agreed to pay in their contract. Cash flow management means always paying bills, payroll taxes, business taxes, workers compensation insurance, liability insurance, filing of Statements of Information with the Secretary of State, business licenses, franchise tax, and timely filing all other government filing requirements, preparing minutes and all formalities required to maintain a *dejure* corporation or LLC.

Strategic thinking also means **"cash flow security."** This requires great caution as who are the signatories on any bank account, and these considerations cannot establish procedures for mere convenience. As the owner, God's Business Servant has to be the sole signatory on all checking accounts which have substantial money deposited and withdrawn for expenditures. If a bank account needs to be set up for workers to obtain parts, nails, wood, etc at one of the supply stores, such as Home Depot, then a special account with a small amount on deposit can be used; and the Personnel Manager can use a debit card, but this account has to be routinely checked each week by God's Business Servant regarding that supply account's use and a strict accounting by the Personnel Manager has to be reported with receipts. Personnel fuel cards also are an area of abuse when company vehicles are driven for both personal use and business use. An area of abuse is service stations allow the fuel cards to be used to purchase food and drinks and other items sold in the stores. Thus, a policy has to be established. If an employee finds a way to steal from God's Business Servant's business, then he or she is a thief and has larceny in his or her heart. As the Pastor of the business, you have to oversee the minds, emotions, and hearts of your Personnel. You do not want to have thieves and liars in your business, because the thief seeks more to steal and the liar becomes habitual and cannot be trusted with company responsibility or secrets. Ephesians 4:28 says, "Let him that stole steal no more: but rather let him labour, working with his hands the thing which is good, that he may have to give to him that needeth." Being honest and truthful are issues of the heart transformation, so the Business Pastor needs to teach his or her employees through studying the word of God. Humility and prayer invites God to purify their hearts. If there is no change replace the employeee.

Strategic thinking involves **"resource planning**," which means God's Business Servants must become God's asset managers, involving:

Strategic thinking involves **"procurement of assets**," so you have the proper resources available for the employees necessary for them to do their part in the business.

Strategic thinking involves **"allocation of assets**," so the building assets are divided that is necessary for each department of the business.

Strategic thinking involves **"deployment of assets**," so the assets are sent and used by the employees needing those assets for their portion of the work required.

Strategic thinking involves **"personnel planning**," which means God's Business Servants must become God's personnel managers, involving:

Strategic thinking is **"Complying with all State and Federal statutes and laws regarding Personnel Rights**," covering immigration law, minimum wage, paid or unpaid vacation times, personal time off, holidays, family death leave, medical emergency leave, pregnancy leave, disability leave, non-discrimination laws, Americans with Disabilities Act, leave for military service, and all laws protecting the rights of employees against discrimination and on the job harassment.

Strategic thinking involves **"Personnel Workplace Safety and Disciplinary Action"** is intended to fairly and impartially correct Personnel behavior and performance problems early on and to prevent reoccurrence. The Personnel must understand and agree that disciplinary action may involve any of the following: 1. verbal warning, written warning, 2. temporary suspension with or without pay, or 3. termination of employment. The Personnel or employee must understand and agree that the type of discipline depends on the severity of the problem, the frequency of occurrence, and if there is a history of discipline of the employee. Strategic thinking must involve establishing a solid base of no toleration for unloving acts, such as physical fighting or other violence, sexual harassment, verbal teasing or harassment, discrimination of any kind under federal and state laws, continuous violations of rules, theft, dishonesty, lying, substance abuse, or any other violation of standards that are not permitted in God's business. Finally, a strict procedure to investigate in a timely manner any workplace allegation of harassment (verbal, physical, or sexual harassment) must be established. This will involve gathering evidence and speaking to relevant witnesses. All parties and witnesses must be interviewed independently and the proper disciplinary measures taken.

Strategic thinking involves "**procurement of qualified personnel**," so God's Business Servants have the properly trained tradesmen and professionals available who can competently perform the services needed for customers or clients.

Strategic thinking involves "**allocation of personnel**," so the qualified personnel is assigned that is necessary for each department of the business to timely perform the services promised to a customer or client.

Strategic thinking involves the timely "**deployment of personnel**," so the personnel sent connects with the assets sent to timely perform their portion of the work or services to fulfill the contractual obligations promised to the customer or client.

The Principle of Incremental Growth

One of the greatest truths in God's Kingdom involving His economic principles in the created universe is the "Principle of Incremental Growth." The principle is that: "All complicated things are built on basic things incrementally constructed according to God's pattern." God matures His Business Servants and the employees by giving them problems to solve daily. As business managers and other employees become responsible and more skilled at handling smaller or simple problems, then the Business Servant should grant more responsibility to manage bigger and more complex problems.

Staying With Your Combat Strategies

As a Business Servant, you should stay with your combat strategies that God reveals to you. Since the wealth of the wicked is laid up for the just, what the wicked have acquired in wealth has to be taken from them as spoils after spiritual warfare. To invade the marketplace with your product or service, you must use God's pattern for strategic thinking. Strategic thinking also means holding to the business plan while you are undergoing spiritual pressure, temptation, or tribulation. Winners in combat are the well-trained soldiers who can stick with their warfare strategies. The wiles of the devil are designed by him to try and make you abandon the business plans and become paralyzed with fear and overwhelming stress.

Business Servants must know the strategies of the enemy. The devil uses the pressures, temptations, and tribulations of life to take the Business Servant away from God's warfare strategies. Satan and his kingdom of darkness ruling in this fallen world designs life's pressures, temptations, and tribulations to take you out of your God ordained business purpose. Sometimes, by your own sinful ways through sowing bad seed, you cause your own pressures, temptations, or tribulations by entertaining natural stimuli from just living in a fallen world. God can use these circumstances to help you lean on Him to walk in the spirit and not in the flesh. Occasionally, when the pressures, temptations, and tribulations of life become habits, God leaves you alone for a season, so you can experience the reaping of these pressures, temptations, and tribulations of life, as God will test you to see how deeply embedded in you are your abilities and willingness to walk in the spirit and not in the flesh. You must not lose your hope, and you must stay steadfast in your allegiance and love of the Lord. You must develop good, spiritually-mature friends who will join you in prayer and not condemn you while you are experiencing these pressures, temptations, or tribulations.

What pressures, temptations, or tribulations will pull you out of your God-chosen prophetic purpose? What pressures, temptations, or tribulations will pull you out of the spirit and have you resort back to your flesh? What is the lesson you must learn as you build God's business or profession as part of God's venue as your ministry for His manifested Kingdom here on earth? The lesson is that God wants to give you His godly model as a pattern to build His business as a ministry, and neither success nor failure will pull you away from God's business plan for you.

The further lesson is that God wants His Business Servants as His ministers with the specific task of maturing His children who work in the business through the daily problem-solving tasks while conducting business. The overall lesson is God wants to use His Business Servants to transplant His Kingdom and His Kingdom principles into the world system through business transactions and relationships. Finally, God's lesson is to train Business Servants as His warriors to tear down the gates of hell that have been established by the Kingdom of darkness, and especially to open gates of opportunity closed to Believers by the god of mammon.

Do not allow apparent success or apparent failure to pull you out of God's business plan for you. Always remain a funnel for money to flow and pour into others and ministry and be a servant to help others with your wisdom, knowledge, understanding, talents, engiftments, and money acquired because you are God's humble Business Servant.

When Satan sees he cannot stop you through frontal assault and pressures, temptations, or tribulations, he will hide behind you and push you through circumstances faster than you can manage your resources in the business as ministry to wear you out and take away your zeal to serve the Lord with your whole heart. Therefore, you need to have discernment and strong relationship with God. David was a man after God's own heart (Acts 13:22).

Building God's Kingdom business with an accomplished salesperson as the CEO may hurt and stall the business unless the business has the accounting and management base to live with what the sales team generates. Yet, trying to run the business with a CEO whose only emphasis is to reduce expenses may also stall the business, because there might be too much attention placed on reducing costs instead of spending for advertisement and greater service by adding on more employees to increase new customers. The best leader of a business is one who knows how to bring balance and coordinate all phases of the business from business planning, sales, asset management, customer service or product fulfillment, and employee management. It is very important to know your customer or client base, their ability to pay, and the quality of product or services they desire to purchase.

Worldly monetary success can be a Christian Business Servant's greatest enemy when it moves him or her away from God's business plan. If one studies the failure story of any once large business, often, you can see biblical principles being violated. Sometimes, the failure can be betrayal within the company. Other times the failure can be caused by the ego inflation of its leaders, which gave them a sense of superiority and careless-ness. There is an old saying, "The further up the ladder you go, the more your behind is showing." When you become successful, you become a target of competitors. Competitors in the world, and Business Servants who are immature regularly become jealous and envious of the success of others.

God's plan for Business Servants is still strong and viable. Spiritually, God's plan for Business Servants was not set aside after man's fall into sin in the Garden of Eden. God had already made provision by begetting His only begotten Son, our Redeemer, prior to the foundations of the World to establish as a pattern of being about the Father's business (Zechariah 1:17-21; Luke 2:49; Colossians 1:15-18; Hebrews 1:2-13; 1 Peter 1:20).

AUTHORITY IS EXTENDED BY GOD AND RECEIVED BY HIS BUSINESS SERVANTS IN SHARING KNOWLEDGE AND RESPONSIBILITY AS GOOD STEWARDS OVER SOME PORTION OF HIS CREATION

Divine healing is the ability to lay hands on someone and the understanding of the authority in Christ that Business Servants have over the material world. So, Business Servants should be about God's business of laying hands on the sick and seeing miracles of healing at the workplace. Divine healing is the understanding that Business Servants can invite the Holy Spirit to bring the spiritual realm into the natural realm to manifest a physiological change. The ability to heal depends on the depth of illumination God's Business Servants have that God has given to the Business Servants authority in the spiritual realm because of what Christ Jesus has already accomplished to effectuate a healing in the material world of a person's body. Submission by God's Business Servants includes obedience in entering God's rest to allow God to bring His good works to operate to mature the Business Servants and through the Business Servants to minister to others. These principles related to divine healing also apply to God's Business Servants regarding their authority over managing God's assets here on earth. All spiritual authority over God's natural creation is activated by humility, submission, and following God's spiritual laws, precepts, principles, and timing.

In this context, "faith" simply is the believing in and inviting God's power and authority in Christ as the Holy Spirit leads to bring about a covenantal promise to fulfill God's Kingdom business purpose. Faith is the ac-ceptance that God has given the Business Servant the power and authority to manage the material world to do His will here on earth. Then, as you are led by the Holy Spirit, you can say, "God prosper me as Your Business Servant, so Your will may be done here on earth as it is in heaven."

Accepting, believing, acknowledging, and moving as God manifests His power and your authority that you have in Christ over the material world is the operation of faith in your life. Whether its praying to rid a sick person of a disease, handling a business problem, changing a material part in a machine, or planting, cultivating, and harvesting a crop on a farm, it can be done by faith in God (Mark 11:23-24). However, true godly dominion over things of this world can only be experienced while acknowledging and submitting to be in Christ, Who has been given all power and authority and rulership over all created things. The clarity you have in believing, understanding, and willfully submitting to acting only by the delegated power and authority in Christ over your assigned place and part of the material world produces spiritual blessings first and then natural prosperity second without any sorrow added to it. Proverbs 10:22 says, "The blessing of the LORD, it maketh rich, and He addeth no sorrow with it."

God's Purpose is to expand God's Kingdom here on earth through the work of His Business Servants using God's knowledge, understanding, wisdom, authority, power, and engiftments over a certain portion of God's natural creation in the material world to conduct God's Kingdom business here on earth (Ephesians 1:18-23).

God's Kingdom will be expanded by Business Servants, as members of the Lord's *Ekklesia,* who faithfully conduct and manage God's business purpose of bringing God's moral and ethical order to God's created natural world. (Genesis 1:26-28; Matthew 11:28 30; Luke 19:13; Romans 8:17; Mark 10:29-30). God's eternal training program begins here on earth and continues beyond the Church Age, through the Kingdom Age, and then throughout eternity. The Lord's *Ekklesia* is both a Kingdom spiritual government assembly and a Kingdom spiritual military assembly. Thus, as members of the Lord's Kingdom government assembly, Business Servants have to become wise under rulers of the Lord. As members of the Lord's Kingdom military, Business Servants can become military strategists as officers to win Kingdom battles against the Kingdom of darkness and the fallen world forces.

Like other Believers in God's *Ekklesia,* Business Servants must accept the fact that we are citizens of heaven, and that we are here in a foreign land trying to fulfill God's purpose of bringing the Kingdom of God here on earth as it is in heaven (Matthew 6:10). Our land where we live belongs to the Kingdom of God. The United States, or the country you live in, is an alien nation to us. Philippians 3:20 says, "Our citizenship is in heaven." Similarly, 1 Peter 2: 11 says that Believers are strangers and pilgrims in a foreign land while 1 Peter 2: 9 proclaims, "But ye are a chosen generation, a royal priesthood, a holy nation, a peculiar people; that ye should shew forth the praises of him who hath called you out of darkness into his marvelous light."

Like other Believers in God's *Ekklesia,* Business Servants have been chosen as Christ's Kingdom Ambassadors here on earth. 2 Corinthians 5:20 says we are government officials in Christ's Kingdom, when Paul said, "Now we are ambassadors for Christ ...." An Ambassador is one who travels to a foreign land representing the country or Kingdom where the Ambassador is a citizen. All Believers owe our first allegiance to Christ, the Son

King of the Kingdom of God. We are government officials in the Kingdom of God, and we all are appointed to represent our Son King and His Kingdom here on earth doing the Father's will of reconciling mankind back to Him and taking possession of the earth back along with the world system to the Father. The entire Godhead lives inside of truly born again Believers to guide us, empower us, and cleanse our souls (John 14: 16 & 23).

Like other Believers in God's *Ekklesia*, Business Servants have been chosen by God to be members of the Lord's Kingdom military as His Ministers in a certain venue here on earth to do a Kingdom work. Speaking of His *Ekklesia* as the Kingdom military, Jesus said in Matthew 16:18-19, "And I say also unto thee, that thou art Peter, and upon this rock I will build my church (military *Ekklesia*); and the gates of hell shall not prevail against it. And I will give unto thee the keys of the Kingdom of Heaven: and whatsoever thou (military *Ekklesia*) shalt bind on earth shall be bound in heaven: and whatsoever thou shalt loose on earth shall be loosed in heaven." Paul said 2 Timothy 2:3-4, "Thou therefore endure hardness, as a good soldier of Jesus Christ. No man that warreth entangleth himself with the affairs of this life; that he may please Him who hath chosen him to be a soldier." Business Servants know there is a transfer of wealth to the Business Servant to use in furthering the gospel of the Kingdom (Matthew 24:14) and repentance and remission of sins (Luke 24:47), so God gives the abundant wealth as spoils of war (Joel 2:18-27; Proverbs 13:22).

BUSINESS SERVANTS MUST LEARN AND PRACTICE SPIRITUAL WARFARE AGAINST THE KINGDOM OF DARKNESS

There is a lot of spiritual warfare in the business world in the natural since Business Servants are going up against the god of mammon, which was the only false god Jesus said competed directly against God for gathering servants to serve it (Matthew 6:24). Just as Wisdom is personified in Proverbs 1:21–33, mammon is personified in Matthew 6:24 and Luke 16:13. Jesus' words here show a powerful contrast between the worship of the material world and the worship of God. Later, writers such as Augustine, Danté (The Divine Comedy), Milton (Paradise Lost), and Spenser (The Faerie Queene) personified Mammon to show the sinister nature of materialism and its seduction of humanity. Mammon is often described as "money," "wealth," or "riches." 1 Timothy 6:10 says, "For the love of money is the root of all evil: which while some coveted after, they have erred from the faith, and pierced themselves through with many sorrows."

For the Lord to use His Business Servants to take the spoils that are in the world for the financing of Kingdom work and to bring back possession of the world system to the Father, Business Servants need to learn to be skilled prayer warriors and spiritual warfare strategists. Paul said in 2 Corinthians 10: 3-6, "For though we walk in the flesh, we do not war after the flesh: (For the weapons of our warfare are not carnal, but mighty through God to the pulling down of strongholds;) Casting down imaginations, and every high thing that exalteth itself against the knowledge of God, and bringing into captivity every thought to the obedience of Christ; And having in a readiness to revenge all disobedience, when your obedience is fulfilled."

Similarly, Business Servants need to put on the full armor of God as they engaged in the world's financial system. Paul said in Ephesians 6:10-18, "Finally, my brethren, be strong in the Lord, and in the power of his might. Put on the whole armor of God, that ye may be able to stand against the wiles of the devil. For we wrestle not against flesh and blood, but against principalities, against powers, against the rulers of the darkness of this world, against spiritual wickedness in high place. Wherefore take unto you the whole armor of God, that ye may be able to withstand in the evil day, and having done all, to stand. Stand therefore, having your loins girt about with truth, and having on the breastplate of righteousness; And your feet shod with the preparation of the gospel of peace; above all, taking the shield of faith, wherewith ye shall be able to quench all the fiery darts of the wicked. And take the helmet of salvation, and the sword of the Spirit, which is the word of God: Praying always with all prayer and supplication in the Spirit and watching thereunto with all perseverance and supplication for all saints."

God's Business Servants are not in a lesser ministry calling just because they are involved in the stewardship of God's physical creation.

God's Business Servants have holy callings, and they can function in the offices of the apostle, prophet, evangelist, pastor or teacher engiftments while operating the businesses as ministry; but their vocation is always as kings, lords, priests, ambassadors, and soldiers in God's Kingdom here on earth.

Their stewardship responsibility from God is for His Business Servants to manage the material world through the spiritual leading of the Holy Spirit in the spiritual world.

God's Business Servants are required to build God's businesses and mature the souls of the employees and co-owners therein, according to God's pattern as contained in the word of God and the leading of the Holy Spirit.

Most Business Servants want profitable businesses with no problems. This is not God's biblical approach to business because God will send the problems with His authority and power to transform their minds, emotions, and wills to mature them to have the character of Christ to manifest the Kingdom of God and the fruit of the Spirit in the marketplace.

In other words, God's pattern is to send you, as His Business Servant, with the authority and power to help you with your responsibility to solve the problems He gives you; so, you can be spiritually transformed and matured into the likeness and stature of Christ, not just to do business to make money to support yourself and your family, but to be a spiritual leader in the body of Christ.

God constantly monitors His Business Servant to see how he or she is using the authority and power He has transferred to him or her to solve the problems He sends. God gives His Business Servant authority and power the old-fashioned way – he or she has to earn it incrementally through competent and adequate stewardship. God makes sure His Business Servant is a good investment before He gives him or her more authority and power, which are always balanced with greater responsibility.

God wants you, as the employer to use the same pattern to train and mature your employees. Using this pattern, Business Servants should ensure an employee proves he or she is responsible in managing the current authority and power before he or she receives any more authority and power. In other words, God's authority and power to get wealth are given incrementally to God's Business Servants as they can handle the responsibility of the wealth, for the wealth is given through them to the Body of Christ; so God can fulfill the covenants God has made prophetically to Abraham, Isaac, Jacob, Moses, David, and His Only Begotten Son, Christ Jesus.

In Luke 15:11-32 is the story of the "prodigal son." This is a parable of when authority, promotion, and responsibility are granted based upon a person's potential rather than the person's faithfulness. How many of you Business Servants have promoted an employee too soon and given business authority and power to a young "dynamo" just to regret it later? The greatest problem is the tragedy of premature promotion in business, giving somebody authority and power, or giving an heir an inheritance before they have the godly character attributes and wisdom to know how to manage that authority and power and wealth. Authority and power in immature hands lead to abuse of subordinates and customers and the waste of assets and substantial parts of family estates through selfishness and inexperience. God chooses Business Servants and asset managers based upon the condition of their hearts not in the potential of their engiftments or talents. God is more concerned with promoting "character" than He is rewarding "charisma."

In other words, God does not give *exousia* authority based upon potential or engiftment, but faithfulness, hard work, and obedience. Unrestrained raw power accomplishes little in God's Kingdom. The exercising of authority and power without compassion and love is not the Kingdom way. Competence is not just meeting the economic goals and the timetables set for accomplishment. God's Business Servant must have competence in handling relationships with employees and customers.

Business problems overseen by employees should draw out of the employees, character traits, consisting of teamwork, courage, creativity, faithfulness, deferred gratification, God dependency, wisdom, knowledge, understanding, patience, compassion, love, and perseverance. Problems reveal areas where godly character has been developed, but also reveal areas where character flaws of self-exist where soul maturation is still needed.

As an employer, and as God's Business Servant, you carefully should be assessing the way each employee performs when he or she oversees problems as opposed to emphasizing the completing of goals. How an employee handles problems reveals the level of maturity of his or her character. If an employee loses his or her temper with subordinates or customers when problems arise, then you should require re-training, anger management, and checks and balances. Does an employee violate ethical mandates or principles just to make a sale, win a discussion or argument, or to look competent in the eyes of the employer? Does a manager or leader insist other employees stop what they are working in their assigned tasks just to ensure the manager or leader finishes his or her work on time? If he or she is unethical in business dealings, then he or she is dishonest. This is a serious character flaw. Dishonesty will lead to theft, excuses for non-performance, and eventually damage the business reputation.

The work of solving problems cleanses people from selfish ambition, presumption, and ignorance. Problems reveal levels of maturity or immaturity. Solving business problems causes employees to conduct business in a way that increases the good will of the business for the enhancement of the employer Business Servant and the stability of the business to ensure employees' continued employment.

If an employee has too high of an opinion of himself or herself, and feels he or she is too skilled to do the menial tasks, let him or her go because he or she will not be a true servant to others as he or she will always first try to determine if the task is part of his or her job description. When this employee is granted power or authority, he or she will eventually turn on you, steal your customers, try to set up a competitive business on the side, always will be talking to other Business Owners for better job opportunities with the promise to bring the trade secrets she or he has stolen from the current employer. Also, he or she may create problems in the business by spreading gossip or by setting up scenarios where other employees will fail and lose favor with the employer. He or she will be motivated more towards self-advancement than being a servant to others. You will not be able to build the business on him or her in the long run.

God always builds from the view what is best in the *long run*, and any employee who has pride, eventually dismiss him or her from employment once it is determined that he or she will not change. If the employee says, "This job is a waste of my talents," get rid of him or her. God's principles work through humble and submissive servants, not egomaniacs, who are obsessively egotistical or self-centered.

Working in a business owned and operated by Christians should be like the difference of going to a Christian school as opposed to a secular school. God's Business Servants must be accepted as part of the Church. Ephesians 5:27 says Christ wants a Church without spot, blemish, or wrinkle, but that she should be holy and blameless. Working in a godly business is like attending a Christian school instead of a secular school. Most Christian parents know it is better to send their children to Christian schools, and Father God is no different. Thus, as the best Father, God's desire is to send His children to work in a business operated by Believers. What better place to cleanse His children from the sins in the world than in God's businesses where His Business Servants are conducting business while applying biblical principles Monday through Friday. Employees will hear the same principles in business as they hear in teachings each week from the pulpit in Church, so they are receiving practical applications of the word preached by the Pastor while conducting business during the week. Eventually, God's children will learn that they have been working in business ministries and that God's Church is also in the marketplace.

How does God sanctify His Business Servants? One of the ways God cleanses His Business Servants is by cleansing and sanctifying them by the washing of water by the word of God (Ephesians 5:26). The Greek in this scripture for "word" is *rhema*, not *logos*. *Rhema* means when God's written word comes alive to you as the Holy Spirit witnesses to you that a particular scripture applies to you personally in the circumstances you are facing in your daily business work. In the context of Ephesians 5:26, the use of the Greek word, *rhema,* means God will personally convict you with His word, which in turn will agitate your rebellious nature. His living *rhema* will scrub you clean. The washing blades in His *rhema* will beat the dirt out of you. Yet, the agitation process is getting rid of the sin, immaturity, and rubble in your life. The debris of your past struggles will be removed by God before the building process can begin. The Holy Spirit cannot lay the solid foundation of Christ in the business unless you clear away the rubble first. Sometimes, God wants you to build His business with burnt stones, those who have been in so many fiery circumstances they have gone through burn out. What the world calls people who are burned out and useless God sees as living burnt stones and worthwhile, which He can use as building material to build a wall to protect God's people. Nehemiah 4:2 says, "And he spake before his brethren and the army of Samaria, and said, 'What do these feeble Jews? Will they fortify themselves? Will they sacrifice? Will they make an end in a day? Will they revive the stones out of the heaps of the rubbish which are burned?'"

Unfortunately, most Believers in business want to get out of the washing machine before the cycle is done. The washing blades of God's activated word discipline Business Servants and set them separate and apart from the world. Then, God will pour on more soap to start the cycle over again in another area of a Business Servant's life He wants to clean. The moment a Business Servant thinks he or she is clean or delivered in a particular area just means God will now go to another area of his or her life to reveal more dirt that needs scrubbing. Most Business Servants do not like this process, and they put up a resistance for a season. When they do, they may be required to relive the season of washing and sanctifying again and again until God makes them clean. When a Business Servant cries out to God and says, "God I never will do that again," and this is truly a heartfelt covenant with God, then God will know His Business Servant is cleansed in that area.

God often will give His Business Servant time to "dry" in a desert place until the Business Servant cries to be delivered from the heat of the desert and beg for water. God gives His Business Servant water. It's the water in His washing machine again. The Business Servant is allowed to drink some of the water before God adds the soap and cleanses him or her in His water that is being agitated for cleansing. Whenever a traveler in a desert comes to an oasis, he will first drink the water, but then he will bathe and even wash his clothes in the pool or stream of water. Most mature Business Servants, after cleansing in several areas of their souls, know that this cleansing is an expression of God's love.

God wants His Business Servant to become a mature man or woman of God that has a pure servant's heart. God then intensifies the Business Servant's spiritual gifts to prosper him or her abundantly because the Business Servant has become a funnel with the gift of giving the wealth of the wicked into God's Kingdom work to preach and establish God's Kingdom in the workplace and preach the gospel of repentance and remission of sins to the unsaved.

Finally, to finance the teaching and cleansing of the saved ones to be spiritually mature, God will use harsher cleansing methods for His Business Servants because the love of money is the root of all kinds of evil. 1 Timothy 6:10 says, "For the love of money is the root of all evil: which while some coveted after, they have erred from the faith, and pierced themselves through with many sorrows." Matthew 6:24 says, "No man can serve two masters: for either he will hate the one, and love the other; or else he will hold to the one, and despise the other. Ye cannot serve God and mammon."

As God's Business Servant, if you are looking to start or purchase an existing problem-free business, you are looking for a dirty business. If a seller represents that he has worked hard to bring morality and hard work in building his or her business, be hesitant in purchasing the business. You will be purchasing a business with ongoing problems that need your hands-on attention for their resolution. If you will submit to God's cleansing of your soul, and be patient, God will pass much wisdom to you and teach you how to spiritually evaluate a business, not based on a balance sheet or an income/expense accounting. After years of solving business problems using God's biblical principles, you will be God's mature Business Servant. Always make it a condition to spend time in the business to personally examine its operation for a few months in order to determine if the seller's representations are accurate or is instead a fabrication and if boasting is involved as to the business' value. If you cannot be at the business, personally, send a trusted manager to do it, and let him come back with a good or bad report. If the business is not as effectively managed or profitable as represented, and you still want the business, then offer a lower price that is closer to its real value. When you acquire biblical principles and wisdom from above, people, saved and unsaved, will come to you with honor and respect, seeking the divine wisdom that you possess from God to solve their problems.

Avoid the "pie in the sky" business opportunities. Especially avoid completely any business opportunity that solicits you to be dishonest or where you know that the businesspersons receiving the capital or loan are going to hurt or jeopardize other people or that causes other people to fall into sin. For example, never buy or invest in a liquor store, a night club, or a gambling casino. You belong to God and His Kingdom, not the world or the Kingdom of darkness, so God will not bless such a business in the long run.

Likewise, avoid involving yourself in broker deals where you introduce people to someone looking to borrow money or requesting capital in the business where you are promised to receive a commission. You have no control as to how the investment or loan money is to be used. If you make those introductions, and the lenders or investors do not receive the return of their money, and if a complaint is filed by any of them, the state Corporation Commission or the Federal Securities Exchange Commission may serve you with a subpoena, which is very stressful. Under the "co-conspiracy law" even if you made just an introduction, there is a potential civil or criminal liability involved. If you are not a licensed securities agent, it is unlawful to receive a referral commission. Also, if the person asking for the money to be paid to him does not have the proper documents disclosing the risks in the transaction and does not qualify the lenders or investors, then a possible securities violation has been committed. You should always seek proper legal counsel first, but money lost by friends by your introductions severely hurts friendships. It is the problem-solving activity and regular product sales, or services rendered, using biblical principles that will keep the business clean and prosperous in the long run. Generally, most extraordinary business deals leave too many loose ends that will later cause serious entanglements that need unraveling.

Thus, godly authority and power is not given through experience or a specific event, but as a result of incremental daily stewardship of God's physical creation and spiritual engiftments that when properly used bring maturity in all people who are involved in promoting and operating businesses with biblical principles. Never try to get rich quick, unless you are sure that God wants you to take the risk in faith. "Get rich quick" deals go against God's work of maturing His Business Servant ministers, along with employees, through the daily incremental problem-solving tasks encountered as Business Servants.

GOD'S BUSINESS SERVANTS ARE GIVEN AUTHORITY
AND POWER TO PROTECT THE FATHER'S BUSINESS
AGAINST THE KINGDOM OF DARKNESS

Jesus said to Simon Peter in Matthew 16:18-19 that "I also say to you that you are Peter, and on this rock (revelation) I will build My church (Ekklesia - military), and the gates of Hades shall not prevail against it. And I will give you the keys of the Kingdom of Heaven, and whatever you bind on earth will be bound in Heaven, and whatever you loose on earth will be loosed in Heaven." God's business man and woman have delegated authority through Christ to bind the Satanic powers of darkness from stealing from the business. As a born again child of God, the business man or woman also has the authority to loosen the storehouse of blessings from the spiritual world to come into the natural realm as he or she is led by the Holy Spirit. This transference of wealth is done through studying God's word, prayer, praise and worship, and faithful obedience to our loving Father God. You have to develop a ear to hear the word of God in order to walk in faith (Romans 10:17)

"How God anointed Jesus of Nazareth with the Holy Spirit and with power, who went about doing good and healing all who were oppressed by the devil, for God was with Him" (Acts 10:38). In turn, Jesus has given His Business Servants His delegated authority and power through the Holy Spirit, Who lives in us, to go around doing good and healing all who are oppressed by the devil. I personally have seen several miracle healings done in my business office as an attorney at law. I have never prayed for a client unless the client requested prayer. Then, together, we are participating in the exercise of freedom of religion that is guaranteed in the First Amendment of the Bill of Rights. God is omnipresent, and He can perform His miracles anywhere. Therefore, pray for the sick right in the business office. God will honor the anointing He has placed in and on you. You will be surprised how readily He is willing to heal people in a business meeting. Again, be courteous and obtain the person's permission before you pray for him or her. Most sick people who are in business do not want to be treated like a victim. They want to be healed and get back to work. They want to be bold, strong, and energized again to be about the Father's business. In your prayer, you can speak about their strength, their servanthood, their good character, the contribution to the business as an introduction to make them come into agreement with you in your prayer of faith for their healing. Sometimes, healing takes time, and recovery from a sickness is still the divine intervention by God (Mark 16:18).

Two words in Greek, which are *dunatos* (God's possibilities) and *dunamis* (God's power entrusted to and used by man), have similar meanings. God uses both *dunatos* and *dunamis* through His business men and women to do His will and to do good works in spreading the Gospel of the Kingdom (Matthew 24:14) and repentance and remission of sins (Luke 24:47), which is righteousness, peace, and joy in the Holy Spirit (Romans 14:17). He also uses *dunatos* and *dunamis* in the exercise of His gifts to heal and prosper His children.

"Behold, I give you the authority to trample on serpents and scorpions, and over all the power of the enemy, and nothing shall by any means hurt you. Nevertheless, do not rejoice in this, that the spirits are subject to you, but rather rejoice because your names are written in Heaven" (Luke 10:19-20). Here, Jesus grants His delegated authority and power to His disciples, some who are business men and women to use them against the forces of darkness. He reminds them that their joy is in the assurance of their eternal life, not in the power and authority granted to them over the devil. A Business Servant should not become enamored with God's granted authority and power. Such comes with responsibility. Stay humble, and God will exalt you to use His greater authority and power in due season as you mature.

"Therefore submit to God. Resist the devil and he will flee from you" (James 4:7). God will not tell Business Servants to do something in business if He has not given them the authority and power to carry it out. It is God's delegated authority and power that operate in them that gives them the victory in business as they submit to Him. Business Servants can never conduct God's businesses by their own authority and power apart from God. Fallen mankind lost his authority of stewardship concerning the things of this world to the devil because of the sin in the Garden of Eden by Adam and Eve. Yet, Believers, especially Business Servants, have delegated authority and power through Christ Jesus' sacrificial offering of Himself on their behalves (Matthew 28:18). Jesus has given Business Servants His authority and power, and therefore Business Servants must conduct business in the name of Jesus, not in the name of self.

2 Corinthians 2:14 says, "Now thanks be to God who always leads us in triumph in Christ, and through us diffuses the fragrance of His knowledge in every place." As Business Servants are led by the Holy Spirit into triumphant business dealings, they overcome the forces of darkness in the world; and God spreads His Kingdom of righteousness, peace, and joy in the Holy Spirit as His business purpose here on earth. Business Servants will have tribulations in this world that are common to all people, but God delivers His obedient Business

Servants from them all through the Holy Spirit because of the redemptive work of Christ Jesus. 1 Corinthians 10:13 says, "There hath no temptation taken you but such as is common to man: but God is faithful, who will not suffer you to be tempted above that ye are able; but will with the temptation also make a way to escape, that ye may be able to bear it." Yet, Business Servants must always give the glory for business success to the Lord Jesus Christ.

Isaiah 54:17 says, "'No weapon formed against you shall prosper, and every tongue which rises against you in judgment you shall condemn. This is the heritage of the servants of the Lord, and their righteousness is from Me,' says the Lord." Since you are in Christ, and if you do all things as an obedient bondservant of Christ, then Satan's weapons and accusatory tongue will be directed at Christ, and not you. Satan already has lost his headship rights as against believers because of the sacrificial work of Christ (1 John 3:8), and the devil attacking Christ's obedient Business Servant, who is innocent of any wrongdoing, will not prevail.

Apostle Paul made his living as a tent maker Business Servant when he was not traveling on the mission field (Acts 18:1-3). Notwithstanding, while he worked in his tent making business during the week, Paul still ministered in the local Synagogues on the Sabbath (Acts 18:4). Paul said in 2 Corinthians 11:9, "...and in all things I have kept myself from being burdensome unto you, and so will I keep myself." While they are not on the mission field, Pastors with a small congregation should develop a business to support themselves and their families, so they are not a burden on the Church. Also, a Pastor can be an example for other Believers in the congregation; and the Pastor, too, can help people in need.

Paul said that he suffered persecution, "And out of them all, the Lord delivered me" (2 Timothy 3:11). Business Servants will suffer various persecutions while doing the Lord's business (2 Timothy 3:12), but they, too, can have faith that God will deliver them. Even if they die, they will still have life because of receiving eternal life through Christ Jesus. As the Lord's apostolic Business Servant, Paul declared, "For to me, to live is Christ, and to die is again" (Philippians 1:21).

In Hebrews 11, there is a wonderful record of our Old Testament forefathers and foremothers who were mostly business men and women. They stood in faith during persecution before the arrival of the Messiah. Hebrews 11 also has the account of a few of New Testament men and women Believers who died as martyrs after Jesus ascended into the Third Heaven.

Business Servants will suffer trials and tribulations in the businesses as they do and teach the commandments of the Lord Jesus Christ, make disciples of all nations, and preach the gospel of the Kingdom (Matthew 24:14) and repentance and remission of sins (Luke 24:47) to all people with whom they come into contact. Business Servants must look to the hope of their final heavenly rewards and then fight the good fight of faith in conducting godly business practices while they remain here on earth.

In addition, God prospers His Business Servants here on earth as they submit to His will, repenting from their rebellion against God. The word "repent" includes confession of sins, but its real meaning is to change one's thoughts in the mind, feelings in the emotions, and beliefs in the heart. Repent also means the way one perceives things and ideas and cognitive thinks, emotionally feels, and heartfully believes about those things and ideas. The word "repent" means to turn around from the sinful direction and start a new direction seeking God intimately. Likewise, God actively prospers families of God's faithful Business Servants, arming them with spiritual weapons to fight against the Kingdom of darkness. Preaching the gospel of the Kingdom (Matthew 24:14) and preaching repentance and remission of sins (Luke 24:47) include the benefit of personal salvation, which is a gift, but it costs a lot of money, effort, and time these days to send the gospel of the Kingdom (Matthew 24:14) and repentance and remission of sins (Luke 24:47) to the people around the world who need it. God's Business Servants are important ministers in the body of Christ. It also costs a financial commitment to send children of God's Business Servants to private Christian schools, so the children can pray, worship the Lord, and bring the Teacher of all truth, the Holy Spirit, into the classroom to train them to live and operate with biblical principles of business and life, itself. The secular university professors may not want to mention the source of the best economic principles in the universe, namely, those in the Bible; nevertheless, God's biblical economic principles should be taught on the university level. Allowing your children to work in God's business during school breaks, and seeing you conduct business, will have a spiritual impact on their lives as they mature into adulthood.

"I can do all things through Christ who strengthens me" (Philippians 4:13). "You are of God, little children, and have overcome them, because He who is in you is greater than he who is in the world" (1 John 4:4). Do God's Business Servants have authority and power from and through God to do His will with the mandate to train His children to live by His biblical principles? Are Business Servants to use this delegated power and authority to do the will of God here on earth? The statement that "I can do all things through Christ which strengthens me" does not mean Business Servants can create galaxies. It just means that whatever God has assigned a Business Servant to do, he or she can do through the delegated authority of Christ and the power of the Holy Spirit to fulfill the will of God in their lives.

John 10:10 refers to the devil as the "thief," who comes to steal, kill, and destroy. How many Business Servants have been "ripped off" in business? In Proverbs 6:31, it says, "But if he (the thief) is found, he shall restore sevenfold; he shall give all the substance of his house." Business Servants need to demand the return what the thief has stolen from them in the businesses, along with a sevenfold return and all that is valuable in his (Satan's) house; so, Business Servants can continue doing the Lord's business.

God is a covenant making and a covenant keeping God. Covenants are contractual understandings based upon committed personal relationships, which God has made with his ministers carrying on His Kingdom business. "And the God of peace will soon crush Satan under your feet..." (Romans 16:20). Whose feet are referred to as "your feet?" "Your feet" refers the feet of the body of Christ. The body of Christ has a covenant with God in

Christ Jesus, and they can totally rely on what He has promised here on earth if they will submit everything to Him. God's Business Servants must be ready to fight daily against the temptations of the god of mammon. Business Servants need to place the god of mammon under their feet where it belongs.

Even if Business Servants die in the business struggles, they still have victory. To be absent from the body is to be present with our Lord Jesus Christ (2 Corinthians 5:8). As one of God's Business Servants, it is time that you repent and change the way you think, emote, and believe the way God does, which will change the way you conduct business Then, through mature Business Servants like you, God can change the hearts of men and women and once again take back the possessory rights of His creation that the devil through fraud stole from Eve while Adam committed high treason in eating the forbidden fruit from the Tree of the Knowledge of Good and Evil.

THE
BIBLICAL
WORK
ETHIC

FIVE

BELIEVER'S VOCATIONAL CALL MAY BE DIFFERENT FROM
HIS ECCLESIASTICAL CALL

Apostle Paul was a Business Servant who was also an Apostle.

Paul's Business: Tent maker

Paul's Ministry: Apostle

Paul worked as a Business Servant as a tent maker where he also shared the gospel of the Kingdom (Matthew 24:14) and repentance and remission of sins (Luke 24:47) to customers and those with whom he came into contact. He was about the Father's business while he worked in business. Paul did not see the difference between his place of business, a home fellowship, or ministering any other place to people. God is omnipresent, and God instructs His servants to spread the Kingdom of God, the goodness of God, and to bring salvation, healing, and prosperity to all people in all places. Paul was primarily the Apostle to the Gentiles and started many fellowships, especially with the Greeks.

Peter's original Business call was a fisherman. After Jesus' resurrection and again after Jesus' ascension at times Peter operated his fishing business as God's Business Servant. At the same time, Peter also ministered the gospel of the Kingdom (Matthew 24:14) and repentance and remission of sins (Luke 24:47) to the unsaved and taught the saved the words and acts of Jesus, while doing healings, as an Apostle of the Lord. Peter left his business to be run by trained employees while he pursued special missionary trips, he attended leadership meetings in the new Church, and he fulfilled God's mandate to go as Christ's witness from Jerusalem, Judea, Samaria, and to the uttermost parts of the known world. Peter had a tremendous anointing. In Acts 5:1-11, Peter sat in judgment over the sins of lying to the Holy Spirit of Ananias, with Sapphira regarding their offering. In Acts 5:15, Peter walked around with healing virtue, "Insomuch that they brought forth the sick into the streets, and laid them on beds and couches, that at the least the shadow of Peter passing by might overshadow some of them."

God is trying to show business men and women their vocational call in the business world is also a ministry outreach for a hurting, dying, and lost people, and as a center where God's wisdom, knowledge, and understanding, truth, and Christ's law of liberty abound. The business as ministry activity is not to be considered as carnal, and the body of Christ needs to sow into businesses where the Business Servants are submitted to Christ, are being led by the Holy Spirit, and are practicing the principles of God's Kingdom motivated by love.

WORK IS A HOLY, ETERNAL CALLING

When Adam was first created, he was placed in the Garden of Eden. Genesis 2:15, 19-20 says, "And the LORD God took the man, and put him into the Garden of Eden to dress it and to keep it . . . And out of the ground the LORD God formed every beast of the field, and every fowl of the air; and brought them unto Adam to see what he would call them: and whatsoever Adam called every living creature, that was the name thereof. And Adam gave names to all cattle, and to the fowl of the air, and to every beast of the field; but for Adam there was not found a help meet for him."

In the Garden of Eden God required Adam to work to dress and keep the garden and take care of the animals. As time passed, none of humanity was sent into the world to be idle. God equipped humanity with cognitive thinking, stable emoting, and Godly believing with a free will, so we would have the innate talents in our souls and bodies to perform work that God directs us to do here on earth. God also gave humanity the earth as our possession, as our place of habitation, and as our place upon which we are to engage in work.

After salvation by accepting Jesus as Savior and Lord, God chose our bodies to be His Temple. Our vocational work as kingdom spiritual Kings, priests, lords, ambassadors, and soldiers is God's mandated holy profession. Thus, as sons and daughters of God as Creator, and now by adoption through Christ Jesus, while we live in this world, and especially after salvation, we have work to preach the gospel of God's Kingdom here on earth and preach repentance and the remission of sins.

The Kingdom service of Business Servant is to preach and teach the benefits from Jesus' death on the Roman Cross and His resurrection, along with seeking first the Kingdom of God and His righteousness. With that foundation, the Business Servant is to provide food, shelter, clothing, transportation, and reasonable luxuries for the Business Servant family and employees. With this mandate, our bodies and souls belong to the Lord, along with our time. If we are transformed in our souls, with our minds renewed, our emotions stabilized, our hearts having purity in beliefs, and our wills submitted, then we will do our Business work as unto the Lord and not for our own self-aggrandizement. Then we will see that stewardship of God's physical creation, and being about the Father's business, as we follow the leading of the Holy Spirit, has the same spiritual value as when we are on our knees praying, studying the Bible, or praising and worshiping the Lord. Being a herdsman or a farmer had great honor as the first professions given by God for man to do (Genesis 9:20; 26:12, 14; 37:7). If you are obedient to God's call, there is true pleasure in working the business God calls you to do. Adam was about the business God called him to do, and he would not have been content if he had been idle.

Work is a holy calling, and God expects every able-bodied man or woman to work, whether as a farmer, chef, waitress, mechanic, construction worker, teacher, lawyer, doctor, tradesman, truck driver, accountant, police-man, fireman, government servant, businessperson, or a stay home mom or dad raising children. God does not like idle people. 2 Thessalonians 3:10 says, "For even when we were with you, this we commanded you, that if any would not work, neither should he eat." 1Timothy 5:8 says, "But if any provide not for his own, and especially for those of his own house, he hath denied the faith, and is worse than an infidel." God wants to employ all His children. God does not want His children to be idle and unhired because God uses work to mature His children and to make them useful servants in His Kingdom. People who continuously collect government unemployment or welfare out of laziness is missing out on God's training that comes through work. What employer will hire you if you do not have work experience? There are jobs everywhere and people do not want them because of the pay. The answer is to work at the low paying job for a few months while looking for something better.

If you have Christian employees, as the Christian employer you should require more from them than the unsaved employees. When you hire Believers, tell them you will fire them quicker than if unsaved because "To whom much is given, much is required" (Luke 12:48). This is how God operates.

SINCE GOD ALWAYS IS WORKING, THEN HE IS THE PATTERN TO FOLLOW. GOD FIRST REVEALS HIMSELF AS A CREATOR, A WORKER, AND THEN AS AN ENTREPRENEUR

Work preceded sin and the fall of man in the Garden of Eden. Work also preceded marriage, as Adam was assigned work before God brought forth Eve. Thus, a young man should be settled in his God ordained work assignment before seeking a God ordained spouse.

Jesus taught that work is eternal. John 5:17, 19-20 says, "But Jesus answered them, 'My Father has been working until now, and I have been working.' ...Then Jesus answered and said to them, 'Most assuredly, I say to you, the Son can do nothing of Himself, but what He sees the Father do; for whatever He does, the Son also does in like manner. For the Father loves the Son, and shows Him all things that He Himself does; and He will show Him greater works than these, that you may marvel.'"

Again, Jesus worked as a Carpenter and Stonemason; but even in His early youth, He knew He had to be about His true Father's business (Luke 2:49).

GOD IS A WORK ASSIGNOR, A REPLICATOR OF HIS ONLY BEGOTTEN SON, A PATTERN BUILDER, A REST PARTICIPATOR, AND A GUARDIAN OF HIS CREATION (GENESIS 1)

A good builder of God's business is a work assignor just like Father God – God's pattern is to assign work to others with accountability. Require your employees account to you daily or weekly as to the work done, whether the work done followed the pattern for the assigned task, and whether the timetables for each part of the work assignment has been accomplished. Delegation of authority without training and supervision of an employee is neglect by the Supervisor.

A good builder replicates the uniqueness that God has given him in his building process. As the artistic Creator, God never makes anything twice, and all things created has in them God's stamp of distinctiveness. God used His only begotten Son Who was in the bosom of the Father as the Pattern to create the spiritual and natural worlds. Hebrews 1:2 says, "Hath in these last days spoken unto us by His Son, Whom He hath appointed Heir of all things, by Whom also He made the worlds." Ephesians 3:9 says, "And to make all men see what is the fellowship of the mystery, which from the beginning of the world hath been hid in God, who created all things by Jesus Christ." God sees everything created as part of His artistic design. God made each human as one of a kind. Even though every human looks, walks, talks, and thinks like a human, every human being is exceptional with a different physical appearance and an individualistic personality.

A good builder of business follows the dictates of the Architect as everything is designed with a pattern to follow. Everything God created came from His patterns, and His patterns are from His artistic designs.

A good builder of business enters rest after the job is completed to restore and maintain the powerful potential to proliferate his talents once again. Genesis 2:3 says, "And on the seventh day God ended His work which He had made; and He rested on the seventh day from all his work which He had made."

A good builder of business guards and protects what he has built to ensure it is used only for the purpose it was built. This includes protecting your ideas by applying for trademarks, copyrights, and patents.

Business Servants should establish the above five principles of work. The promise of a work free Third Heaven, work free earth during the Millennium, and work free Kingdom age at the time the New Jerusalem comes down to earth is aberrant theology at best and interferes with God's work of maturing the saints at worse.

Nowhere in the Bible does it say that the Third Heaven, back here on earth during the Millennium, or at the time the New Jerusalem comes down to earth will be work free.

God says that the Third Heaven, back here on earth during the Millennium, and at the time the New Jerusalem comes down to earth are places where work is done more efficiently because the devil is removed. During the Millennium, the devil is thrown into a pit for a thousand years, and then at the White Throne Judgment Seat he is thrown into the Lake of Fire with the Kingdom of darkness, death and the grave, along with those unsaved (Revelation 20: 11-15). The removal of the devil will be to God and His work as is the removal of debris from the tracks of a running train. God's work will be unhindered by the devil, yet God will still have to deal with people born in sin here on earth during the ages to come whom are descendants of Adam (Revelations 21: 24,27; 22:15). Thus, those who have died and are resurrected are here on earth in the Kingdom Age continue doing the work of the Lord reigning and ruling with Christ over the people of the earth. Revelation 5: 9-10 says, "And they sung a new song, saying, 'Thou art worthy to take the book, and to open the seals thereof: for thou wast slain, and hast redeemed us to God by thy blood out of every kindred, and tongue, and people, and nation; And hast made us unto our God kings and priests: and we shall reign on the earth.'" Similarly, 2 Timothy 2:12 says, "If we suffer, we shall also reign with Him...."

The Third Heaven, back here on earth during the Millennium, and at the time the New Jerusalem comes down to earth, and the ages to come thereafter are not going to be the final retirement center for the saints of God. God's Kingdom in Heaven or Earth is not the ultimate weekend fun in the sun experience where you relax on the beach or a mountain retreat, but it is a place where we co-labor with Christ eternally. Ephesians 2:10 says, "For we are His workmanship, created in Christ Jesus for good works, which God prepared beforehand that we should walk in them."

THIS TEACHING OF A WORK FREE THIRD HEAVEN, BACK HERE ON EARTH DURING THE MILLENNIUM, AT THE TIME THE NEW JERUSALEM COMES DOWN TO EARTH, AND THEREAFTER, REVEAL PRESENT DAY BELIEVERS' ANTI-WORK ETHIC

This laziness affects the entire economy in American society. The current accounts deficit and the import export deficit in the United States are evident of the prevailing anti-work ethic. The problem is these two economic indicators in the U.S. are growing in other countries. It now is expanding into Japan and Korea and other in Southeast Asia, although the work ethic is much stronger in these competitive economies. We are not going to be able to deal with the current accounts deficit and import export deficit without a major change in the American work ethic. There are blocks of people in the U.S. who want a Socialist, cradle to grave support because they do not want to work. We should recapture the strong work ethic in America that was instilled in the foundation of American beliefs and came primarily from the Puritans. It will be hard for Americans to compete with the Japanese, Koreans, Chinese, Vietnamese, and Germans who still have better work ethics, unless we get back to the biblical work standards upon which many of the Great Industrialists conducted business, and which, for the most part, were originally predicated.

The Church is partly responsible for the problem of teaching the antiworker attitude because the Church leaders are fearful of urging that work is required of the Believer after initial salvation, for fear that some Believers will interpret this teaching to mean that work is required to receive the initial salvation of the Lord unto eternal life. The Church Leaders have misunderstood the differences in the audiences that Ephesians 2:8-9 addresses unsaved man cannot be saved by works, lst he boast while Ephesians 2:10 addresses a saved man is God's workmanship created as a vessel for God's good works. Also, Paul is addressing already saved Believers in Philippians 2:12-13 when he writes that a Believer must work out his salvation or maturation of his soul with fear and trembling by allowing God's works to operate in him and through him. Similarly, James 3:17 requires the Believer to combine work with faith by saying that faith without works under God's authority and power is dead. Likewise, Ephesians 4:12 encourages the Believer to do the work of ministry, as the job of the apostle, prophet, evangelist, pastor and teacher in Ephesians 4:11 is for the equipping of the rank-and-file saints for the work of the ministry as stated in Ephesians 4:12. Thus, work after initial salvation is commanded by God, but it must be done under the leading of the Holy Spirit. Working out one's own salvation means that work is used by God to cause one's spiritual maturation and must be done in accordance with biblical principles and by the leading of the Holy Spirit.

As God's Business Servant, like all other Believers, you are designed by God to put your life into your work with excellence and zeal (John 1:27). Only the true biblical work ethic can activate Believers in any culture or nation. Work is an issue of the heart, where your will resides. The heart is a place where the foundation of your belief system directs your actions. You will do what your heart believes is right as opposed to what your mind thinks is a good idea. Sometimes, the spiritually right thing to do may make no sense in your mind because the wisdom is from above and not from this natural world. Yet, later on you usually learn why the Holy Spirit instructed your heart instead of your mind, as it was a spiritual matter and not a natural matter. It is only through the Christian faith in Christ Jesus that mankind can have an intimate relationship with the true Creator who uses work as a tool for maturation of His children (John 14:6; Ephesians 2:10; Philippians 2:12-13). You must know the truth from God's word, and obey those principles of truth, before you can be set free from the bondages of this world and sin of slothfulness (John 8:31-32).

God puts His *zoe* life in His natural work. All natural living things with its natural life were made alive with God's *zoe* life from His spiritual dimensions. When Jesus instructed His disciples how to pray in Matthew 6:10, He said, "Thy Kingdom come. Thy will be done in earth, as *it is* in heaven," He taught His disciples to pray that God's spiritual Kingdom from the Third Heaven come to the natural world and bring *zoe* life here on earth, which is life abundantly. God's Kingdom is a working Kingdom that works in Believers' lives. For this reason, Believers are commanded to seek first the Kingdom of God and His righteousness, and all things here on earth would be added to them (Matthew 6:33). Believers need to repent of this anti-work ethic and accept and inculcate in their lives God's work ethic. When Believers start doing God's work assigned to them, they will find His purpose, plan, and a better and more fulfilling life.

We have promoted an anti-work ethic in the Church by teaching from the pulpit that the Third Heaven, back here on earth during the Millennium, and at the time when the New Jerusalem comes down to earth, into the "ultimate weekend playtime." This is simply an unbiblical teaching.

Why are the "Crown of Life" (James 1:12), "Crown of Glory" (1 Peter 5:4), "Crown of Exultation" (2 Timothy 4:8), "Incorruptible Crown" (1 Corinthians 9:25), and "Crown of Rejoicing" (1 Thessalonians 2:19) given by our Lord at the Judgment Seat of Christ? It is to reward those for their ministry work done here on earth, and it is to promote those who have become spiritually mature through obedient work to rule and reign with Christ throughout eternity in the Kingdom Age back here on earth when Jesus comes and sits on His Throne in the

New Jerusalem. The Third Heaven is not run by a Socialist or Humanist philosophy. Our Lord is a benevolent, loving King. God promotes those into higher authority who have become obedient to His call here on earth before they die to work with godly obedient character.

The Kingdom of God under the rulership of our Great King is not built upon the principle of Socialism or Humanism, as God rewards those who are faithful and who diligently seek Him (Hebrews 11:6). God's heart is full of grace and mercy, institutes giving and receiving as His economy, and decrees love and justice for the faithful and humble.

There was an injection of "Reformation Theology" in the American economic psyche in the 1600's through the Puritans. Part of the Puritan ethic was the work ethic. This Puritan work ethic played a major role in the Great Industrial Revolution of America. America's greatness economically was at its height in the Industrial Revolution which caused tremendous wealth in many industrial families such as the steel magnate, Andrew Carnegie, the automobile mogul, Henry Ford, the banking investor, J.P. Morgan, the oil tycoon, John D. Rockefeller, and the railroad builder, Cornelius Vanderbilt, which are five of the great Industrialists that laid the foundation for America to become the greatest free enterprise society in history. Before the Industrial Revolution, the United States was more of a second world country, with most people living in farming communities, but these Great Industrialists ushered post–Civil War United States into the industrial modern era that outdid all European countries at that time.

However, it was in the early 1900's in the U.S. that the popular concept of the workers' escape from problems and going to a work free Third Heaven. To attract members into church this work free heaven anemic teaching became the popular sermons preached from the pulpits in churches.

The American people in the early 1900's began to view in a deeper way work as a curse and the ultimate pleasure weekend as the goal of the acquisition of business and income. Before the early 1900's, work was seen as a godly virtue which caused maturation, good character, good parentage examples, and good citizenship. In those days, you worked to increase your talents, to become a mature person of character, to be a godly Business Servant, to make a better life for your family, to have a family dynasty of several generations, and to be a respected voice in your community and church because of your charitable giving.

If you examine the obituaries in newspapers in the late 1800's with those after the turn of the Century in the early 1900's you would find in the late 1800's that when someone died, he was described as being a good man with good character, his religious background, and what was his reputation in the community. After the ideas of Socialism expounding the rights of the proletariat became the cry of the workers, then when someone died, his obituary would list what he did as a business, profession, or worker, which class of society he belonged, what part of town he lived, and the fact he was married with the number of children. The fact that he was a good man, a church attendee, the good he did for the community, or his charity work often would not appear in the obituary.

Promoting new business startups by promising bigger houses, expensive cars, yachts, expensive vacations, and a work free lifestyle is not biblical. Proverbs 21:17 says, "He who loves pleasure will be a poor man; he who loves wine and oil will not be rich."

Look at most of the business startups advertised on the internet. What do they promote as ideas to motivate people to buy their package for starting a new business or joining their marketing company? They use the lifestyle of the rich and famous as being big homes, new cars, yachts, vacations, ocean cruises, and basically self-indulgence as motivating people to work short term instead of work being a holy lifetime calling of service and a maturing process of God.

The world ideas teach that we should spend our *capital on recreation* instead of spending our capital in discovering ways of the following:

Working better,
Increasing skills,
Carrying out God's purposes,
Capturing a market share for the next generation,
Putting money into research and development to ensure that your children's children have the latest inventions with which to sell, and
Setting aside money in savings for future expenditures to avoid debt.

The Church leaders should teach the biblical principles of God's economics once again to bring back a good work ethic in America as a biblical obligatory heartfelt belief. You should work because it is a holy calling of God.

Americans are not going to see a fundamental lasting change in the economic situation of America, or any nation, until the Church repents of its anti-work attitude and views work as a blessing and divine calling which Believers are motivated to put their lives into to have an estate to pass on to their children and children's children as mandated in Proverbs 13:22, just like God puts His life into His work for the benefit of His children. Socialist Politicians are trying their best to bring Socialism into the mainstream of acceptable political thought in the U.S. and in other nations. Socialism is anti-biblical, anti-God, but is also antichrist.

If Christian business leaders can instill the revelation of the godly concept of the work ethic to employees and other church members, then they will cause a financial revival in this nation. Subsequent generations will praise them for doing their godly duty. Perhaps, Business Servants can recapture the greatness God intended for this country, a melting pot of all other nationalities. "One nation under God...." that is establishing God's

Kingdom and doing His will here on earth as it is in heaven.

WHAT GOD DOES NOT LIKE IS UNHIRED PEOPLE DOING NOTHING!

Matthew 20:1-15 is the parable of the "unhired men" whom the owner of the vineyard found in the marketplace.

The world in their Socialist and Humanist mindset complains that at the end of the day the workers who worked through the heat of the day got the same wages as the men hired near the end of the day.

Socialists and Humanists read into this parable the injustice of higher wages for less work.

However, from God's perspective, the tragedy was idle lives that were "unhired" and not working. Idle lives are unproductive, immature, without developed talents, and without provision. Titus 3:14 says, "And let ours also learn to maintain good works for necessary uses, that they be not unfruitful."

What we need to come to as church leaders, Business Servants, and fathers and mothers is to see the misfortune of men and women's engiftments rusting away because no one has hired them and called them to perform up to their potential to fulfill their purpose in Christ.

God dislikes the fact that Believers come to church and just sit in chairs or pews, listen to a teaching or sermon, drop some money in the offering plate, leave the building, and do nothing to enhance the Kingdom of God during the normal work week. A lot of this complacency is because Believers have not been activated and told that there is a holy calling to work for the Kingdom after initial salvation.

Everyone has to work in God's Kingdom. Angels work as ministering spirits to the heirs of salvation here on earth (Hebrews 1: 14). God commands His children to be His Ambassadors here on earth and to spread the promise of reconciliation (2 Corinthians 5:19-20). Thus, Believers, especially God's Business Servants, are working ministers, not spectators.

Leaders who teach a message there is no work for Believers to do after initial salvation except to come to church, listen and pay for a teaching each Sunday morning, and just wait for the Rapture, is aberrant theology. God's discipleship of His Business Ministers is not done just in a lecture hall called a church building. God's discipleship is on the job training at home, in the marketplace, in school, and in government. Dicipleship training is done with one-on-one fellowship, then in a group setting, but always under the leadership of the Holy Spirit.

Paul came against those Believers who set around doing nothing while waiting for the Lord's return, who went from house to house to live off other people. 2 Thessalonians 3: 10-12 says, "For even when we were with you, this we commanded you, that if any would not work, neither should he eat. For we hear that there are some which walk among you disorderly, working not at all, but are busybodies. Now them that are such we command and exhort by our Lord Jesus Christ, that with quietness they work, and eat their own bread."

The Church leaders need to activate people into their God's appointed work assignments. This will help when church members are sent into the marketplace looking for a job. In order to accomplish this, church leaders need to preach and teach both a pluralistic Kingdom gospel and an individualistic Kingdom gospel. Church leaders need to preach and teach also repentance and remission of sins, as relevant herein, the sin of laziness. We are saved into God's family and have work responsibilities. We are saved into the Kingdom of God and are subjects, or citizens, for our King, Christ Jesus. We are not saved just to receive eternal life and go to a vacation spot called Heaven. The gospel of the Kingdom (Matthew 24:14) and repentance and remission of sins (Luke 24:47) mean you are mandated to be about the Father's business here on earth seeking the unsaved in need of salvation and maturing those already saved children who are doing God's business in the marketplace. Jesus instructed His disciples to preach the gospel of the Kingdom and repentance and remission of sins here on earth while you are alive. Jesus taught God's Kingdom come and God's will be done in earth as it is in heaven (Matthew 6:10).

God's Kingdom rules regarding work carry their own results, which operate under the agrarian principles that govern sowing and reaping, that forbid sowing mixed seed, that require the responsibility of sowing into good soil, that mandate good stewardship over the seed entrusted, that command care and cultivation as the seeds grow into mature plants for proper harvesting of the fruit or grain, and that call for extraordinary work at time of harvest to ensure a "profit" is made for the business of God and God's children. God is in the business of harvesting souls. Jesus said in Luke 10: 2, "The harvest truly is great, but the labourers are few: pray ye therefore the Lord of the harvest, that He would send forth labourers into his harvest."

POSSESSIONS AND INCOME GAINED BY WICKEDNESS WILL BE LOST, AND THE WICKED WILL SUFFER

"Wealth gained by dishonesty will be diminished, but he who gathers by labor will increase" (Proverbs 13:11).

"The righteous eats to the satisfying of his soul, but the stomach of the wicked shall be in want" (Proverbs 13:25).

"A faithful man will abound with blessings, but he who hastens to be rich will not go unpunished" (Proverbs 28:20).

"The labor of the righteous leads to life. The wages of the wicked to sin" (Proverbs 10:16).

"He who works deceit shall not dwell within My house. He who tells lies shall not continue in My presence" (Psalms 101:7).

HE THAT IS SLOTHFUL MAKES EXCUSES NOT TO WORK

"The lazy man says, 'There is a lion outside! I shall be slain in the streets'" (Proverbs 22:13).

"He who is slothful in his work is a brother to him who is a great destroyer" (Proverbs 18:19).

"The lazy man will not plow because of winter; he will beg during harvest and have nothing" (Proverbs 20:4).

"In all labor there is profit, but idle chatter leads only to poverty" (Proverbs 14:20).

"He who has a slack hand becomes poor, but the hand of the diligent makes rich. He who gathers in the summer is a wise son; he who sleeps in harvest is a son who causes shame" (Proverbs 10:4-5).

God has called Business Servants to work with Him in building wealth, which includes character, skills, and relationships that will pass on to the next age into the Millennium, the age of the coming of the Holy City from Heaven, and the ages of eternity thereafter, whatever they will be.

Paul tells us in 1 Corinthians 3:9-15, "For we are God's fellow workers; you are God's field; you are God's building. According to the grace of God, which was given to me, as wise master builder I have laid the foundation, and another builds on it. But let each one take heed how he builds on it. For no other foundation can anyone lay than that which is laid, which is Jesus Christ. Now if anyone builds on this foundation with gold, silver, precious stones, wood, hay, straw, each one's work will become clear; for the Day will declare it, because it will be revealed by fire; and the fire will test each one's work, of what sort it is. If anyone's work which he has built on it endures, he will receive a reward. If anyone's work is burned, he will suffer loss; but he himself will be saved, yet so as through fire."

First, God enlists fellow workers to manifest and establish His Kingdom here on earth. Second, God sees your heart as a field where He plants His word which grows and produces faith, spirit, life, harvest of good works, good character, and fruit of the Spirit. Third, God has a building plan to build His temple, which is inside members of the body of Christ, and His business is to transform their souls to make them acceptable places for His dwelling and to be spiritually minded, spiritually emotional, spiritually believing, and spiritually willful in all they do.

Each person's work will be tested by fire in this life, but judgment is after death. In the context of Scripture, the work described here is the building of relationships, which is a far greater work than the work of making money. Making money is considered by God as a "little thing" (parables of the talents and minas) as far as eternal rewards are concerned, although the Master expects you to be faithful in this "little thing" of the matter of handling money. In Matthew 23:23 Jesus said, "Woe unto you, scribes and Pharisees, hypocrites! For ye pay tithe of mint and anise and cummin, and have omitted the weightier matters of the law, judgment, mercy and faith. These ought ye to have done, and not to leave the others undone."

If you build on the foundation (Jesus Christ) represented as gold, silver and precious stones, you will be rewarded, but if you build on the foundation (flesh) represented as wood, hay or straw, you will suffer loss through fire. You will still be saved, but the teaching by Paul is a reference as to how much rewards you will receive at the Judgment Seat of Christ.

You must be concerned whether your work passes through the fire. This means whether you have built the business according to God's pattern as being a place primarily to mature His children, expand His Kingdom through economic evangelism, and bring the wealth of the wicked into the hands of the just. Establishing lasting relationships and being about the Father's business of maturing yourself, the business partners and your employees are what God considers as gold, silver, and precious stones. From that place and work as God's Business Servant, you can start making disciples of all or ethnic groups, starting in the business.

When you die, if the Lord tarries, the only things you will take with you is the work you did according to God's pattern and the godly character and skills you obtained by being obedient to your God ordained calling, along with the people you brought into the Kingdom and made disciples of them into the use of godly managerial and entrepreneurial leadership skills as teachers who will teach others to teach (2 Timothy 2:2). This work is the gold, silver, and precious stones of the Lord.

If the work is in the spirit, it passes through the testing of fire, which are the circumstances encountered in life. If the work is of the flesh, it does not pass through the testing fire but burns up and does not last multi-generationally nor throughout eternity.

What God is looking at when you come in front of the Judgment Seat of Christ is not the perishable assets you have accumulated through your labors, but those entrepreneurial leadership skills you will have acquired and have taught others to acquire in building God's business according to His pattern.

The question is: "Did God's Business Servant who died take with him 'eternal work skills,' so Father God can use him in applying those work skills in the next phase of his eternal life beyond the grave?" OR "Was the person who died a 'Christian businessman' who just made a lot of money?"

God has no problem in giving and sharing His material wealth to those who will build His business according to God's pattern in Christ. He is more interested in the **incremental maturing process** that managing God's creation as a good steward is doing to His children as they have relationship with Him and with each other. God is interested in how many other Believers His Business Servant trains with management and entrepreneurial teaching skills, as well as bringing in new Believers into His Kingdom.

Hebrews 6:10 says, "For God is not unrighteous to forget your work and labour of love, which ye have shewed toward his name, in that ye have ministered to the saints, and do minister."

The goal of God's Business Servants should be to start an economic revival in the local, businesses, and communities through the local Church, first, and then inclusive of your nation, and then all other through the Christian Community. The second revival in Joel 2, commencing with verse 17 and going to verse 27 is the pouring out of the wealth that is in the to finance the end time revival where the Spirit is poured out on all flesh (verses 28-29) to wind up the age. Thus, the Joel 2 revival started on the Day of Pentecost, as Peter stated that the Day of Pentecost was the fulfillment of Joel 2: 28-29, but there is an end-time intense move of the Holy Spirit to wrap of the Church Age before the coming of the Lord. There have been continuous moves of the Holy Spirit during this end-time dispensation. The goal of the Lord in these end-times encompasses the activation of Christian business and professional men and women in business as ministry to be God's Business Servants. These activated business and professional servants will learn and then teach and activate others in God's economic stewardship training principles. Economic stewardship training principles include the teaching that Believers must build God's business according to God's pattern personally in their own local sphere of influence, and then expand this teaching and training nationally and internationally to finance the further expansion of God's Kingdom through economic evangelism and individual maturity for the edification of the entire body of Christ.

God's pattern is that He wants to build in us, His Business Servants, His character to teach others, and impart eternal motivations in our character and skills to expand His multi-peopled business that He calls His Church and the Kingdom of God. God's pattern is for His Business Servants to impart this God chiseled character and skills into their God directed businesses because only these godly character traits and skills establish the firm foundation of godly relationships will pass through the fire.

Those characteristics that are developed in you, and whatever characteristics you stimulated in others that are managerial and entrepreneurial in their nature, remain as permanent attributes that will pass through death as treasures in the Third Heaven, back here on earth during the Millennium, and at the time the New Jerusalem comes down to earth, or the ages to come thereafter, to your account at the Judgment Seat of Christ.

The Lord is not after only profit, but more so after individual character and managerial skills which He can use to build His Ekklesia and Kingdom here on earth.

Obedient work that is commissioned and approved by God will transcend death because such work creates in your soul godly character and skills.

Material possessions do not pass through death; only character and skills do, which is why we should not be motivated only by financial profit. Those character traits and skills are defined as:

Having godly motives as character.

Being guided by godly ethics in all transactions.

Recognizing your limitations.

Knowing your working gifts.

Staying focused on service to others.

Developing leadership management skills; and

Being a good steward of God's assets.

There are many difficulties and problems Business Servants handle in business which rob us of our time. Likewise, the pressures to perform and obtain results for money tend to take us out of our godly purpose of character and skill maturation process. However, what God wants to happen in the middle of that daily grind process is:

The continual worship of Father God as the purposeful true Owner of the business.

With the hunger to be used as Jesus' disciple, seek the Holy Spirit and request, "Holy Spirit, teach me how to handle these problems according to God's word and will."

Seek the Holy Spirit, and pray, "Holy Spirit, give me the direction and proper application of the way you want to train me in the midst of all of these circumstances bearing down on me in this business and help my faith grow."

When it is all said and done, what is important is the degree you have imparted those God developed character traits and skills to yourself, and those with whom you work. All of that development is permanent change in character which will pass through the fire.

Christian business activities and goals mean a lot more than just being a recipient of "the wealth of the wicked that is laid up for the just" (Proverbs 13:22). In order to obtain the spoils from the enemy, you cannot be a spoiled Christian yourself.

Life is a vapor of smoke. It appears for a while and then it is gone. "Come now, you who say, 'Today or tomorrow we will go to such and such a city, spend a year there, buy and sell, and make a profit;' whereas you do not know what will happen tomorrow. For what is your life? It is even a vapor that appears for a little time and then vanishes away" (James 4:13-14).

Can you imagine a nation that is impacted by ten million of Christ's business servants who have this kind of Christian work ethic? We are talking about a powerhouse of God's anointing falling on those obedient children because they will know how to manage the power to obtain God's wealth and how biblical economics really operate for the expansion of the Kingdom of God.

God's Business Servants will radically impact everything they touch with their hands, character, and skills. Their labor will generate a lot of profit because they will never work harder than when they work for the Lord for their rewards, looking forward to when they stand before the Judgment Seat of Christ. Business Servants, and people in general, work harder when they are needed; and being needed by other gives them something to work for, which changes your time here on earth from mere existence to life abundantly.

Therefore, God's pattern is for you to establish as your goal to encourage as many people working as unto the Lord for their own maturity in their God ordained work in your God ordained business. Godly profit will automatically follow toward this godly service and godly activating goals.

God's stewards of His businesses will be the recipients of the wealth of the world because employees have received a motivation to work by the wisdom from the One who created them. Godly work that causes a maturation of character traits and work skills is the primary purpose of work in the Kingdom of God. God will give you a work assignment that is designed to bring you the problem-solving opportunities that directly confront you with your ungodly character traits, just as Jesus gave Judas the task of handling the money collected because Judas had a problem with money, like the Rich Young Ruler. One would ask, "Why did the Lord, always being a perfect steward with what His Father gave Him, give the job of treasurer to Judas when He obviously knew that Judas had theft in his heart?" Jesus followed His Father's instruction in employing Judas to be the treasurer. Seeing wickedness in Judas' heart, God knew that Satan would put into Judas' heart the motivation to betray Jesus, which was part of God's plan to allow Jesus to be falsely accused, arrested, beaten, and crucified. God gave Judas many opportunities to be convicted by the Holy Spirit to repent and get right with the Lord. Eventually, Judas betrayed Jesus for thirty pieces of silver, the price to redeem a female bond slave. Judas' betrayal was part of the redemptive process under the Law of setting free the Bride of Christ. However, the redemption of the Bride of Christ was purchased not with silver or gold, but with the grace afforded by the precious blood of Jesus (1 Peter 1: 18-19).

Family businesses work best because the natural authority flows down from the parents to the children. In Nehemiah 3 & 4, Nehemiah did not say go over and build the wall and die for God, nor did Nehemiah say, "Let's go build a wall for God." He said essentially, "Work for God and work for your own vested family interest. Build the wall and fight for God, and build the wall and fight for your spouse, children and your land God has given you." Nehemiah 4:13-14 says, "Therefore I positioned men behind the lower parts of the wall, at the openings; and I set the people according to their families, with their swords, their spears, and their bows. And I looked, and arose and said to the nobles, to the leaders, and to the rest of the people, 'Do not be afraid of them. Remember the Lord, great and awesome, and fight for your brethren, your sons, your daughters, your wives, and your houses.'" Likewise, every work assignment was headed up by a "father" which is the family business concept of the Lord in His Kingdom.

God knows what motivates people, and God is the recipient of the good works derived from that kind of motivation. God has no problem rewarding people large amounts of wealth for the God ordained work assignment in handing down the wealth through the family. Abraham, Isaac, Jacob, David, and Solomon established family dynasties.

WHEN SETTING BUSINESS WORK GOALS, CONSIDER
THE USE OF GOD'S UNLIMITED POWER AND
ECONOMIC PRINCIPLES IN THEIR ACHIEVEMENT

Most people in business (even Believers) set goals that they think can be accomplished with only man-made natural power and abilities. Few set business goals hearing first from God. If they did, we would see miracles in business which will lead to miracles of finance.

If Business Servants rely on their own limited natural talents and human energies to accomplish their individual goals, then they will limit their goals to non-spiritual economic agendas they think they can achieve. God plans are impossible in the natural.

Business Servants need to set work goals where they consider the utilization of God's unlimited power. The truth is that the Lord Jesus Christ has big plans for you and other Business Servants as an integral, important part of His eternal plan to make ready Christ's Church and Bride.

Proverbs 21:5 says, "The plans of the diligent lead surely to plenty, but those of everyone who is hasty, surely to poverty." Why do most Business Servants quickly turn to the world standards in setting monetary goals instead of spiritual goals?

All work business goals must be structured to please the Lord and not to please men. "And whatever you do, do it heartily, as to the Lord and not to men, knowing that from the Lord you will receive the reward of the inheritance; for you serve the Lord Christ" (Colossians 3:32-34).

Matthew 6:33 says, "But seek first the Kingdom of God and His righteousness, and all these things shall be added to you." Jesus did not say seek first the world's remedies for the problem, seek first your own ideas for new inventions, seek first the best universities for your children to be successful in life, or seek first the economic textbooks written by university professors for the best wisdom. What God is saying is that you should seek His unlimited power, knowledge, and wisdom in His Kingdom, and your need will be provided a whole lot easier than seeking the things with only our own natural talents, education, and power (Philippians 4:19).

The reason why you should seek first the Kingdom of God and His righteousness is because economics has a spiritual element to it. The tithe is holy unto the Lord (Leviticus 27:30-34).

Many Christian parents think the best answer for their children's success in life is to pay to have them attend the greatest liberal universities with the highest prestige and reputation in the world, so their children can obtain a good education and a good career upon graduation. Yet the secular universities teach non-biblical principles of economics, life principles, and strong Socialists philosophies; and secular university professors brainwash the students to discard their Christian upbringing. What parents should be teaching their children is to find the best Church, whose leaders are teaching and activating men and women to enter the business world with biblical principles of economics and start their own businesses as God's stewards in the market-place. The amount of money for tuition and on-campus living is in the tens of thousands every year. Instead, take this money and use it as seed investment into starting a biblical-based business for your children after they have thoroughly mastered the biblical economic principles that are in the Bible and in this book.

Following the biblical principles of economics is better than the success instruction books written by non-biblitarians. Some so-called economic advisers say, street knowledge is better than book knowledge. That may be true, depending on the book being read or taught. Facts about investments and economy are in the world, but the truth principles about God's Kingdom economy are in the Bible. If you want to be successful, follow God and His economic principles, not the principles in the world system.

THE BIBLICAL WISDOM OF PSALMS 37

"Fret not thyself because of evildoers, neither be thou envious against the workers of iniquity. (2) For they shall soon be cut down like the grass, and wither as the green herb. (3) Trust in the LORD, and do good; so shalt thou dwell in the land, and verily thou shalt be fed. (4) Delight thyself also in the LORD; and He shall give thee the desires of thine heart. (5) Commit thy way unto the LORD; trust also in Him; and He shall bring it to pass… (7) Rest in the LORD and wait patiently for Him: fret not thyself because of him who prospereth in his way, because of the man who bringeth wicked devices to pass. (8) Cease from anger and forsake wrath: fret not thyself in any wise to do evil. (9) For evildoers shall be cut off: but those that wait upon the LORD, they shall inherit the earth… (16) A little that a righteous man hath is better than the riches of many wicked…(23) The steps of a good man are ordered by the LORD: and he delighteth in his way. (24) Though he fall, he shall not be utterly cast down: for the LORD upholdeth him with His hand. (25) I have been young, and now am old; yet have I not seen the righteous forsaken, nor his seed begging bread. (26) He is ever merciful, and lendeth; and his seed is blessed. (27) Depart from evil, and do good; and dwell for evermore. (28) For the LORD loveth judgment, and forsaketh not his saints; they are preserved for ever: but the seed of the wicked shall be cut off. (29) The right-

eous shall inherit the land, and dwell therein forever. (30) The mouth of the righteous speaketh wisdom, and his tongue talketh of judgment.... (34) Wait on the LORD, and keep his way, and he shall exalt thee to inherit the land: when the wicked are cut off, thou shalt see it. (35) I have seen the wicked in great power and spreading himself like a green bay tree. (36) Yet he passed away, and, lo, he was not: yea, I sought him, but he could not be found. (37) Mark the perfect man and behold the upright: for the end of that man is peace. (38) But the trans- gressors shall be destroyed together: the end of the wicked shall be cut off. (39) But the salvation of the right- eous is of the LORD: He is their strength in the time of trouble. (40) And the LORD shall help them, and deliver them: He shall deliver them from the wicked, and save them, because they trust in Him."

SIX

POVERTY IS USUALLY THE ECONOMIC CONSEQUENCES OF SPIRITUAL DISOBEDIENCE

THERE ARE UNSEEN SPIRITUAL PATTERNS FOR GOD'S BUSINESS SERVANTS TO FOLLOW

Hebrews 9:23-24 says, "It was therefore necessary that the *patterns of things* in heaven should be purified with these; but the heavenly things themselves with better sacrifices than these. For Christ is not entered into the holy places made with hands, which are the figures (patterns) of the true; but into heaven itself, now to appear in the presence of God for us."

The spiritual world is far greater than the natural world. The difference is the comparison of the size of the earth with the size of the universe.

Ephesians 1:3 says, "Blessed be the God and Father of our Lord Jesus Christ, who has blessed us with every spiritual blessing in the heavenly places in Christ." Your spiritual blessings come from heavenly places in Christ. God's Business Servants often look to earthly sources for their blessings.

Since Believers' born again spirits live in the spiritual reality of God's Kingdom, speaking with God daily, Believers' spirits live in higher dimensions than can be visualized in the natural by our bodies. There are higher thoughts in God's spiritual Kingdom which God speaks to our born again spirits. Isaiah 55: 8-9, 11 says, "'For my thoughts are not your thoughts, neither are your ways my ways,' saith the LORD. 'For as the heavens are higher than the earth, so are my ways higher than your ways, and my thoughts than your thoughts... So shall my word be that goeth forth out of my mouth: it shall not return unto me void, but it shall accomplish that which I please, and it shall prosper in the thing whereto I sent it.'"

Believers' bodies can only hear and see the sounds and things in this natural four-dimensional world. Believers' souls must walk by faith in God, not by sight to experience spiritual reality. Believers must walk in the truth. John 16:13 says, "However, when He, the Spirit of Truth, has come, He will guide you into all truth...."

How do God's Business Servants see and hear the thoughts of God that come in higher dimensions than the dimensions of the natural world? The Holy Spirit will lead Business Servants into His spiritual reality of higher dimensions, so they may know the patterns God has designed to build His businesses through His Business Servants here on earth.

Since everything has been created by God, He makes no preference in importance in scripture between His created inward spiritual reality and His created outward physical reality. All things in the spiritual and natural worlds were created as God's artistic design. God created both worlds primarily for His only begotten Son, Christ Jesus, and He declared the physical reality to be good (Genesis 1). Jesus came to share the importance of these two worlds with Believers. Jesus came to be about His Father's business, and Jesus has commissioned His Business Servants to collaborate with Him to be about His Father's business to bring the spiritual principles of the Kingdom of God into the Kingdoms of this natural world, which are currently under the rulership of the prince of this world, the devil. John 14:30 says, "Hereafter I will not talk much with you: for the prince of this world cometh, and hath nothing in Me."

Although you cannot work your way to heaven, you were created to do good works here on earth after initial salvation (Ephesians 2:8-10). In other words, Business Servants were called into business to touch God's spiritual reality and be led by the Holy Spirit into character prosperity, which then leads into financial prosperity in this natural physical reality.

As a Business Servant, and as a member of the body of Christ, you are mandated by God to walk and deal only in the truth. Otherwise, you will not be in God's spiritual reality. What is then this spiritual reality? John 4:24 says, "God is Spirit, and those who worship Him must worship Him in spirit and truth." The word "truth" can be interpreted as God's spiritual reality, which is personified in Christ Jesus (John 14:6). Thus, God's truth is spiritual reality, not just a four-dimensional natural world reality. God wants this truth inside your soul, so Christ can be all in all in your life (Ephesians 1:23).

God's eternal truth is not the things of this natural world which are subject to the Law of Entropy, or the law of sin and death, which means everything in the world is headed toward decay and death because of Adam and Eve's original sin. In God's Kingdom and spiritual realm, there is no decay or death, and everything lives in eternity. Although subject to the law of sin and death, God's physical creation still testifies of the invisible attributes of God, the Creator (Romans 1:20).

If you fail to enter God's spiritual realm at your place of business, then you will not encounter the spiritual reality of God's Kingdom. Until you touch the spiritual reality of the Holy Spirit, you will not know Who is the Personified Truth, and in turn will not experience intimacy with Him and the true freedom in and from the Lord. The patterns for business are in God's spiritual reality. Without truth, you will be confused, without wisdom, will do things by trial and error, will be attacked by the devil, and will be subject to the fallen nature in the world system if you do not touch God's spiritual reality in the business. You need know Jesus, intimately, because Jesus is the power of God and the wisdom of God personified (1 Corinthians 1:24).

Since you are called as God's Business Servant to manage, dominate, and multiply God's material creation and participate in the spiritual maturation process of those with whom you work, then it is imperative to touch God's spiritual reality daily to receive blessings and be a funnel of blessings to others. It is imperative that you gain the knowledge needed to touch the spiritual reality of God's Kingdom in the business. It is necessary that you have an intimate relationship with Jesus.

Every created physical thing has its own spiritual reality in God's Kingdom. If you merely touch this spiritual reality, you will know increasingly more about God's creation and how you can build the business here on earth according to the patterns of God in His spiritual realm.

1 Corinthians 15:38-44 says, "But God giveth it a body as it hath pleased Him, and to every seed his own body. All flesh is not the same flesh: but there is one kind of flesh of men, another flesh of beasts, another of fishes, and another of birds. There are also celestial bodies, and bodies terrestrial: but the glory of the celestial is one, and the glory of the terrestrial is another. There is one glory of the sun, and another glory of the moon, and another glory of the stars: for one star differeth from another star in glory. So also is the resurrection of the dead. It is sown in corruption; it is raised in incorruption: It is sown in dishonour; it is raised in glory: it is sown in weakness; it is raised in power: It is sown a natural body; it is raised a spiritual body. There is a natural body, and there is a spiritual body."

If you only touch the outward appearance of the business, only deal with issues as to how they affect you economically, and seek after only money, then you will be subjecting yourself and the business to the rise and fall of the market. You will suffer the stress of the roller coaster ride of the forces of this economic fallen world and the god of mammon.

In order to tap into the spiritual reality of God's blessings in the business, become active in multiplication in the business, and minister as a shepherd toward the goal of maturation of your employees and others you contact in business, then you focus to learn to touch the spiritual reality of God's Kingdom, which is spiritual and which must be manifested consequentially as physical reality for you to prosper in business.

Although spiritual realities must be expressed in words, unless the words are the *rhema* of God, they have less manifested spiritual reality, as they lack requisite faith. When you are led by the Holy Spirit to pray earnestly in and for people in the business or led by the Holy Spirit to read the word of God for wisdom about business matters, then you are bringing God's spiritual realities into the business. God's patterns for the business will be revealed to you; and the Holy Spirit will then lead you into that spiritual reality. Whenever you touch God's spiritual realities, then you hear the voice of the Spirit, speaking the words of Jesus, and obtain spirit and life, along with faith (John 6:63; Romans 10:17). If you are obedient to what you hear from God, you will then be about the Father's business in the business He has assigned to you.

Legalistic formalities are not spiritual realities. Man's traditions can make void the Commandments of God, and you will not receive the *rhema* of God. When the word of God remains only *logos*, it is the dead letter of religion instead of the spirit. Likewise, human performance is not by itself spiritual reality; yet, faith without the Holy Spirit led works is dead. You are directed to learn how to hear God and then submit to what God tells you to do. Intimacy with the Holy Spirit is required to have a personal relationship with Him to touch spiritual reality, because the Holy Spirit brings spiritual reality of God's Kingdom into your daily living. The Holy Spirit is in your workplace, your business, your home, your voting booth, and your church fellowship.

Thus, God is Spirit, and everything that you do in the business must relate to God in the spirit and not just in the natural. The lust of the flesh profits nothing (John 6:63). The Spirit of Truth is the Spirit of spiritual reality.

Spiritual reality is that which transcends the natural in business. Once your belief system moves away from the leading of the Holy Spirit, it becomes letter and form and loses its spiritual reality. If you do not touch spiritual reality in the business, you are disobedient, and the Holy Spirit will not prosper your character, as you will not be about your Father's business.

Therefore, as you are led by the Holy Spirit in the business, as you hear the still small voice of the Holy Spirit, and as you obediently walk in the Holy Spirit, then you will experience spiritual reality of God's truth which activates God's covenant promise to prosper you in your character, relationships, and finances.

God is more interested in transforming your soul to be spiritually minded in the daily operation of the business, than to bring you money, assets, or opportunities in the business. Also, if you touch His spiritual reality, He will cause you not to fall into the devices of the devil or the entrapments of this world system. In God's spiritual reality is God's spiritual protection.

In God's spiritual reality is also God's abundant life. If you want more life, and if you want the business to prosper financially, you must touch spiritual reality.

As a Business Servant, you should accept the spiritual reality that there are evil forces in the spiritual realm that you cannot see that affect you and the business. Until you enter God's Kingdom and worship in spirit and truth as your reality, you cannot have the forethought, the prophetic word, the wisdom, the spiritual knowledge, or God's wisdom of what is best to do in business. You will not understand the seasons for a given thing or the time for a chosen purpose.

John 16:13 instructs you how to enter this spiritual reality to find the truth in God's patterns for business. You have to be revealed what is God's spiritual reality and must have the resolve to be guided by the Holy Spirit into that spiritual reality or truth. "But when He, the Spirit, comes, He will guide you into all truth (or spiritual reality)." God's Spirit and Truth go together. You cannot have the Truth you need to prosper and fulfill your ministry calling until you start seeking and coming to God in spirit.

The two greatest services of the Holy Spirit are revealing of this spiritual reality and His guiding discipline. The Holy Spirit reveals the spiritual reality, while His discipline leads you into that spiritual reality.

The goal of the Holy Spirit is to reveal to you the spiritual reality and truth of God's patterns for business, and then to lead you into that spiritual reality; so that the work you will do as a Business Servant will last multi-generationally and will accomplish the spiritual purposes God called you into business for in the first place.

If you will allow the Holy Spirit to take control of your life, then you will find yourself seeking God's will in every business decision. Rest assured, every day the Holy Spirit seeks every opportunity to reveal to you His spiritual reality and God's patterns for business. As you acknowledge the source of this divine wisdom, then the Holy Spirit tries to lead you into that spiritual reality for you to experience life abundantly in God's Kingdom.

THE ECONOMIC NATURAL WORLD AND MATERIAL CREATION ARE GOVERNED BY SPIRITUAL LAWS THAT BUSINESS SERVANTS MUST HAVE IN THEIR FOUNDATION OF BELIEFS

John 1:10 says, "He (Incarnate Christ) was in the world, and the world was made through Him, and the world did not know Him." This is the fundamental truth and pattern for every Business Servant to consider.

Christ Jesus has dual natures of perfect humanity nature and His divine nature as God the Word. His humanity nature is/was the image of the invisible God and is and was the pattern through Whom all things in the beginning were created and have continued to consist.

Colossians 1:15 says, "He is the Image of the invisible God, the firstborn over all creation." Since the verse is speaking about the "Image of the invisible God," then the Author is referring to Christ's humanity nature, which is the "express image" of His divine nature, God the Word. Colossians 1:16 says, "For by Him all things were created that are in heaven and that are on earth, visible and invisible, whether thrones or dominions or principalities or powers. **All things were created through Him and for Him.**" Since the author of the Scriptures used the pronoun "Him," then one must accept he is referring to the same person to whom He was referring in verse 15. Therefore, "Him" is referring to the "He" who "is the Image of the invisible God," not God, Himself. Thus, verse 16 is referring to the humanity nature of Jesus Christ. Consequently, Christ Jesus, God's only begotten Son, the sinless Seed, was the Image or Pattern used by God to create all things in the universe, both visible and invisible.

If the pre-manifested sinless Seed was the "Image" by which "all things were created that are in heaven and that are on earth, visible and invisible," then the pre-manifested sinless Seed was the "Firstborn over all creation" because His humanity nature was the Pattern used to create all things. The Pattern is also the only begotten Son born before time began Who is the Figure, Model or Design from which all other things and beings were created. Colossians 1:17 says, "And He is before all things, and in Him all things consist." The dual natures of Christ Jesus, with his humanship nature living before the creation of all things in the spiritual and natural worlds and God the Word, as One Person was needed for creation itself and to make the universe operate and consist perpetually.

John 1:1-5 also shows how God the Word, indivisible but unconfused with the sinless humanity nature of God's only begotten Son, was in the beginning and was used in the creation of all things. "In the beginning was the Word, and the Word was with God, and the Word was God." In verse 2, however, the author of the scriptures changed to the pronoun "He," and was referring to the sinless humanity nature, which was the only begotten Son of God in His Seed potential form with His dual natures. John 1:2 says, "He was in the beginning with God." The phrase "with God" means Jesus' humanity nature. God the Word was personified in the premanifested only begotten Son of God, even before He was manifested by becoming flesh and dwelling amongst mankind (John 1:14). John 1:3 says, "All things were made through

Him, and without Him nothing was made that was made." The phrase "through Him" refers to Jesus' humanity nature. Again, this is a definite reference to the sinless humanity nature of God's only begotten Son, which was both sinless humanity and God the Word. Finally, John 1:4 says, "In Him (Jesus' humanity nature) was Life, and the Life was the light of men." John 1:14 says, "And (God) the Word became flesh and dwelt among us, and we beheld His glory, the glory as of the only begotten of the Father (sinless humanity nature), full of grace and truth. John bore witness of Him and cried out, saying, 'This was He of whom I said, "He who comes after me is preferred before me, for He was before me."'" John the Baptist said that even though Jesus' humanity nature was born after him, He really lived before him in eternity past.

Hebrews 1:1-13 is a scripture passage referring to the only begotten Son who was begotten before the foundation of the world as the Pattern or "Express Image" of God by which and through which all spiritual and natural realities were created. Hebrews 1:2-4 says that God "has in these last days spoken to us by His Son, whom He has appointed heir of all things, **through whom also He made the worlds**; who being the brightness of His Glory **and the express image of His person**, and upholding all things by the Word of His power, when He had by Himself purged our sins, sat down at the right hand of the Majesty on high, having become so much better than the angels, as He has by inheritance obtained a more excellent name than they." Again, this scripture supports the truth that Jesus' humanity nature, as the only begotten Son of God, was the Pattern or "Express Image" of God by and through whom the worlds were made. This is the same manifested humanity nature of Christ who after He had "...by Himself purged our sins, sat down at the right hand of the Majesty on high...."

Furthermore, Hebrews in the first chapter continues to explain Who it was through whom the worlds were made. Hebrews 1:5-6, 8-10, 13 says that "For to which of the angels did He ever say: 'You are My Son, today I have begotten You?' And again: 'I will be to Him a Father, and He shall be to Me a Son.' But when He again brings the Firstborn into the world, He says: 'Let all the angels of God worship Him.' ...But to the Son He says: 'Your throne, O God, is forever and ever; A scepter of righteousness is the scepter of Your Kingdom. You have loved righteousness and hated lawlessness; therefore God, Your God, has anointed You with the oil of gladness more than Your companions.' And: 'You, Lord, in the beginning laid the foundation of the earth, and the heavens are the work of Your Hands.' ... but to which of the angels has He ever said: 'sit at My right hand, till I make Your enemies Your footstool'?" Without doubt this passage of scripture in Hebrews 1:2–13 refers to the only begotten Son of God in both His Pre-manifested Incarnate form before He was born of the Virgin and as the manifested Son of Man and Son of God as the Word made flesh by being born from the woman. This passage of Scripture also refers to the only begotten Son of God after His death, resurrection, ascension, glorification, and enthronement.

Therefore, all that we do as Business Servants must be patterned after the work of Christ. Also, the economic policies of a nation must be based upon the moral principles of God and His Kingdom. Whatever we do as Business Servants, it must be the expression of agape love as we are led by the Holy Spirit. 1 Corinthians 13:3 says, "And though I bestow all my goods to feed the poor, ... and have not charity, it profiteth me nothing."

THE FALSEHOODS IN THE WORLD
THAT HAVE NO BIBLICAL BASIS,
BUSINESS SERVANTS MUST AVOID

FALSEHOOD NO. 1: It is false to say that poverty victimizes people, i.e., poverty just happens to them without any cause. Socialism treats poverty as a disease, something to be treated with money from collected taxes or government loans from the U.S. Federal Reserve.

FALSEHOOD NO. 2: Civil Government is morally compelled to reduce the inequality of wealth caused by cultural differences, instead of based upon the condition that a particular race has been deprived of capital because of outright discrimination as Afro-Americans have suffered historically.

FALSEHOOD NO. 3: Civil Government in society is to be a buffer zone or protector between people and the consequences of their own disobedience to the will of God.

GOD'S TRUTH: POVERTY IS PRIMARILY THE CONSEQUENCE
OF SPIRITUAL DISOBEDIENCE

TRUTH PRINCIPLE ONE: Business Servants must understand this very important principle of God. Since prosperity comes through obedience to God's principles, word, and the leading of the Holy Spirit, poverty comes as a result of disobedience of God's principles, word, and to the leading of the Holy Spirit. God's grace and mercy are a part of His economic principles, as can be seen by the following exceptions:

Exception 1: Children born into a family of spiritually disobedient parents are true victims for a season and deserve financial support that leads to enablement but not generational enslavement as welfare recipients.

Exception 2: Afro Americans in inner cities are true victims for a season of several generations. Poverty from the results of multi-generational disintegration of the family unit from the horrible degradation of slavery and discrimination requires a season of favor, grants, priority for employment by society to allow them to catch up educationally, financially, and politically. The United States, along with many other parts of the world, had deprived the Afro-Americans of capital accumulation generation after generation. Yet, there are Afro-American movie stars and professional sport participants that are multi-millionaires, so they do not need a handout just because they are Afro-Americans. Additionally, a blanket incentive program for all minorities is a racist policy since it would not take into consideration the economic disadvantage history of the race. For example, many Asians coming in from foreign countries do not have a history of being deprived of capitalization. Many foreigners, who technically become minorities in the country, brought substantial riches and wealth with them when they came into the country. Likewise, many foreign minorities do not have a history of being culturally deprived of equal opportunities in business and education to the same extent as the Afro Americans have been deprived in the United States historically.

TRUTH PRINCIPLE TWO: Getting people out of poverty is not going to be resolved just by giving them money without instituting a program of educational and economic opportunity enablement back into the workplace. The government grants must be used to teach them, as it were, how to fish. Throwing money at poverty without a training program for enablement in employment and business principles is like throwing water on a gasoline fire, it spreads the fire but does not stop it.

TRUTH PRINCIPLE THREE: Money can reward behavior that causes poverty. Rewarding people who are impoverished, without retraining and helping them to enter and earn money in the marketplace, can make them remain impoverished. Making people responsible for the money granted leads them in a practical way to become mature, while at the same time helps them to escape from historical poverty.

TRUTH PRINCIPLE FOUR: Risk is necessary because the possibility of failure is needed in society for maturity. People must learn there are consequences to their actions. Granting money to people without training them that loss or gain results from the consequences of one's stewardship is unbiblical.

GOD HAS HEAVENLY PATTERNS WHICH BUSINESS SERVANTS ARE
REQUIRED TO FOLLOW IN ORDER TO PROSPER AND HAVE SUCCESS
IN CHARACTER DEVELOPMENT AND FINANCIAL REWARDS

Again, Hebrews 9:23-24 says, "It was therefore necessary that the *patterns of things* in heavens should be purified with these; but the heavenly things themselves with better sacrifices than these. For Christ is not entered into the holy places made with hands, which are the figures (patterns) of the true; but into heaven itself, now to appear in the presence of God for us."

2 Corinthians 4:1, 2 & 18 says, "But we have renounced the hidden things of shame, not walking in craftiness nor handling the word of God deceitfully, but by manifestation of the truth commending ourselves to every man's conscience in the sight of God. While we do not look at the things which are seen, but at the things which are not seen. For the things which are seen are temporary, but the things which are not seen are eternal."

Business Servants must start discovering God's spiritual realities that are unseen to receive the patterns for businesses that are seen. Business Servants must touch the spiritual reality of God's Kingdom, which is their place of provision, wisdom, knowledge, and understanding of God's ways. God's heavenly things are eternal patterns for Business Servants to build their businesses here on earth in this dispensation.

God has made it easy for you, as His Business Servant, to understand His principles. He always gives you a pattern to duplicate, so you are in obedience to His word. God does not believe in trial and error. He does not want you to go through trials or tribulations, nor make errors in judgment. He tells you what to do and how to do it by a pattern He provides.

I remember that in July 1974, I took a hard six-week State Bar review course to study for the State Bar of California exam to be licensed as a lawyer. The instructors informed us law school graduates that if we followed the pattern of study that they laid out for us, listen to the lectures, and take the practice exams daily, that they guaranteed that we would pass the State Bar exam the first time. I believed what they said, and I followed what they said precisely; and I studied and followed their instructions averaging 18-20 hours a day. By being totally obedient, I passed the State Bar exam in the first time sitting. It was hard precision work, but I trusted what they promised; and I was able to build myself up with the needed knowledge and skills to pass the two-and-a-half-day exam. Yes, I had law school training from a very good, prestigious school, Pepperdine University, but I passed the Bar Exam because I followed the pattern with strict compliance. This is how God wants His Business Servants to study and learn the biblical principles of economics to fulfill God's Kingdom purpose. Romans 8:28 says "And we know that all things work together for good to them that love God, to them who are the called according to His purpose. For whom He did foreknow, He also did predestinate to be conformed to the image of His Son, that He might be the firstborn among many brethren."

THE LAWS OF NATURE ARE, IN FACT, ORDERED RESPONSES TO THE MORAL GOVERNMENT GOD HAS BUILT INTO HIS CREATION

God as Creator has built His rules into His entire spiritual and physical worlds, and these rules, laws, principles, and God's will are the guiding purpose behind all movement in His spiritual and physical universes.

God has activated His Kingdom rules, laws, principles, love, grace, mercy, gifts, and will run His created spiritual and natural worlds to fulfill His purpose.

Colossians 1:17 says, "And He is before all things, and in Him all things consist." In other words, God has put His spiritual and natural laws to work to make sure the universe runs with His order.

Also, God upholds all things by the power of His word in the active sense of history. In other words, God has a plan for mankind, and regardless of what man does or what the devil does, God's plan will still prevail.

Poverty can be the result of family curses that have roots of iniquity or rebellion handed down by your forefathers and foremothers. Poverty is one of the curses of the law. These family curses can be broken by forgiving your forefathers and foremothers, and by the application and pleading of the Cross as Jesus redeemed us from the curse of the Law when He became a curse for us by hanging on a tree (Galatians 3:13). When someone violates God's spiritual laws, it will manifest itself in the material world multi-generationally until the effects of the violation are cut off. Thus, unprincipled people live in poverty and pass this poverty generationally to their children as a curse to the fourth generation unless it is cut off by pleading the Cross daily until it disappears. Being a Believer, God determines your soul's seriousness to rid yourself and family of curses of the law by how much you accept the finished work of grace by Jesus' sacrificial death on the cruel Cross. Your born again spirit is perfect and sinless but your soul as a Believer is in the daily process of being pruned, washed, sanctified, and the deeds of the flesh mortified out of the soul.

Business Servants must understand and learn the ways of God. God's ways of justice are embedded in His laws that are activated for or against you by your free will choices. Iniquities and thus curses can be passed down to the third and fourth generation (Exodus 20:5). Conversely, blessings can be passed down generationally as well. Deuteronomy 7:9 says, "Know therefore that the LORD thy God, He is God, the faithful God, which keepeth covenant and mercy with them that love him and keep his commandments to a thousand generations."

GOD HAS BUILT HIS UNIVERSE WITH A GOOD HARVEST FOR GODLY OBEDIENT BEHAVIOR AND A BAD REAPING FOR UNGODLY DISOBEDIENT BEHAVIOR

It is not an issue of award or punishment for obedience or disobedience. You obey God's word because you love God and trust Him as a covenant making and covenant keeping God. God's word works spirit and life when it is obeyed and works poverty, sickness, and death when it is disobeyed. The word is a seed that is planted in your heart where the foundation of your beliefs resides (Mark 4:14-15). Your obedience and disobedience to the word of God is the care you take of the word into your soul and release of the word into your environment. Do you nurture the seed or word of God, or do you allow it to not reap a harvest within you? Thus, God's word either works for you, or you ignore the word of God; and the world's promise of sin and death by default will work in your life. You reap what you sow (Galatians 6:7).

Yet, this is not God actively judging you. You cannot say God is judging you if you rob a bank and are arrested and go to jail. You just violated one of God's activated laws forbidding the commandment, "Thou shall not steal."

God is your Abba Father (Romans 8:15), and He loves you, and nothing can separate you from the Father's love (Romans 8:38-39). He wants to restore things that have been stolen from you. He wants to heal you and give you divine health. God is wealthy, and in God's house there are many mansions (John 14:2). Your Heavenly Father takes pleasure in the prosperity of His servants (Psalm 35:27). In other words, God enjoys when He prospers you, especially His obedient Business Servants.

In Luke 18:1-8 Jesus tells the parable of the persistent widow before the unrighteous judge to contrast with the readiness of Father God to affect justice and mercy in the lives of His children who diligently seek Him. Jesus saw a lesson in the parable of this courtroom scene to teach His disciples to persistently seek their righteous heavenly Father for justice. The woman pestered the unrighteous judge to grant her petition. It was a lot of work for the widow to keep going back to the unrighteous judge time and time again. The decision of the unrighteous judge could affect her financially the rest of her life, so this was very serious business. The woman prevailed because she diligently and persistently pestered the unrighteous judge who out of exasperation granted her petition, not because the judge feared God or man to do justice. Jesus concluded in Luke 18:7, "And shall not God avenge His own elect, which cry day and night unto Him, though He bear long with them?" Business Servants have this hope that God will personally send out a decree for His angels to aid them to collect money owed them. God's angels are ministers to the heirs of salvation (Hebrews 1:14). If someone steals from you, God demands that the thief repay you sevenfold, along with everything in his house (Proverbs 6:31).

SOME OF THE LAWS OF
GOD'S ORDERED UNIVERSE

LAW OF "GRAVITY:" If you jump off a ten-story building and kill yourself, you cannot say you are a victim of the law of gravity or a victim of God just because He did not send His angels to catch you. God's laws do not victimize anybody, as they are no respecter of persons. We victimize ourselves by disobeying God's laws.

LAW OF "SIN AND DEATH:" Paul wrote in Romans 8:2 the Law of Sin and Death what Newton called his Second Law of Thermodynamics, which says basically "the material world is tending toward dissolution." Sin brought death into the world, so afterwards everything tends toward entropy or is in the process of dying or headed toward dissolution. We are not victimized by that law; it is something that our forefather Adam caused to happen by the fall, which was man's original sin. We were all in the loins of Adam, so his sin of high treason passed to all of us. We were all born naturally into sin. We cannot blame God just because Adam and Eve were disobedient which caused God's justice in His law of sin and death to become operational.

LAW OF THE "SPIRIT OF LIFE IN CHRIST JESUS:" Jesus brought a new spiritual law into the world, which is called the law of the "Spirit of Life in Christ Jesus." Romans 8:2 says, "For the law of the Spirit of Life in Christ Jesus has made me free from the law of sin and death." Jesus is Life personified (John 14:6).

LAW OF "SUPPLY AND DEMAND:" The business world is built on this law that the value of a thing is based upon its availability and utility. Gold, silver, and other precious metals are considered valuable because their supply is low and hard to mine.

LAW OF "SERVICE AND SUCCESS:" Whoever serves becomes successful. This law God put into His created universe as a law to motivate His people to serve the Lord and one another in love.

LAW OF "SOWING AND REAPING:" Genesis 8:22 says, "While the earth remains, seedtime and harvest, cold and heat, winter and summer, and day and night shall not cease." Galatians 6:7-10 says, "Do not be deceived, God is not mocked; whatever a man sows, that he will also reap. For he who sows to his flesh will of the flesh reap corruption, but he who sows to the Spirit will of the Spirit reap everlasting life. And let us not grow weary while doing good, for in due season we shall reap if we do not lose heart. Therefore, as we have opportunity, let us do good to all, especially to those who are of the household of faith." Reaping what you sow, whether of the spirit or flesh, is one of God's economic laws. However, the good news is that God can cancel out a bad crop upon true repentance of sins. Jesus' blood wiped out all our past sins or seeds of rebellion sown when we were saved, and He still does this work ongoing. God's mercy endures forever. However, our souls not being totally transformed, still sin, and we must repent and seek forgiveness daily in our souls even though we already have eternal life (I John 1:8-9).

LAW OF "BREAKING AND RELEASING:" God will break you to release His potential in you. God will break you, so your carnal nature will be subdued to release His godly influence and holiness that is deep within you. The breaking of a seed planted in the ground releases the God-created potential inside the seed, and new life springs forth. God's word that has become rhema to you or a prophetic affirmation planted in your heart will die and resurrect with new life that will become a spiritual fruit bearing tree for the spiritual nourishment of others. A fruit tree does not eat its own fruit and is a servant to others. The fruit tree bears fruits that have seeds that when planted participate in God's multiplication and expand God's Kingdom by adding Believers who become mature fruit bearing trees themselves. God's law of reproduction operates to release new life in this method while Believers' souls are being transformed unto spiritual maturity. Revelation 13:8 says that Jesus as the sacrificial lamb of God was, "slain from the foundation of the world."

LAW OF "PERSISTENCE:" Thomas Edison did hundreds of trial runs before he found the right metal for the light bulb. God waited with patience for four thousand years to bring the Savior. You persistently must wait expectantly for the return of the Lord. You persistently must wait expectantly for the fulfillment of your prophetic words. If you persist without quitting God will reward you. This is part of God's law of deferred gratification. This is part of God's educational process. This is the development of the fruit of the Spirit called patience."

LAW OF "CAUSE-AND-EFFECT:" This Law in God's physical and spiritual universes is similar to the Law of Sowing and Reaping. This also sometimes is referred to as the Law of Causality. There is a relationship between an action or event (the *cause*) and an action or event that naturally or spiritually flows from that action or event (the *effect*). The first action or event is responsible for the second resulting action or event. Thus, God's Law of Cause-and-Effect states that every cause has an effect, and every effect becomes the cause of something else. This law suggests that Believers living here on earth are always in motion and always in progression in their lives from a chain of events. With every mental thought, emotional expression, or willful action that is transmitted by a Believer, the Believer sets into motion a natural or spiritual chain of effects which was generated from the Believer's spirit and soul to the entire cellular structure of the Believer's body and then out into the Believer's environment. God put into His law effects that correspond to actions which are the causes.

God has set in motion all events at the time of creation, so He is the true Definer of causes and their resulting effects. However, God expects Believers to learn His laws and avoid the bad consequences for violation thereof and promote the good consequences thereof by obedience to God's laws.

If the Believer does evil actions, then the effect will be destruction of finances, relationships, and sometimes even incarceration. If the Believer does good deeds, then the result usually is that good deeds are sent back to the Believer by others.

Titus 3:8 says, "This is a faithful saying, and these things I will that thou affirm constantly, that they which have believed in God might be careful to maintain good works. These things are good and profitable unto men."

Matthew 6:33 says that if a Believer seeks first the Kingdom of God and His righteousness, then the effect will be that the Believer will receive all things that pertain to life and godliness. 2 Peter 1:3 says, "According as His divine power hath given unto us all things that pertain unto life and godliness, through the knowledge of Him that hath called us to glory and virtue."

The economy of the Kingdom of God is giving and receiving, while the economy of the world is buying and selling. In order to benefit the Believer, himself, his family, associates, church, and society as a whole, the Believer should use his free will of choice to perform good deeds with the awareness that what he thinks, speaks, and acts will affect his own life and the lives of others. Proverbs 18:21 says, "Death and life are in the power of the tongue: and they that love it shall eat the fruit thereof." The prosperity of life is created by the Believer's own expressions in being a servant to others through thoughts, speech, and actions. A Believer's spoken affirmations given to others, or the Believer's kindness bestowed on others through actions, will have the effects that God has established as appropriate results, according to God's divine justice involved in His Law of Cause and Effect. For example, Luke 6:38 says, "Give, and it shall be given unto you; good measure, pressed down, and shaken together, and running over, shall men give into your bosom. For with the same measure that ye mete withal it shall be measured to you again."

There are many other laws God has activated here on earth such as the "Law of Floatation," the "Law of Relativity," the "Law of Polarity," the "Law of Fluid Dynamics," "Faraday's Law of Induction," or Newton's "Laws of Motion," but these laws do not have the relevance for this study in this book. Yet, these laws are interesting to the scientific field.

SEVEN

THERE ARE ECONOMIC CONSEQUENCES TO OUR MORAL CHOICES

GOD THINKS AND PLANS IN THE
LONG RUN, NOT SHORT RUN

GOD'S PRINICPLE: A Business Servant has freedom to choose his or her business transactions and decisions, but the Business Servant does not have the freedom to choose the consequences of his or her business dealings and choices.

Thus, the business servant must take more effort in studying the word of God which will reveal the consequences of a particular business decision.

Consequences are the authority and decision of God to declare. Yet, God in His grace and mercy can cancel a bad business crop you have sown. Personally, I have had to experience God's grace and mercy to cancel the crops of the bad seeds I had sown when I was younger. At the time of sowing those bad seeds, they appeared to be good seeds that would give me a great harvest. Now, I pray over the seed as to whether I should sow it in the first place. You need the help of the Holy Spirit to make business decisions when ideas are only in seed form. The Holy Spirit will see the resulting harvest when you cannot. This is wisdom. This is practicing teleology, as God does.

The economic consequences from making bad or good moral choices become visible in the long run. In the short run, you can appear to get away with sin, disobedience, or failure to follow God's biblical principles in business, but not in the long run. On the other hand, the consequences of a life of right, moral decisions and choices will result in godly character, good reputation, and financial prosperity because you did not enter a transaction based upon greed or covetousness.

Psalm 37 answers David's question: Why do the wicked prosper and righteous suffer all day long? However, David essentially said he was envious until he saw what happened to the wicked in the long run by violating God's principles.

God's principle is that wickedness does not prosper in the long run, only appears to prosper perhaps in the short run. God's laws of justice grind slowly, but they do grind on, and God's justice is finally done unless God's grace and mercy intercedes.

THE WORD "ECONOMICS" LITERALLY MEANS
"HOUSEHOLD FINANCIAL MANAGEMENT,"
"BUSINESS FINANCIAL MANAGEMENT,"
AND "GOVERNMENT FINANCIAL MANAGEMENT"

Civil Government officials cannot manage a nation's economy different than you manage a household or business economy. "Nation financial management" is an extension of the same economic laws and principles of "household financial management" and "business financial management."

Only the Politicians and the wealthy banking families believe that you can cut up paper at the U.S. Treasury, or in a print shop, call it money and thereby produce wealth. The Politicians and the wealthy banking families believe that when you become a Civil Government, or the bankers for a Civil Government, somehow new "mystical economic laws" supersede "God's economic laws of household and business financial management." Much of the government Socialist Bureaucrats and Politicians plan the government budgets by increasing further debt through the issuance of U.S. Treasury Bonds, and on the state and local levels through the issuance of Municipal Bonds in exchange for money. The governments keep increasing their debt. God's covenant of wealth includes a debt-free lifestyle, as debt nullifies the Lord's liberty because debt creates bondage. Families are forced to go on a tight budget when the income does not meet the monthly debts. Parents do not increase their children's allowances if money becomes very tight. Many families save money for vacations and Christmas, and for emergencies. Yet, if the government wants more money, the Politicians do not shrink the government, and especially do not decrease the staff of needless agencies. The Politicians simply raise the taxes and/or sell more Treasury bonds and increase the national debt. The U.S. would be declared to be bankrupt, and it would be placed in receivership if the U.S. was a private corporation or business. When will this non-biblitarian practice of debt financing by the government stop?

As of the time of this writing, the U.S. Federal Reserve Dollar is really "fiat money." Fiat money has no inherent value, which means there is nothing of true value backing up the currency. Fiat money is a deception into which most economists and Politicians have accepted as the purpose of government, and they have accepted that they should use governmental authority to decide on economic power to obtain wealth instead of following the principles of true power to obtain wealth as delineated in the Bible (Deuteronomy 8:18). Fiat money is a lie on the people. It is Humanism trying to replace God's will and economic principles. Fiat money is man declared power to get false wealth, yet only God can create lasting wealth. Only God has the discretion to give power to obtain wealth. Fiat money is mere paper that is not backed up by assets which have a limited supply naturally created by God, such as gold, silver, oil, or other valuable natural minerals.

BIBLICAL ECONOMICS: "Biblical economics" can be described as the ability and management of production, distribution, and consumption of goods and services as directed by the Holy Spirit for the expansion of the Kingdom of God and the furtherance of God's will here on earth.

GOVERNMENT EXPLOITATION: "Governmental exploitation" can be defined as "a confiscation of all or some of one's property, business, or income by a government, for the government's own self-preservation, consumption, re-distribution, and/or empowerment." According to Socialists, who disdain profit motivated businesses, exploitation in the business world is by employers against wage earners. Economic exploitation in the Socialist false philosophy is that value is intrinsic in a product only according to the amount of labor that has been spent on producing the product, not the money invested to manufacture the product or getting it to the market. Socialists believe that money for labor is greater than profits realized from investment of capital, production of products, and taking steps necessary to get those products to the marketplace for purchase by consumers. Thus, Socialists think there is no exploitation when there is confiscation against business owners or property owners for the greater public good, or just because the greater taxes can be realized. For example, Kelo v. City of New London, 545 U.S. 469 (2005), was a case decided by the Supreme Court of the United States involving the use of eminent domain to transfer land from one private owner to another private owner to increase the real property taxes for the local municipality.

BIBLICAL JUSTICE: "Biblical justice" means people receive what is due them or what they deserve. It also means reaping what people themselves have chosen to sow, unless a crop is cancelled by God's act of grace, mercy, and love.

BIBLICAL VICTIM: A true biblical victim is suffering innocently because of that which has been sown by another.

BIBLICAL LOVE: "Biblical love" is not something you fall into as in Hollywood movies. The biblical definition of agape love is the promotion of someone else's good at your own expense for the furtherance of God's principles of good stewardship and acts of mercy.

BIBLICAL JUSTICE AND GRACE: "Biblical justice and grace" balanced together govern God's biblical economics contrary to popular belief in the world. Yet, the Father shows His love in His discipline, pruning, and chastisement to bring His children into maturity and obedience.

FELLOWSHIP OF CHRIST'S SUFFERING: Entering the "fellowship of Christ's suffering" means that we participate or do our part. We do not have to personally die on the Cross and go to Hades or Abraham's Bosom for three days and nights. That was Jesus' part. Jesus paid the price for our rights to salvation, eternal life, blessings, healing, and prosperity from the Father. We suffer and are obedient to the Lord to maintain our blessings, healing, and prosperity, but not our initial salvation. Jesus suffered and died that we may obtain our born again spirits and eternal life. We must suffer the task of submitting our wills in our souls to our spirits and Holy Spirit for the maturation of our souls, and we must stay humbly obedient to God while doing His will of being about His business here on earth.

SPIRITUAL CAUSES THAT UNDERLIE

POVERTY IN THE "LONG RUN" WHICH

ARE ENEMIES OF WEALTH

FEAR: "Fear" is the inability to take risks because of the lack of trust in an ordered spiritual creation under the rulership of Almighty God. Fear is different than caution, as caution is needed to research any potential investment or business opportunity. Being cautious is prudent.

BUSINESS, SCIENCE, AND LEGAL SYSTEM: "Business" moves products to consumers, business serves the public, and business servants are rewarded for their work based upon laws of servanthood. "Science" as we know it is predicated upon the biblical, Christian faith, which is founded on the truth of a covenant making and covenant keeping God. If there are laws that operate in earth and in the universe, there must be a law Creator and a law Enforcer for the laws to consistently work. God's laws of predictability based upon a covenant making and covenant keeping God is the basis of our American/English Judicial legal system.

PAGANISM: Historically, "Paganism" does not have a world view of an ordered universe where systematic laws operate because of a covenantal God. All pagan philosophies, including the Greeks, who prided themselves on their rationality, are based on capricious gods who were continuously changing the rules to fit their own whims.

WESTERN SCIENCE: "Western Science" is based upon the law of predictability and the law of cause and effect that exists because of a covenant making and covenant keeping God. Scientists assume that if you cause something to occur; it is predictable that a certain reaction will happen. Science as we know it is totally rooted in biblical predictability.

PREDICTABILITY: God's "law of predictability" can also be seen in the legal system. American and English Judicial systems have stability in their legal systems based upon predictability of law because of their judicial adherence to precedent called *stare decisis*. Valence is the unique value an individual places on a particular outcome. Legal stability has a moral valence insofar as it assures persons living in the country that like cases in the future will be treated equally because of *stare decisis*. The Courts do not always follow strict *stare decisis*, such as when the U.S. Supreme Court passed *Roe v. Wade* in 1973 and made abortion on demand a Constitutional right. Currently, *Roe v. Wade*, being a predictable legal precedent has changed based upon more evidence that a baby in the womb is a life that should deserve legal protection. The law in America regarding abortion on demand has divided the country. Americans have allowed almost seventy million babies killed based on the reasoning that a woman has a right over her own body. Yet the law states that a woman does not have a right over her own body to make money as a prostitute, does not have a right over her own body to take illegal drugs, and does not have a right over her own body to attempt committing suicide. Thus, the legal foundation of *Roe v. Wade* is flawed.

The Supreme Court in *Dobbs V. Jackson Women's Health Organization*, No. 19-1392, 597 U.S. (2022), overturned *Roe v. Wade* (1973) and *Planned Parenthood v. Casey* (1992), by holding that the U.S. constitution does not confer a constitutional right to abortion. The Court failed to declare that the unborn child is a person entitled to Constitutional rights of being deprived of life, liberty, or property without due process of law. Instead, the Court returned to every state the power to regulate any aspect of abortion not protected by Federal law. The Court did say, "Abortion presents a profound moral question." At least the Supreme Court in Dobbs gave Prolife Believers the ability to argue on a state level to outlaw abortion completely as it is murder under God's law. Thus, God gave the battle for life of the unborn back to Believers to stand up as Biblitarians to protect the innocent, as abortion is unlawful homicide that reaps bad consequences for our nation. For example, abortion is the hatred of a nation's posterity. The national debt is the same spirit as abortion; it is the hatred of our posterity.

Since Dobbs, the State of Idaho passed the "Fetal Heartbeat Preborn Child Protection Act," Title 18, Idaho Code, and Section 18-8702 (1), which says, "The life of each human being begins at fertilization, and unborn children have interests in life, health, and well-being that should be protected... (6) The fetal heartbeat, when detected, presents a clearly identifiable point at which the preborn child in the womb has a greater than ninety-five percent (95%) chance of survival when carried to term. (7) The presence of a human heartbeat is a more reliable indicator of life than the medically uncertain concept of "viability" and whether that preborn child is "potentially able to live outside the mother's womb. (8) Therefore, the State of Idaho has a compelling interest in protecting the life of a preborn child at all stages of its development, including after the preborn child has a detectable heartbeat, which signals rhythmically and without pause the presence of a precious and unique life, one that is independent and distinct from the mother's and one that is also worthy of our utmost protection."

Many people in America are prolife to the unborn. If a baby in the womb is killed in a traffic accident by a drunk driver, the perpetrator is not guilty of illegal homicide because a fetus is not a person that has constitutional rights to life with that crime. Yet, in more violent crimes a fetus is considered a person who has constitutional rights to life. This makes no sense at all. How can a baby in the womb be a person under one law but not another law? President Bush on April 1, 2004 signed into law the "Unborn Victims of Violence Act" of 2004 (Public Law 108-212), wherein this United States law recognizes a "child in *utero*" as a legal victim, if he or she is injured or killed during the commission of any of over 60 listed federal crimes of violence. The law defines "child in *utero*" as "a member of the species homo sapiens, at any stage of development, who is carried in the womb." The "Unborn Victims of Violence Act" was strongly criticized by most pro-abortion organizations on grounds that the U.S. Supreme Court case of *Roe v. Wade* had as part of its reasoning that the human fetus was not a "person" under the Fourteenth Amendment to the Constitution, and that if the fetus was a Fourteenth Amendment "person," then he or she would have a constitutional right to life. [At least they were thinking logically in their criticism.]

Today, the laws of 34 states also recognize the human fetus as the legal victim of homicide (and often, other violent crimes) during the entire period of pre-natal development (24 states) or during part of the pre-natal period (10 states). Legal challenges to these laws, arguing that they violate *Roe v. Wade* or other U.S. Supreme Court precedents, have been uniformly rejected by both the federal and the state courts, including the Supreme Courts of California, Pennsylvania, and Minnesota.

The highly publicized Laci and Conner Peterson murders, where Scott Peterson, the husband and father, was found guilty of two murders under the California "Fetal Homicide State Law." The Legislature and Governor of Alabama made national headlines in 2019, enacting the most extreme pro-life legislation in the country, known as the "*Alabama Human Life Protection Act.*" This State of Alabama law makes it a felony for a doctor to perform an abortion at any time during a pregnancy, with no exceptions for rape or incest. The law was scheduled to take effect in November but has been challenged in court. After signing the law, Republican Governor Kay Ivey issued a statement saying, "To the bill's many supporters, this legislation stands as a powerful testament to Alabamans' deeply held belief that every life is precious and that every life is a sacred gift from God."

Now, back to the Law of Predictability, as it is a fundamental Law of God. Arabs and Assyrians came close to this divine covenant science by inventing arithmetic and the predictability of numbers.

Likewise, empiricism came out of the Christian culture based upon a covenant making and covenant keeping God.

"The just shall live by faith" (Romans 1:17). Faith is premised on the simple idea that God has created a universe and holds it in predictability as a covenant with His creation. God is not a man that He would lie (Numbers 23:19). He is a rewarder of them that diligently seek Him (Hebrews 11:6). Faith is the conviction and knowledge that you live under the covenant of your Creator Who wants to reward you with the good things of life with *predictability.*

If you do not submit under the covenant of a good, loving Creator, you will not be able to invest in business opportunities in the future because the future is going to be in your mind too unpredictable, or a false god is going to be capricious, and the rules will keep changing. The Christian free enterprise system is premised on the concept of making an investment of current resources into the future based upon the predictability of your covenant-making and covenant keeping God to give a just return.

AMERICAN INDUSTRIALISTS: Most of the early Industrialists of the United States believed that if you invested money, worked hard with your time and talents, lived properly in covenant with God with godly character, God would reward your investment, labor and disciplined lifestyle. The Rockefellers, Du Ponts, and Fords perpetuated the family wealth from generation to generation by passing on successful attitudes and values. Many of the industrial giants used Biblical economics to acquire great wealth. They did not always have good character, but people like Rockefeller tithed as a youth and kept this practice as an adult. Rockefeller handed out a dime to everyone he met after he recovered from a severe illness, claiming that he had heard from God to start giving away his fortune, less he die. The more he gave, the more was returned to him, and his family kept getting wealthier. In fact, it was Rockefeller's influence alone which started the "March of Dimes" when he rode in his limousine and laid down dimes one after another for one-mile down Wall Street. These supposed "robber barons" did a lot of things contrary to scripture, as well. In contrast, the models available to the poor are usually not wealthy, successful businesspeople. God does honor His laws, so if someone follows His laws, then God allows the good sowing and consequential good reaping to prove that His laws are in operation and work.

The whole concept of free enterprise in the United States came out of a predictable covenantal relationship with God Who actively makes His laws work in favor of them who obey His laws.

If the United States continues to grow in not applying biblical economic principles or laws, the effect will be the reduction of investments in the future because Paganism brings with it a lack of faith in the true God; and a lack of a predictable future based upon covenant with the Creator causes fear and mistrust and stifles investments. Currently, business investors exhibit confidence in American business economy. Currently, the S&P 500, the broad measure of stocks of the 500 largest US companies, is up 29% since 2017. This means the S&P 500 returned more than 50% before Covid-19, according to data from Bespoke Investment Group dating to 1928. Also, the Bellwether Index gained more than 28% this year, well above the average 12.8% return.

How can you invest if you have no covenant assurance that if you obey God, He will predictably, out of the laws of causality, give you positive returns on your investment?

Paganism guarantees a cessation of investments in business and private property. Thus, biblically based culture and society will cause wealth to flow because of Business Servants' submission to God.

THE ANEMIC ECONOMIC EDUCATION IN OUR UNIVERSITIES

God's laws of predictability of returns on business investments caused by a covenant making and covenant keeping God was taught in history in our universities. Today, the economists never talk about faith in America of a covenant making and covenant keeping God as part of free enterprise. The classes taught are devoid of our Christian heritage. The whole concept of free enterprise is based upon a causality relationship in the universe and the predictability of a covenant making and covenant keeping God. Yet, this is never taught at secular universities as the historical economic beliefs of the so-called Great Industrialists. Hebrew 10:23 says, "Let us hold fast the profession of our faith without wavering; for he is faithful that promised."

Professors as a whole in universities do not even introduce the concept. They could have said Christians believe in this thought, and we can see the economic fruits of this way of thinking in history.

Generally, the students in college today are taught to ridicule the "Protestant work ethic" and the seemingly lack of Socialist government philosophy in Christian beliefs in the Kingdom of God. Max Weber, a Socialist, was one of the chief critics. The professors never really introduced the foundational concepts of Christianity as the basis of the free enterprise system. Because of this, secular universities have hidden the truth from their students by keeping them away from biblical truth. They never taught the biblical foundations of American economics.

A new breed of re-educated college graduates who will re-instill Christian truths to the next generation are in the Christian businesses today, and they are becoming vocal in turning back to the predictability of economy based upon a covenant making and covenant keeping God. In order for the wealth of the wicked to come into the hands of the just to finance the end time revival, the true economic principles of God will have to become the prevailing thought of mainstream Business Servants once again.

THE SPIRITUAL CAUSES OF POVERTY
COME FROM GREED AND COVETOUSNESS

The motivation that demands rewards beyond what is just, and loving money, is the sin of greed and covetousness. Greed is wanting more than you have, while covetousness is wanting what someone else has.

The theft, covetousness, or guilt associated with ill-gotten property or gain can also have its roots in generational carnal materialism and the love of money. 1 Timothy 6:10 says, "For the love of money is the root of all evil: which while some coveted after, they have erred from the faith, and pierced themselves through with many sorrows."

.

POVERTY RECURRENTLY COMES FROM LAZINESS

BIBLICAL LAZINESS: "Biblical laziness" means the lack of godly self-government, which results in a failure to energetically and wisely acquire and apply skills, labor, and resources in the Kingdom of God. God's mandate is for Believers to find work to do as a holy calling while submitting to God's discipline for Believers' souls to be transformed in the image and likeness of Christ. Taking dominion over the earth as God's business servant leaders, especially His Business Servants, requires full employment.

LAZINESS: "Laziness" is mismanagement of business, property, and investment. Laziness can take the form of escapism and is a way of thinking that an unpleasant or boring experience is voidable by directing your mind on something more exciting. Laziness is also seen in Freudianism, which is where a lazy person believes he is a victim and does not need to achieve much, or work hard, and believes he should be excused from normal maturation. However, laziness without physical or mental disabilities is sin. Laziness can further be seen in welfare free rides, where you accept a poverty lifestyle to live off of government subsidies such as government paid health care, Section 8 housing, or food credits or food stamps, instead of pursuing higher education, a profession, or training in a trade.

God's approach to life is to give His children special problem-solving tasks in the family, job, business, school, government, and all other social interactions to obtain maturation.

POVERTY OFTEN COMES FROM IDOLATRY

The worship of false gods, which often are values of taking upon oneself the attributes of enthronement reserved only for God, is a major cause of poverty in some countries in the Far East. You become what you worship. You can worship money. You can also worship your presumed self-worth based upon your wealth, fame, or accomplishments.

Belief in false religions, distorted values, rejection of limits (e.g., fiat money, politically managed inflation, national debt incurred to stimulate economy), dualism (emphasis of the spiritual over natural or the natural over the spiritual) or cultural heritage ("I'm an American") or profession ("I'm a lawyer or medical doctor"). All these beliefs tend to produce poverty in your life if you adopt these ideas over your worship and love of God. Oftentimes, these beliefs are founded on pride and cultural traditions. Jesus said in Matthew 15:3, "...Why do ye also transgress the commandment of God by your tradition?"

POVERTY IS PRIMARILY A SPIRITUAL PROBLEM, NOT AN ECONOMIC PROBLEM

India has sacred cows because of Hinduism, and one can see the consequence of poverty caused by this religion. Cows eat seven times more food than humans, and it is illegal to stop a cow from eating your crops. Rats infest most cities in India because it is unlawful to kill them, as Hindus believe the rat may be somebody's past relative.

Mexico and Central America: Some Mexican and Central American citizens have a poverty mentality – "I am only a peon." "I am unworthy to receive rewards." Too little self-worth or too much self-worth is both bad. True worth is who you are in Christ Jesus.

PAGANISM PRODUCES POVERTY

Obedience to the word of our covenant-making and covenant keeping God produces wealth. Those who do not believe in God, or His word, practice Paganism and are subject to the law of cause and effect, which produces poverty for most people because the ruling prince of the world system is a malevolent evil spirit and his Kingdom of darkness goal is to do harm to humanity.

REJECTION OF GOD'S "LIMITS" BY POLITICIANS
BRINGS POVERTY TO A NATION

Biblical economics calls for real material wealth as standards for backing a nation's currency, i.e., silver and gold or some commodity must have a one to one relationship of real material asset behind paper currency. Originally, the framers of our Constitution followed this biblical principle by requiring in the Constitution that no money may be printed by the government unless backed by gold or silver. By allowing a non-governmental entity called the Federal Reserve to have authority to print and handle the U.S. Currency, this allowed them to print fiat money that was not backed by a hard asset with a limited supply, namely gold or silver, as mandated by the U.S. Constitution if the U.S. Treasury itself printed the money. However, if the U.S. Treasury established the value of the dollar and printed the currency, the U.S. government would not have to issue Treasury Bonds to send to the Federal Reserve to obtain needed currency for its spending. Thus, if the U.S. Treasury printed the U.S. government's money, there would be no national debt.

It is no accident that the U.S. eventually started heading to the goal of getting off the gold standard when fractional reserve banking came in with John Maynard Keynes with the Roosevelt New Deal, and it was finally consummated by President Richard Nixon in the early 1970's. In the 1970's an agreement between the U.S. and Saudi Arabia for Saudi Arabia to deposit its currency with the Federal Reserve who would issue a bank account in New York of U.S. dollars to purchase U.S. Treasury Bonds. Then it was agreed that all other nations had to purchase Saudi Arabia oil with U.S. dollars. This enriched the Federal Reserve with petro-dollars. Every country had to purchase U.S. Treasury Bonds. This caused the Federal Reserve to be rich, while the U.S. went into debilitating socialist and military spending and debt.

The gold standard behind currency would keep Politicians within limitations and fiscal responsibility based upon the supply of gold and silver, products that are scarce and created by God. God wants mankind to live with a constant reminder of man's mortality and mankind's creaturehood and God's eternal divinity and unlimited power, which require mankind's total dependence upon a limitless, all-powerful Creator and close relationship God.

Only God can create true wealth, which consists of businesses, real property, precious metals, precious stones, livestock, food growth, energy resources, and all things created by God. Man must be given the power to obtain wealth by God (Deuteronomy 8:18) as man cannot create wealth. Man should invest in the things of God's wealth assets instead of man's riches (stocks, bonds, Notes, Insurance Products, Guaranteed Investment Contracts, and the like).

Mankind's obedience to God's commands grants mankind the use of God's authority and power to obtain and use God's wealth as God's steward. This means God's Business Servant is energized with God's power or he or she is given the anointing to spoil the institutions of the world under the sway of the Kingdom of darkness to acquire wealth for the Kingdom of God to fulfill the covenants made to the fathers of our faith. God wants to give wealth to those who will do His will here on earth. Sometimes unsaved man is given wealth by God because that person is following God's principles but not necessarily is in the perfect will of God. God often will use their obedience to His principles to be broadcasted to His children that wealth comes to principled obeying people. For examples; Donald Trump invests in real estate, and he professes to be a Believer. Bill Gates started an industry with personalized computers which has increased knowledge to mankind, but not morality; but I do not know whether Bill Gates professes to be a Believer. Notwithstanding, Donald Trump's real estate investments and Bill Gates computer businesses are wealth assets instead of riches, and each of these men have altruistic agendas that motivate them to give a part of their accumulated wealth away to what they believe are good causes. Whether the causes they give follow God's principles and will is a different discussion, but the pattern for giving by Believers is there. God wants wealth assets to be acquired by His Business Servants, and He desires that His Business Servants be funnels of the money derived from that wealth, which God wants to be given as the Holy Spirit leads them.

When the United States took the dollar off of a one-to-one ratio of a limited commodity of gold or silver, then politicians were trying to play God by creating a paper wealth, which is serving the god of mammon to finance man's Socialist experiments.

NO RESERVES: Similarly, when the banks in 1980 were allowed to start lending out the same money on deposit repeatedly without keeping a reserve, then the failure of the banks became a certainty. This was fractional reserve banking without the requirement of any reserves. This is the biggest scam on the public, especially since most of the retirement money in America and Europe is placed in the banks. In the United States the Federal Deposit Insurance Corporation (FDIC) would immediately file bankruptcy upon the failure of the banks. This is a legal fraud on the American people and an economic failure that is destined to happen.

The U.S., and all other countries in the creditor-debtor-fiat-money system, unless a way out is discovered, are headed for an economic crash because their whole money and finance system has violated God's laws of economics. There is going to be either a crash of world economies or a total global currency reset where each country's currency is backed by God-created hard assets, such as gold, silver, oil, or land that is produced within each country. God's mandate for each country's currency must be based upon a limited reserve system where the legal tender is backed by hard assets created by God.

If each country's currency is backed by hard assets created by God (wealth assets), then the Civil Government can no longer play God by its monetary fiscal policies and no longer can finance its Socialist experiments with borrowed fiat money. Debt enslaves a people while spending limits free people.

Every family household must know that the family must live within a disciplined budget and not live off credit. Living a debt-free lifestyle provides more money to live life abundantly. Most Believers work to pay their bills. Most Believers live month to month. Most Believers use their credit cards for vacations and Christmas, and then they work harder and struggle more to pay off those debts incurred. Why do people struggle to keep a good FICO score of over 700 in the U.S.? It is to have a good credit rating, so they can buy things on credit to go into the bondage of debt. Believers must save money and buy things with cash and not credit. It would be better to just establish a savings for future expenditures and make sure credit card usage is a thirty-day expenditure which is paid off every month. Personally, I stopped using credit cards years ago, and I use my debit VISA card where the money is taken out of my account the moment a transaction with my debit card is used. I do not have to make payments on credit cards each month, and this practice restricts my spending habits. I do have credit cards only for emergencies, such as a sudden death in the family, and I have to pay for a plane flight and hotel expenses. That is okay, but I do not use credit cards for anything else. I believe what the bible says that the debtor is slave to the creditor (Proverbs 22:7).

THE MAJOR CAUSES OF POVERTY IS OFTEN
THE "SINGLE GENERATION CONSUMPTION"

The single generation consumption is misuse of resources properly belonging to the next generation. This is what we have in the United States, and in most countries, today, influencing governments, businesses, and families. Most businesses and families in America are ninety days from bankruptcy.

Malachi 4:4-6 is a mandate to change short run thinking because short run thinking is a hatred of our posterity: Sins of abortion, adultery, divorce, and homelessness are all anti-family and therefore destructive to the family as the primary carrier of God's blessings in a nation.

"I'm spending my children's inheritance." Some people have this as a bumper sticker on their cars. The Bible says parents ought to store up wealth for their children's children (Proverbs 13: 22). That is wealth used by at least three generations. Thus, part of what people in the world are spending belongs to their children and their children's children. God's mandate is for wealth to be passed down multi-generationally.

The U.S. national debt is a spiritual outrage. The National Debt is $36 Trillion in November of 2024 and is increasing another $Trillion about every four months. Additionally, the Federal Government already has committed to future debt which raises the National Debt to approximately $120 Trillion. President Trump says that he will start paying off the National Debt by down-sizing the Federal Bureaucracies and increasing the production of Oil to be the largest producer of oil in the world and using some money to pay off the National Debt. It is the same spirit as connected with abortion. It is the hatred of our posterity, our children

God's wealth assets increase in value by multiplication when God's economic principles are being followed. The pressure on corporate leaders in America by investors to create a greater return in the short run is depleting businesses in America of needed capital and causing Business Servants to be disobedient to God's Kingdom principles of business as a wealth asset. American Business Servants find it more and more difficult to compete in the global markets with countries who think multi-generationally through investment for preserving resources, for maintaining saving accounts for future needed expenditures, for research and development, and for capturing greater market shares.

Historically, the Great Industrialists of America and the Japanese, South Korean, Chinese, Vietnamese, and German cultures are not concerned as much with short run dividend returns as they were and are with the following principles:

1). Obtaining a greater market share.
2). Setting up savings accounts for future business expansion capital and for future needed expenditures to avoid debt.
3). Research and development, and
4). Laying up an inheritance for future generations.

The above four concepts are long term future oriented and follow the pattern established by God. He is the God of Abraham, Isaac, and Jacob, and always thinking and instituting at least a three generational plan in His purpose and goals for His business here on earth. God's plans always take at least three generations to fulfill. Today the United States has the lowest amount in these four categories than the other familial based societies at the present time. We must pray that investments in these four categories increase in the business minds and hearts of American Business Servants.

God's Business Servants must stop following the world's methods of doing business, as they must stop being short run thinking and single generation consumption motivated. God's methods always think and plan with long run principles of growth, not consumption. The diligent, hard working ants gather food for the winter months during the summer, so they have food for the winter. "Go to the ant, thou sluggard; consider her ways, and be wise." (Proverbs 6:6).

Short run consumption habits in society teach stockholders to demand short run returns, and this phenomenon is the biggest psychological reason for the mergers and asset acquisitions. In other words, mergers and asset acquisitions are fueled and driven by short run thinking. This mindset continually causes businesses to cut themselves out of the market share because the business leaders cannot afford to expend money to capture a market share while at the same time meeting the stockholders' demands for short run dividends.

These business owners, entrapped in short run thinking, need more and more cash to keep the machinery running in the short run to give short run stock dividends.

In government, the local municipal bonds issuance is based upon short run thinking. The government is also fueling a runaway train of theft of families' future. This irresponsibility must change. We will start seeing more financial train crashes in municipal bonds and failed companies after the mergers in the future if we do not wake up to biblical economics. The U.S., and other countries, should abandon short run thinking to turn around their country's economy from a debtor nation to a wealth nation.

Business Servants must stop using the government's short run methods of economics as the pattern to operate the businesses. When the government goes year after year into further debt to spend for military and social entitlements, it will lead to financial suicide for the nation. Often, just seeing what the Socialist and Humanist Civil Government Politicians and Bureaucrats do and doing the opposite will cause the Business Servants to be more in line with God's biblitarian principles of business and economics.

Company leaders have been pressured to show short term profits to encourage the buying of their company stock by the public and as investments by employees' pension trustees. In order to fuel their need for additional capital to meet expenditures, this short run returns mindset added pressure that caused worldly business executives and board of directors to defraud their employees by devising a plan for the pension trustees to continue purchasing the company's own stock with their 401k pension money. When the company's stock goes down then the value of the employees' 401K pension plan goes down. If the company goes bankrupt, then the pension plan of the employees is totally wiped out. This is the result of short run thinking and short run investment returns.

When companies in the world system go bankrupt, bond holders usually are wiped out, stockholders lose the value of their stock investment, retirees often see their pensions and benefits vanish, and employees lose their jobs. Oftentimes, CEOs and other top executives of large public companies that go through Chapter 11 receive higher salaries, stock bonuses, and a package of other benefits. Sometimes these executives earn more than they did before the company went through bankruptcy. In the wake of corporate catastrophes such as Enron, Congress passed legislation focused on preventing companies from paying retention bonuses to executives of large companies going through Chapter 11. Yet, this still goes on throughout America. Why should CEO's and top executives be rewarded for violating God's principles of economics and destroying the financial security of bondholders and stockholders, while annihilating the pensions and the lives of the employees?

Like the private sector who wiped out employees' pension plans, local governments who file bankruptcy wipe out government employee pension plans because the government leaders violated God's economic principles. In October 2014, a federal judge ruled that California Public Employees Retirement System (CalPERS) pensions could be cut in a bankruptcy proceeding filed by a City like any other debt of the City. He rejected the argument that the giant pension system is an "arm of the state" with pensions protected by federal law and two state laws on contracts and liens. In July 2012, the City of San Bernardino, California filed for bankruptcy without first trying mediation with their debtors, municipal bondholders, and employees. When the City of San Bernardino found it was in danger of not making payroll, it decided to forego all payments to CalPERS for a year. The failure to make payments gave CalPERS grounds to terminate its contract with the City, triggering a deep cut in pensions for the City of San Bernardino's current workers and retirees. Firefighters and police had their salaries cut. All these woes were caused by the Civil Government not following God's biblical principles of economics. If Civil Governments followed long run thinking, stayed out of debt, managed assets with wisdom, and provided savings to meet expected future expenditures, then government employees would not be injured; and taxpayers would not have their taxes increased.

God's biblical principles always mandate Business Servants to act with truth, not with fraud and deception. The public at large needs retraining in biblical economic and ethical principles before they invest, as their vetting should be if the business owners in charge are following God's economic laws of wealth creation and ethical laws of honesty. Wealth creation includes proper company investment in long run planning in research and development, capturing a greater market share of business, retaining capital to pay off costly debt, continuous training of employees, building up a savings for unexpected expenditures, ensuring the stability of employees' retirement investments, expansion of satellite businesses to increase profit, and seeking the best Believers of the next generation.

EIGHT

BUSINESS SERVANTS ARE CALLED TO BE BIBLITARIANS

THE BIBLITARIAN IS A BELIEVER WHO APPLIES THE BIBLICAL

TRUTHS ABOUT GOD'S ECONOMIC PRINCIPLES TO RUN
GOVERNMENTS, BUSINESSES, SCHOOLS, FAMILIES, CHURCHES,
AND INDIVIDUALS' LIVES

The Holy Spirit uploaded the word "Biblitarian" to me in the spring of 2004, and many people now are using this word as if it has been written in the dictionary. I probably should have filed a copyright to protect the word, but since God gave it to me, it belongs to all Believers, especially God's Business Servants. I have used this word many times in my other books and written sermons, which have been given copyright protection. I like the fact that this word is being used by Believers, in the business and political realms, and I would like the word to be used in families, in churches, and by individual Believers.

The issue is: "What are the ideas and thoughts that make up the principles or rules of economics by which we are going to function the government, manage family spending and investments, operate family-owned businesses, and fund the church community of any nation and society?"

Our Founding Fathers of the U.S. were Biblitarians, with some like Thomas Jefferson were deists. Individual Biblitarians should follow God's biblical principles in the family, Church, business, Civil Government, and the voting for individual Politicians at election times. Biblitarians believe in personal liberty balanced with personal responsibility, stewardship of real property and businesses, maturation through a strong work ethic, minimal government regulation and promotion of responsible free enterprise, an emphasis on local government instead of national government to solve people's problems, and embracing all the issues discussed in this book regarding long run thinking, teleology, godly self-government of each individual, and following God's biblical principles of economics.

Any ideas or thoughts that are contrary to the principles and truths in the Bible are outside the will of God. When Believers adopt these worldly untruths as the prevailing thoughts in society and debate, and particularly in their businesses, they will be seeds that in the long run will be damaging to the stability of a covenant people whohave joined together for God's blessings in government, business, family, and church. The thoughts and ideas of this fallen world, and the Kingdom of darkness, are contrary to God's word, and are designed to steal, kill, and destroy you, your business, your ministry, your family, and your society.

2 Corinthians 10:4-5 says, "For the weapons of our warfare are not carnal but mighty in God for pulling down strongholds, casting down arguments and every high thing that exalts itself against the knowledge of God,

bringing every thought into captivity to the obedience of Christ."

A person can be a good debater, sound wise, have great understanding about the world problems; but if his or her solutions are not biblically based, then he or she is not a practicing Biblitarian, even though he or she may be saved. If he or she is not a Biblitarian, his or her solutions will not be good and wise in the long run, although they may be a temporary solution in the short run. 1 Corinthians 1:19 says, "For it is written, 'I will destroy the wisdom of the wise, and bring to nothing the understanding of the prudent.'"

A Biblitarian does not love the things of this world, nor adopts the principles of this world system as the foundation of his or her beliefs. 1 John 2:15-17 says, "Do not love the world or the things in the world. If anyone loves the world, the love of the Father is not in him. For all that is in the world, the lust of the flesh, the lust of the eyes, and the pride of life is not of the Father but is of the world. And the world is passing away, and the lust of it; but he who does the will of God abides forever."

A Biblitarian believes in limited government, moral free enterprise that believes in a covenant making and covenant keeping God and, long run thinking and planning led by the Holy Spirit, equal opportunity for all races, religions, cultures, national origin and genders, lives debt free or is working to become debt free, primarily invests in wealth assets, believes work is a holy calling, sees the family as the basic unit of society, promotes churches and families caring for the needy with tax incentives instead of the Civil Government going into debt to provide cradle to grave, womb to tomb welfare, encourages mature self-government following God's biblical principles, works to permeate God's Kingdom in every area of society, and recruits and trains the next two generations to become Biblitarians.

THE SOCIALIST AND HUMANISTIC CIVIL GOVERNMENT AND
ITS POLICY OF DEALING WITH "ECONOMIC INEQUALITY"

The economic policies of Socialist and Humanist Civil Government Politicians and Bureaucrats are sometimes just legalized theft because they are prefaced on the following notion:

Due to the disparity of wealth between various groups in society (which it is assumed is caused by overt or tacit exploitation by wealthy people, businesses, and organizations to the lower class population), the Socialist and Humanist Civil Government Politicians and Bureaucrats believe that they (as self-appointed arbitrators and dispensers of wealth and riches) are morally responsible to spread and equalize the wealth of all people through higher tax rates for the industrious Business Servants along with strict regulations that limit freedoms and free enterprise. The Civil Government regularly exempts its agencies and Bureaucrats from being bound by the same laws it imposes on the citizens, families, and private businesses in the nation.

Once Socialist and Humanist Politicians and Bureaucrats in charge of the Civil Government decided to be as

God or elite philosophers, they then found themselves making life decisions for people in a natural environment they did not create. God's universe and environment are filled with inequalities and discrepancies from the point of view of the Socialist and Humanist Civil Government Politicians and Bureaucrats, which they could not explain and wanted to eradicate under their Humanist and Socialist mindsets, agendas and laws. Therefore, the Socialist and Humanist Civil Government Politicians and Bureaucrats had to construct an explanation for the differences in God's created order by saying Business Servants are bad because they exploit consumers and employees in their acquisition of profits and are the cause of poverty to so many in the nation. Basically, the mindset or philosophy of the Socialist and Humanist Civil Government Politicians and Bureaucrats is that Business Servants are less important in society than those working in civil government, as civil government makes no income or profit and exists simply to help persons in the country. In truth, the agenda of the Socialist and Humanist Civil Government Politicians and Bureaucrats is the acquisition of more and more authority and power to obtain personal wealth and to rule over people as an oligarchy, which is the establishment of an elite ruling class mostly concerned with protecting their own power. Socialist and Humanist Civil Government Politicians and Bureaucrats try to make themselves exempt from all laws that they pass and force upon the people.

Actually, the career professional Bureaucrats in the U.S. Federal government believe they are the actual ruling class for the nation because Presidents and Members of Congress come and go, but the career Bureaucrats live on and rule over people through their participation in writing legislation and regulations for the Legislative Branch and the execution of the those laws and regulations by the Executive Branch. In the establishment and execution of these laws and regulations, and in developing an explanation of the many differences and inequalities in God's created order, the Socialist and Humanist Civil Government Politicians and Bureaucrats invented their Humanist and Socialist sense of justice, which is earthly demonic wisdom (James 3:15) to attempt to bring "equality" of wealth to the masses when God created diversity and inequality of those in sports, medicine, law, education, and the trades. The Socialist and Humanist Civil Government Politicians and Bureaucrats are not satisfied with regulating equal opportunity for the masses as one of the ultimate virtues of their Humanist and Socialist philosophies but want to confiscate and overtax the money earned from God's Business Servants, and give it to the masses thinking that is the fair thing to do.

The mindset of Paganism is to try to make equal what God has created unequal, or what God has permitted to become unequal based upon physique, intellect, hard work, education, or being a member of a wealthy family. The Bible is for equal rights under the law and opportunity for all people. Everyone should have equal opportunity for education, health, sports, scholarships, grants, and any other rights afforded by law. God never made one race better than another race. God loves variety and diversity. Yet, some people have a greater athletic ability to play sports than others. Some people are more intelligent than others. This does not give them more rights, but it may give them an opportunity to participate which requires qualifications. If anyone has prepared a resume, then the one knows that the one with the most education and experience usually gets the job. The job should not be denied or given just because of race. A godly Believer who is spiritually mature is living up to his God ordained potential in Christ. There is a period when special favors and benefits should be given to any race which has been deprived of business capital, opportunity, and favoritism for several generations through government and cultural discrimination. Special favors and benefits for any deprived race because of tacit discrimination are okay and justified for a season to correct historical wrongs.

The Socialist and Humanist Civil Government Politicians and Bureaucrats have adopted the false religion of Socialism and Humanism as the philosophical altruistic principles to guide their decisions in running the affairs of government and society. The Socialist and Humanist Civil Government Politicians and Bureaucrats look at the different economic strata in society, and they presuppose that if somebody has more than somebody else, he or she had to have ripped off the other or has received special favors. They ignore that a successful wealthy Believer had followed God's biblical moral principles, and followed God's principles of biblical economics discussed in this book.

Why do the Socialist and Humanist Civil Government Politicians and Bureaucrats presuppose this prejudice against those who have become wealthy as Business Servants through hard work, use of developed unique talents, and taking risks with their capital for business startups? The reason is the whole concept of rewards because of obedience to God's covenantal voice from the word of God has been taken out of the social order and the principles by which the businesses, government, and people are supposed to operate and live have been removed or relegated to being irrelevant to the acceptable world standards.

Without submission to God, and His life enhancing rules, precepts, and laws, what is left in society is Paganism. Paganism cannot explain differences in wealth being a result of honest labor, business skills, investment of risk capital, and following biblical economics because it does not have a concept of the covenants the Hebrews and Christians have with God, which were once the accepted foundational basis of our American culture.

Pagans along with Socialist and Humanist Civil Government Politicians and Bureaucrats see the economic inequality and the proponents of these philosophies conclude, "This is wrong. Why should these people be wealthy, and these people be poor?" Pagans along with Socialist and Humanist Civil Government Politicians and Bureaucrats believe that the industrious wealthy should pay a higher percentage rate of taxes to government to help pay the government welfare programs and other expenditures. Also, the Socialist and Humanist Civil Government Politicians and Bureaucrats believe they are justified even to confiscate the assets of the super wealthy when the government needs extra money for the poor. This is theft by the Socialist and Humanist Civil Government Politicians and Bureaucrats who, as servants of the people take an oath to uphold the Constitution, which is based upon God's principles of economics, fairness, and rights.

The Fifth and Fourteenth Amendments forbid the taking of life, liberty, and property without due process of law. Theft is theft. Taking by the government from a small group of wealthy people should be unconstitutional, as it is unbiblical. A tax law singling out only wealthy citizens offends the Supreme Court's repeated invocation that the primary purpose of the Takings Clause is "to bar the Government from forcing some people alone to bear public burdens which, in all fairness and justice, should be borne by the public as a whole" [Armstrong v. United States, 364 U.S. 40, 49 (1960)]. Thus, the notion by the Socialists and Humanists that taxes are never takings is wrong. Also, the court held in Armstrong v. United States that taxing "named individuals or easily ascertainable members of a group" might be unconstitutional on grounds that it is a forbidden Bill of Attainder, as it imposes punishment. The Court in United States v. Lovett, 328 U.S. 303, 315 (1946), discusses the Bill of Attainder Clauses, which are stated in U.S. Const, Art. I § 9 cl. 3 (barring Congress from passing bills of attainder) and Art. I § 10 cl. 1 (same for State Legislatures). The Supreme Court has stated that "confiscation of property" is a form of punishment for purposes of the rule against Bills of Attainder Nixon v. Administrator of General Services, 433 U.S. 425, 474 (1977)]. Taxation of one person or a small, identifiable group might amount to a Bill of Attainder and is therefore unconstitutional.

For example, the city of Los Angeles passed by voters by ballot initiative in 2022 what is called the "Mansion Tax", which is a special transfer of ownership tax for owners who own five million dollar fair market value or more. The additional transfer tax is 4% of the sale price if the real property is valued at five million. The additional transfer tax is 5.5% of the sale price if the real property is valued at ten million. Thus, a five million house owner has to pay an additional two hundred thousand dollars on top of real property taxes and the county transfer tax. This tax is only in the city of Los Angeles. So far, the City of Los Angeles has won in the trial court, but the case is on appeal. If the City wins on appeal, this case could be a standard for other cities and counties in California to charge extremely high transfer taxes that are called "Mansion Tax." Yet, the average three bedroom (2,500 sq. ft.) track homes in greater Los Angeles have appreciated to two million dollars. The City of Los Angeles will most likely put the minimum home value to one million which means they consider almost every homeowner will be punished with the Mansion Tax. Socialists' rulership method is to tax and spend. With more money they can continue their cradle to grave monetary support to those who will continue to vote them in office, without denying support based upon their status as immigrants. In my legal opinion, this Mansion Tax violates the Constitution prohibitions against Bills of Attainder under U.S. Const, Art. I § 9 cl. 3 (barring Congress from passing bills of attainder)] and Art. I § 10 cl. 1 (same for State Legislatures). Bills of Attainder are when an easily ascertainable member of a group are punished with extraordinary taxes when other people do not have to pay.

Higher rates on those earning higher incomes confiscate the property of top earners in our nation. Strictly proportional rates (i.e. a "flat" tax) would satisfy this version of the Takings Clause. Furthermore, the common use of a property tax to fund education should be unconstitutional as all citizens should be paying for school expenses, not just the real property owners. A Biblical analysis is that since God owns all real property because the earth is the Lord's (Psalms 24:1), then all real property should be exempt from taxation. This is the same reasoning for allowing Churches to be non-profit organizations and exempt from taxation because the Churches belong to God.

If the wealthy person is a true Biblitarian, then God promises wealth as a reward for obedience in following His biblical principles. What the Humanists and Socialists should ask is, "What have these wealthy Biblitarians done to accumulate this wealth, so their thoughts and actions can be taught to the poor; and what have the poor done or failed to do, so their thoughts and actions, or lack thereof, can be avoided?"

The Bible says, "To him that has, more shall be given" (Luke 19:26, Matthew 13:12) because he has the covenantal skills, character, and blessings from God, Who is the Chief Wise Investor in all creation, both natural and spiritual. God rewards the industrious Business Servants by giving them more to steward.

God as King of His Kingdom, expects a good return on His investment. See Matthew 25: "Parable of the Talents" and Luke 19: "Parable of the Minas." God is the most itelligent Investor. God invests in Believers who He trains through daily incremental problem-solving in business and those who pray for wisdom to run the business and invest in wealth assets.

Jesus collected the leftover bread and fish, so that nothing would be lost after He fed the five thousand (Matthew 14:13-21). Jesus was training His disciples on the principles of good stewardship. God's biblical principle is as follows: "Whatever God multiplies through His spiritual anointing, God wants to preserve the anointing and hold it in storage for future use."

Jesus had the unlimited power to create wealth, multiply the bread and fish, or cause a miracle of multiplication here on earth, but He practiced the principle of His Father of good stewardship over the increase given by having His Apostles picking up the bread and fish leftovers. This work showed the Father's nature. "Whoever I find that used my biblical principles, I'm going to bless him or her and give him or her more to care for." God hates waste and expects good returns on His investment. True Biblitarians practice this principle.

"You've been faithful with ten minas, I'm going to make you ruler over ten cities" (Luke 19:17). Because God is the best Ruler, He looks to where He can find faithful stewards here on earth who will give Him increase to rule over cities. To those who misuse what God has given them, He takes it away (Luke 19:26). Before God makes you a Shepherd of people, He will transform your soul by teaching you His word. At the same time, God wants to train you to be a good steward of things like money or running a business. Thus, the principle is if you are going to be chosen as one of God's rulers, then you must learn how to multiply as a Believer what God gives you. Most all Politicians or Bureaucrats do not think about investing taxes collected to multiply the tax money. They see the government as a non-profit organization, while they see themselves as rulers over people. Yet, in God's Kingdom, if you cannot make a profit through good stewardship, you are not entitled to rule. Politicians and Bureaucrats in America only think about spending money, not making profit. For example, when the U.S. and its allies won the Iraqi war, why did not the U.S. take assets from Iraq, such as oil, as part of the spoils of war? Why did the U.S. Politicians and Bureaucrats spend Trillions of dollars in the war in Iraq and not demand at least reimbursement? Why did President Biden order the military to leave 83 billion worth of arsenal of military equipment, armored vehicles and weapons. This includes the following left to the Taliban terrorists: 22,174 Humvees, 1,000 armored vehicles, 42,000 pick-up trucks and SUVs, 64,363 machine guns, 358,350 assault rifles, 126,295 pistols, 200 artillery units, and state of the art military helicopters, warplanes, and other aircraft. This constituted a waste and violated biblical principles. Biden gave our enemy the spoils of war.

God does not like to sow seed into bad soil. God will choose healthy, good soil to plant His word. God is a good Sower and chooses good ground (Mark 4:13 20 parable of the four soils). The hearts of trustworthy Believers are the good soils in God's created order whom God will sow His good seed (the word of God) into. God chooses people by the condition of their hearts, not their engiftments.

However, God requires compassion and love by those who have, to those who have not if those who have not are truly victims of society (Matthew 25:35 46). This is not runaway confiscation by government to equalize wealth through over taxation of the industrious or confiscation. People who are poor need capital to start a business, or to find a job in the private sector.

The Civil Government should not be the biggest employer in the culture because the government collects taxes, but pays full salary to government employees, along with many benefits, not normally received in the private sector. Thus, assuming that taxes are at 34% for someone who earns $100,000, the government employee pays nothing in the Social Security fund and pays $34,000 (if no deductions) in income tax. Federal government employees have a high compensation package that includes benefits that still cost the taxpayers who have paid taxes and get nothing from the government financially, except roads to travel on, schools, and military. Here are the federal government employee benefits in addition to salaries:

Salary — The Federal Government offers competitive base pay, with most positions using the General Schedule (GS) pay system. Some highly competitive jobs, such as entry-level IT specialists, provide higher special pay rates.

Federal Student Loan Repayment — Federal Agencies help repay Federally-ensured student loans up to a maximum of $10,000 a year or a $60,000 lifetime maximum.

Incentives and Awards — In addition to salary, a federal hiring agency may offer monetary recruitment, relocation, or retention incentives and performance awards.

Ten paid holidays per year.

Vacation, Personal, and Sick Time

Pay and Leave Flexibilities

Leave to Care for Family Members

Child Care Subsidies

Child Care Workplace Flexibilities

Commuter Subsidies

Continuing Education and Professional Development

Health, Dental and Vision Insurance

Life Insurance

Long-Term Care Insurance

Elder Care Workplace Flexibilities

Employee Assistance and Referral

Flexible Spending Accounts

Reasonable Accommodations

Retirement Benefits

Volunteer Activities/Community Service

The problem with a Socialist government is the more the government tries to take over from families, churches, and local business, the more employees the Socialist government has to employ, and the greater expense to taxpayers. In an article entitled, "Reforming Federal Worker Pay and Benefits," written by Chris Edwards, dated August 2, 2019, he wrote the following: "The federal government employs 2.1 million civilian workers in hundreds of agencies at offices across the nation. The federal workforce imposes a substantial burden on America's taxpayers. In 2019 wages and benefits for executive branch civilian workers cost $291 billion. Since the 1990s, federal workers have enjoyed faster compensation growth than private-sector workers. In 2018 federal workers earned 80 percent more, on average, than private-sector workers. And federal workers earned 47 percent more, on average, than state and local government workers. The federal government has become an elite island of secure and high-paid employment separated from the ocean of average Americans competing in the economy. Spurred by large budget deficits, policymakers imposed a partial freeze on federal wages from 2011 to 2013, which saved billions of dollars. However, further savings are needed. Policymakers should turn their attention to the overly generous benefit packages received by federal workers. They should also cut the size of the federal workforce by terminating low-value programs and reducing layers of management."

Trends in Federal and Private Pay: In 2018 federal civilian workers had an average wage of $94,463, according to data from the U.S. Bureau of Economic Analysis (BEA). By comparison, the average wage for the nation's 118 million private-sector workers was only $63,306.... The Bureau of Economic Analysis provides data on the average value of federal and private sector benefit packages. In 2018 federal workers enjoyed average annual benefits of $41,508, which compared to average benefits in the private sector of just $12,075

Susan Walsh, Reporter for the "Associated Press" wrote on February 12, 2018, "The 2019 Presidential Budget proposal includes a pay freeze for federal employees for the federal fiscal year, and documents the administration's intention to rely more on 'pay for performance' structures than the standard pay increase schedule. The existing federal salary structure 'rewards longevity over performance,' according to budget documents, which pointed specifically to tenure-based 'step-increase' promotions 'that white-collar workers receive on a fixed, periodic schedule without regard to whether they are performing at an exceptional level or merely passable.' Employee union groups, however, have labeled the pay-for-performance structure, and the corresponding

removal of poor performers, as an attack on due process for federal employees. 'Federal workers shouldn't be hired or fired on the whims of political appointees whose allegiance is to their political party, not the country's best interests,' said American Federation of Government Employees national president J. David Cox Sr."
Apparently, Socialist Bureaucrats truly believe they serve the country's best interest while the Politicians serve only their political party's best interest. This is the elitist view of the Socialist Bureaucrats who believe that big government is in the country's best interest. Mr. Cox did not say the Bureaucrats are the ones who serve the American people's best interest, especially the American taxpayers, and he did not criticize that the Politicians do not serve the people who elected them. Bureaucrats are mostly sold-out Socialists, not proponents of free enterprise or biblitarian principles of economics.

Matthew 25: 35-46 does not "mandate" governments to feed the hungry, give drink to the thirsty, provide homes for the homeless, clothes for the naked, visit the sick, or go minister to those in prison. It says the individual Believers in the Church are supposed to do this as expressions of love. If people obey Jesus' commandment in John 13: 34-35 to love one another, then this giving and helping of others less fortunate than them should be a lifestyle of every Believer; and government employees and government expenditures can become smaller and decrease the need for more income taxes. It would be better for the tax code to be changed to give tax deductions or tax credits to those who support the needy than for the government to use income taxes to hire government employees to dispense money to the poor where most of the taxes are used for big government not people in need. Today's non-profit organizations spend between seventy to ninety percent on administration expenses and Administrators' salaries instead of giving the money to the less fortunate which was advertised as the purpose the non-profit organization was formed and the purpose for which the donors contributions were to be used. Non-profit organizations should be vetted, before anyone gives them any amount, as to how much money donated reaches the needy.

Yet, there is a difference between the rewarding of disobedience and God's way of showing compassion to the have nots while enabling the have nots to become productive members of the community once again. God's welfare program is to have compassion while you enable, not to reward disobedience of God's principles of economics and successful living. Giving someone a helping hand is giving them bread and fish while they are being discipled as farmers who know the law of sowing and reaping and fishermen who know how to bring to the marketplace what the "fishes" or consumers really want to bite or purchase.

BIBLITARIAN ECONOMICS INFUSED INTO SOCIETY WILL CHANGE
SOCIETY FOR THE BETTERMENT OF ALL CITIZENS, FAMILIES, CHURCHES,
BUSINESSES, AND GOVERNMENTS IN A NATION

God's rule is that if you give charity, expect nothing in return.

If God impresses you to give with compassion in such a way to enable someone, you are investing in someone;

and God wants a return. Through you, God will give seed for the person to sow and bread to live on while waiting for the harvest to come (2 Corinthians 9:10). God helps people and especially Believers to get back on their feet to re-enter the work-force, so He can continue in His spiritual maturation process where the Believer becomes a good servant son or daughter in the Lord's Kingdom. God dislikes idle people, as work is the primary method, He uses to mature His children.

Enablement forces people to deal with the implications of their own actions. This requires supplying resources with accountability. The Socialist and Humanist Civil Government Politicians and Bureaucrats have been doing the opposite. Small children and the permanently disabled should receive help, but under a system that keeps the family responsibility to the individual as a condition precedent. Educate, train, and then put the able body poor to work. Being a welfare recipient cannot be a life's profession.

Love is not supplying dope to a junky. Love is helping the junky emotionally, economically, and spiritually to go through withdrawal, so he or she is no longer addicted to that which is destroying him or her. A good government or society follows the Bible when they reward the industrious, have compassion on the needy for a season, provide ongoing help to those who are permanently disabled from working, but insists that the able are retrained and brought back into the work field. Likewise, the industrious are not Business Servants whose motive is to destroy his or her competition or to become a monopoly. The industrious Business Servants merely must want a fair share in a particular industry. God's Business Servants do not circumvent, do not steal customers or contacts, do not rip off others through deceit, and do not take unfair advantage of another smaller, struggling God's Business Servant.

The Socialist and Humanist government Bureaucrats and Politicians promote ongoing disobedience through laws which try to make everybody equal in their economic positions in society, instead of just requiring biblical economics to be the moral compass and principles to operate the businesses. Big is not always best. Local businesses run by families are the ideal, as they become known as a fixed part of the community and operate efficiently through the application of biblitarian principles by Business Servants with godly wisdom and thanksgiving in their hearts to be God's chosen servants to manifest God's goodness and love to his or her family, along with the church community and neighborhood.

However, the Bible promotes laws that grant across the board equal access to all opportunities to reward those who are talented and diligent with what God has graced them. These laws are good. Yet, laws which give unfair advantage to one group of society over another, except real victims for a season such as Afro-Americans or Hispanics or others in the inner cities who have been deprived of capital through discrimination for several generations, need to be changed. Notwithstanding, not all minorities have been denied capitalization for several generations and thus should not be given the same advantage. Also, nothing is spoken about the underprivileged orphans whose parents died an early death. They are often discriminated against and are forgotten and have little if any chances of being recognized as entitled for grants as others that are underprivileged in society. The underprivileged need a helping hand, not just a handout. They need capital to start their own businesses, along with business biblical training, so they too can prosper through the applications of biblical principles in God's Kingdom. It is wrong that foster children are cut off financially when they become eighteen. They are sent out to live on the streets to fend for themselves. Often they sell drugs or some get into prostitution.

The Socialist and Humanist Civil Government Politicians and Bureaucrats are called by God to promote godly obedience, godly justice, godly love, godly principles to promote the equalization of opportunity in education, business startup grants and low interest loans, access to political offices, and equality in all other areas of society. The Socialist and Humanist Civil Government Politicians and Bureaucrats are not called to make equal what God has made unequal. The Civil Government is not called to reward those who do not follow God's principles of wealth acquisition and the stewardship of God's creation.

Theories that say otherwise are built on the presupposition that the Humanist or Socialist Bureaucrat and Politician working in Civil Government is to be as God, redesigning and changing God's principles, and leveling human differences in skills, efforts, faith, family traditions, and the like, in their re-defining the phrase that "all men are created equal," without emphasizing that this statement in the U.S. Declaration of Independence and as applied in the U.S. Constitution refer to rights before God, government, and society to have the equal opportunity to live toward one's potential with life's tribulations bringing forth the risk of failure and the maturity resulting therefrom, along with a strong work ethic.

THE TRANSFER OF WEALTH FROM THE PRIVATE SECTOR TO THE PUBLIC SECTOR IN AN ATTEMPT TO EQUALIZE WEALTH INHERENTLY IS SELF-DEFEATING IN THE LONG RUN

Since the Socialist and Humanist Civil Government Politicians and Bureaucrats do not practice biblical business principles generating profit through innovation, risk, return, efficiency, or the stimulation of profit-sharing proprietorship, the Civil Government is the wrong entity to regulate wealth acquisition and distribution. This regulation should be done by families and communities joined together in personal covenant for their mutual benefit, mutual protection, and mutual enhancement of God's spiritual *zoe* life and *agape* love. Economic management should be done by local, faith-based family Businesses Servants who apply God's biblitarian economic principles and agape love.

Instead, the Socialist and Humanist Civil Government Politicians and Bureaucrats cause an involuntary transfer of capital, assets, riches, money, and wealth to the Civil Government, who in turn spends too much of these tax revenues in salaries for government employees and expenditures and lessens the amount of money used to meet the needs of people who are true victims. The Socialist and Humanist Civil Government Politicians and Bureaucrats also spend far too much on wars at the detriment of our society. Maintaining a very strong military is a deterrent to enemy attacks but spending money from loans and taxes on wars to promote policing around the world is a bad policy. With all the money spent by the United States on actual military conflicts, it has not made the people in the United States any safer. In fact, it has caused the opposite, as countries being attacked by the United States want to fight back, not conform to the way of life of the culture and values we cherish in the United States. These foreign countries and cultures have their own cherished traditions and mores, and they do not want to become Americans, necessarily. Taxes paid to the government are not a capital investment that brings about a return on investment, as government does not make profit. Therefore, extremely high taxes result in economic stagnation and exploitation in society, not long term returns on investments. A better approach is to give private businesses tax credits for building schools, libraries, roads, bridges, and infrastructure, and to give tax credits to families who take care of the welfare needs of the needy. It would be far more efficient and less costly.

Also, centralized Socialist and Humanist Civil Government Politicians and Bureaucrats are not the best authority to solve local needs. God always brings power and life from the ground up, not from the top down. God starts with a seed, plants it in fertile ground, lets it die, watches it resurrect as a new plant, waters it properly, protects it from the weeds, promotes its growth, and causes it to produce a bountiful harvest. All life forms released at creation go through this cycle of life. More efficiency could be experienced in government by granting incentives for local governments interacting with local businesses and families to help solve local problems. Under God's Kingdom, the local problems in the family are to be solved by the Families, Church Leaders, and Business Servants, but not government. God's moral laws are to be infused into the hearts of His children, especially those who have supervisory responsibility or stewardship of His creation. Once God's moral laws have been infused into a culture, people become Biblitarians as God's principled people. The Socialist and Humanist Civil Government Politicians and Bureaucrats compete with God and establish their own rules that are often devoid of biblitarian principles of economics and true freedom.

CURRENT PHILOSOPHY RUNNING CIVIL GOVERNMENT IS INHERENTLY ANTI FAMILY AND AGAINST MORALLY-INFUSED FREE ENTERPRISE THAT RESULTS IN POVERTY

The policy of creating dependency on Civil Government entitlements instead of the promotion of God's principles of honoring parents, preserving family units as that which is best for children, building estates to pass on to posterity, operating family businesses, stewarding family real estate, and covenantal commitments, undermine the family, which is God's basic unit of society through which He sends His blessings and wealth from one generation to the next. God wants Believers to establish Christian family dynasties through family managed businesses, and wealth assets stewardship, which are passed down generationally through trusts for wealth accumulation in the long run for Kingdom work and Christian family blessings.

Civil Government through death taxes penalizes generational transfer of covenantal wealth to the posterity of families. Death taxes are inherently unfair and anti-family because the assets of an estate of a deceased person were purchased already with after income tax dollars. Taxing the transfer of these assets to the next generation is double taxation and unfair. Death should not constitute a taxable event. The testator's death was not an incident where labor, riches, money, or wealth were created or realized by the testator at his or her death. The assets were already in the family from labor or investment, and income taxes had already been paid on the gain or income realized; so, the Civil Government has just arbitrarily passed a law to confiscate property from families just because someone died. Is this a reward for the testator who has been diligently following godly principles to lay up an inheritance for his children and children's children? I do not think so. Thus, death or estate taxes work against God's principles, which abhor single generation consumption. The Civil Government gets involved with too high of income taxes and then participates in confiscating the assets in a single generation through death taxes.

THE PRESENT SOCIALIST AND HUMANIST CIVIL GOVERNMENT
POLITICIANS AND BUREAUCRATS' POLICIES REWARD SIN

The Socialist and Humanist Civil Government Politicians and Bureaucrats promote fornication or adultery by the welfare mother with illegitimate children by allowing the mother to collect welfare only if no man lives permanently in the home as a traditional family. The welfare mother is encouraged to divorce and to have illicit affairs because she is paid to do it by the Civil Government, under the alleged "Constitutional right" of freedom of association. The sin involved in such activity is ignored completely.

Socialist and Humanist Civil Government Politicians and Bureaucrats reward theft and insolence by its over-protective policies for the rights of the criminal and justify disobedience with the excuse of being one of the "culturally disadvantaged." In other words, the criminal's excuse is, "I did not have the requisite mindset and am not responsible for my own actions because the culture in which I live has caused me to break the law." This governmental guiding policy violates God's mandated principles of godly self-government by His children being discipled also to become godly self-governed.

Socialist and Humanist Civil Government Politicians and Bureaucrats do not promote godly self-government or personal responsibility but promote financial dependency to "buy votes" and to justify governmental intrusion into the private lives of individual citizens. There are no governmental programs that reward people for following biblical principles of economics.

Socialist and Humanist Civil Government Politicians and Bureaucrats allow economic differences in society to be the acceptable basis as excuses for disobedient anti- biblical behavior.

WELFARE REFORM WITHOUT A BIBLICAL COMPASSIONATE BASE IS WRONG. Welfare reform must include aid to dependent victims, but only according to the biblical pattern, i.e., for a limited time to promote enablement, unless someone is permanently disabled. Job training and education should be a mandate for anyone on welfare. The policy should be to educate, train, and prepare them for work to remove them from the welfare role, not create a lifestyle of government financial dependency from cradle to grave or womb to tomb.

There must also be tax reform based on biblical principles such as a "flat income tax of less than ten percent" or a "universal consumption tax." The "flat tax" is God ordained, which we see with the tithe or flat tax of ten percent, paid by one and all. The Bible says a nation brings bondage upon itself and its people when its income tax is equal to or above the amount "taxed" by God (1 Samuel 8:15 17). The "consumption tax" would be fair to all persons, regardless of income bracket, because it would be based upon the consumer's purchase of goods and services throughout the year, which anyone can control. Assume the consumption tax is nine percent. Those who buy one billion dollars of goods and services for the year will pay ninety million dollars in consumption tax. Those who purchase ten thousand dollars of goods and services for the year will pay nine hundred dollars in consumption tax. Thus, it is fair to all people. The rich and wealthy pay more because they buy and consume more. The poor pay less because they buy and consume less.

THE PROGRESSIVE INCOME TAX, which punishes the diligent, skill oriented, long run thinking business and industrious individuals, is anti-Bible and thus antichrist in origin. The philosophy of the Socialist and Humanist Civil Government Politicians and Bureaucrats is that taxing the income of the poor takes away their food, shelter, clothing, and transportation, but taxing the rich does not affect their ability to pay for these necessities. Yet, it makes Business Servants want to take their business to another country where there are more favorable income tax laws, which would cause a loss of jobs for the poor or middle class. Therefore, the consumption tax would be fair to all people in society. The more they spend, the more they pay. The rich and famous live to spend; they will pay taxes daily, and they will pay much more, but it is fair.

Ministering to the poor is not an ongoing trough of feeding, medicating, housing, and clothing them while they remain disobedient to God's principles of economics. This non-biblical, non-accountable, non-enabling, non-incentive welfare system is rewarding people for disobedience to God's Kingdom economic principles. It also is encouraging them to remain in sin, enslavement, and dependent on the government idol, which is government feeding programs, housing programs, and medical programs without any incentives to obtain training and education to qualify for a job to stop receiving taxpayers' money from the government or causing the government to go into debt by selling Treasury Bonds and Municipal Bonds.

Socialist and Humanist Civil Government Politicians and Bureaucrats recognize that the family is its chief competitor in caring for people. The real reason or explanation for governmental intrusion into private family lives is that the Socialist and Humanist Civil Government Politicians and Bureaucrats want to take over the family responsibility because people pay taxes and are voters who vote Politicians into office. Furthermore, government department size in personnel and importance is based on the size of the group of people over which the governmental Chief Bureaucrat supervises. The more votes a Politician receives, or the more people a Chief Bureaucrat supervises, the more power the Bureaucrat has in government. If the Socialist and Humanist Civil Government Politicians and Bureaucrats can train up the children to espouse its secular, Socialist and Humanist religion, then when they become adults, they will vote to keep their "priests" in office. The problem with any program in government, once the bureaucracy is established, is it usually continues to grow and exist, even though the purpose for the bureaucracy has long since gone.

For example, President Jimmy Carter had good intentions, I believe, for wanting the consumers to cut back on fuel consumption, and in his speech of April 18, 1977, he said he was proposing to establish the Department of Energy which would oversee the following goals: "Cut in half the portion of United States oil which is imported, from a potential level of 16 million barrels to six million barrels a day. Establish a strategic petroleum reserve of one billion barrels, more than six months' supply. Increase our coal production by about two thirds to more than 1 billion tons a year. Insulate 90 percent of American homes and all new buildings. Use solar energy in more than two and one-half million houses. We will monitor our progress toward these goals year by year. Our plan will call for stricter conservation measures if we fall behind." On August 4, 1977, President Jimmy Carter signed the Department of Energy Organization Act, and he centralized the responsibilities of the Federal Energy Administration, the Energy Research and Development Administration, the Federal Power Commission and other energy-related government programs into a single presidential cabinet-level department. The Department of Energy went into existence on October 1, 1977. Although the new Department of Energy was responsible for long term planning to reduce the U.S. dependency on foreign import oil, import oil purchases increased steadily over the years while the Department of Energy continued to grow in personnel and budget expenditures. The Department of Energy was also responsible for long-term, high-risk research and development of energy technology, federal power marketing, energy conservation, energy regulatory programs, a central energy data collection and analysis program, and nuclear weapons research, development, and production. However, no alternative energy was developed by the government. When it was originally established, the Department of Energy had about 20,000 employees. Although it has totally failed in its mission, it is still in existence. Today, it has about 16,000 permanent employees and about 100,000 contract employees, who work in the national laboratories and other facilities. Currently, the U.S. Secretary of Energy oversees a budget of approximately $23 billion and more than 100,000 federal and contract employees. Its original budget was $944 million in 1980. Figures on the number of initial employees remain allusive. Although the Department of Energy has completely failed in its mission to stop the dependence on foreign oil, it is still in existence. No one is sure what its function really is today, as many other departments have been formed to handle energy related issues. Since the Department of Energy's inception in 1977, the U.S. uses over 45% more now, of foreign import oil.

Thus, this is an example of the unnecessary waste of taxpayers' money by government Socialist and Humanist Bureaucrats who are inefficient to achieve real progress. Notwithstanding, in just two years under a conservative business-minded President, Donald Trump, the U.S. became a net exporter of oil. Why didn't the Department of Energy make the U.S. a net exporter of oil since 1977 after 41 years spending government money of almost one trillion dollars? The Department of Energy lost its purpose, so it tried to redefine itself and began to focus on environmental remediation of past actions, including cleaning up its own contaminated weapons facilities. Department of Energy budget requests for funding had 85% earmarked for Environmental Quality, with only 15% earmarked for Energy Resources. To a large extent, politics stopped the U.S. from being energy independent. In November 2015, President Obama was influenced by the environmentalists to reject the proposal to build the Keystone XL pipeline from Alberta to the Gulf Coast because of domestic environmental concerns over water quality as well as the general antipathy of the environmental movement to pipeline building, and the production practices in the source (the Athabasca oil sands). Only days after President Trump was inaugurated, he signed an executive order aimed at reviving the Keystone XL and Dakota Access pipelines, and by March 2017 a permit was granted for construction of the Keystone XL pipeline, calling it "the first of many infrastructure projects" that he intended to approve in order to put more Americans to work.

THE SOCIALIST AND HUMANIST CIVIL GOVERNMENT POLITICIANS AND BUREAUCRATS SPENDING ON WARS ARE ALSO OUT OF CONTROL AS WELL. The more the U.S. promotes itself as the policeman of the world, the more debt the U.S. creates to pay for the military complex and the private contractors who make billions for making weapons of war or the private mercenaries who act as a police force or who are paid to modify armaments for the protection of soldiers on the field of the battle. Biblitarians believe in a strong national defensive militarily. However, the U.S. has been in constant wars since WWII, which have all been paid for by government going further into debt. The Civil Government spending on unnecessary wars is totally out of control. The U.S. must have a strong defense, but continuously spreading our troops and military weapons throughout the world diminishes our ability to marshal our military personnel if we are attacked. Presidents and Members of Congress regularly and historically engage our county in wars that contribute heavily to our ever-increasing national debt. American politicians should stop causing conflicts with other countries because it causes our country to go into further debt to fight wars. We need to strengthen our defenses and stop going to war. Why cannot the U.S. be more like Switzerland who has not been in a war in 500 years and signed the Paris treaty of 1815 declaring its neutrality, and the League of Nations formally recognized Switzerland's neutrality on February 13, 1920.

The Afghanistan and Iraq wars lasted longer than the Vietnam War, and trillions of dollars have been wasted. It has cost the U.S. States hundreds of billions of dollars to try to make Afghanistan and Iraq democratic countries like the U.S., but they have their own history much older than the U.S.; and they like their culture the way it is. They do not want to change. Only God can change human hearts, not governments.

ALSO, THE POLITICIANS AND BUREAUCRATS THAT RUN
THE CIVIL GOVERNMENT HAVE DONE EVERYTHING THEY CAN DO TO
UNDERMINE THE REALITY AND THE FOUNDATION
OF THE TRADITIONAL GOD ORDAINED FAMILY UNIT

Some of these anti-family and anti-business laws and actions by government are:

Easy "no fault divorce."

Redefining the family to include any non-biblical relationships.

New State laws since Dobbs, allowing children to have abortions and sexual aids without parental knowledge.

Not allowing the father of an unborn child to have any right to protest the killing of

his unborn children through abortion.

Government funding abortion clinics which practice what could be defined as Eugenics.

Taking away parental rights to choose their children's education.

Penalizing family units through taxation.

Strictly regulating where and when Churches can meet and worship.

Defining more people as victims, so they can receive government subsistence and financial enslavement and become Socialist voters.

Defining recipients of welfare as only those who do not live in a traditional mother, father, and children family unit.

TAXING SMALL BUSINESS SERVANTS AT THE SAME RATE AS EXECUTIVE EMPLOYEES: When the executive employees do not earn their income by risking their own capital as do small Business Owners, then this is a reason to tax the Small Business Owners at a lower level, or at least have a special tax credit for risking their capital. Taxing the industrious Small Business Owners at the same tax rate as executive employees is the "Robin Hood Mentality" and unfair since the executive employee did not risk his own capital to earn the same amount.

Allowing super wealthy people who are not elected, who have ungodly agendas and motives, by funding politicians and District Attorneys to prosecute political opponents become the ones making governmental decisions and policies instead of duly elected representatives who are supposed to be the servants of the people. This should be illegal. Prosecuters should not use criminal complaints with non-supportive evidence or packing a Grand Jury with only same political party jury which is potentially unfair.

The answer to social needs is to empower the families, once again, as having the authority as the base institution of the society. Family law and juvenile courts need to change the fundamental policy from "what is in the best interest of the child" to "what is in the best interest of the child and the preservation of the family unit."

If the U.S. government was following biblical principles, then the slogans to those who have specific needs should be:

Go home for care and welfare.

Go home for wealth creation.

Go home for building a family based Biblitarian business with fair taxing laws to give incentives to small Business Servants for taking financial risks.

Go home for housing the homeless.

Go home for laying up of wealth for your children's children, who are God's Kingdom citizens.

THE TRUTHS

God's biblical economic principles in the Kingdom of God reward the faithful, industrious, and diligent, not the fearful, lazy, and disobedient. He who is faithful with what he has, God gives more to manage. He takes from the have nots who are able to work but are slothful and hands it to the haves who are faithful and obedient and industrious servants.

This is God's biblical economics as seen in Luke 19:26 in the parable of the minas. The Socialist and Humanist Civil Government Politicians and Bureaucrats try to counter God's biblical economics with their demonic man-made philosophy espousing relativism, pluralism, Socialism, Humanism, and economic "equality" by punishing the industrious with higher taxes, punishing the Business Servants who employ people with choking business regulations, and confiscation of assets to divest families of estates that should be passed down to subsequent generations.

The Socialist and Humanist Civil Government Politicians and Bureaucrats punish the faithful, hard working small business entrepreneurs by making them underwrite new health insurance requirements, clean up the environment, and pay for most every other social ill, even though small Business Servants employ about seventy percent of the work force in the U.S. while receiving small incentives for taking the risk of failure with their own capital investment.

The Socialist and Humanist Civil Government Politicians and Bureaucrats reward those who practice anti-family values, non-biblical social behavior, and exempts government from all "OSHA" safety requirements to protect government employees, exempts "EPA" regulations regarding the polluting of the environment, exempts "SEC" regulations regarding the sale of U.S. Treasury bonds or state municipal bonds, and exempts government from being sued without its permission.

The Socialist and Humanist Civil Government Politicians and Bureaucrats rescind Constitutional protective rights from forfeiture and the due process of law when empowering the IRS and the state taxing authorities in collecting taxes against income earning persons in the country. The Civil Government non-elective Bureaucrats are exempted from accounta bility requirements and Social Security (which is a tax, not a retirement fund) along with a host of other protective, self preservation regulations.

NINE

RISK AND POSSIBILITY OF FAILURE ARE ESSENTIAL FOR GROWTH AND MATURITY

GOD DESIGNS EVENTS IN OUR LIVES WITH THE
POSSIBILITY OF FAILURE TO MATURE US

God takes Business Servants through difficult situations that present the possibilities of failure to mature His Business Servants. While Business Servants try to operate their businesses as places of ministry, the reality is they operate their businesses in a fallen world; and there is never a perfect financial or business transaction that will allow the Business Servant to get rich quick. God uses the daily problem encountering and problem-solving requirements in the business to not only mature the employees but also the Business Servant owner. Everything God does causes growth in the souls of His Business Servants.

The world system is full of bad people, sin, false philosophies, disappointments, covetousness, greed, and traitors like Judas. It is challenging work to maintain biblical principles when it seems people in the world are making money with less than good and honest ethics. Business difficulties will cause stress, but God uses the opportunity to encounter the risks of failure to train His Business Disciples to make wise decisions, be accountable, and not allow failure to stop operating their business as their place of ministry. All these experiences of possibility of failure and great difficulty are designed to cause His Business Servants to lean closer to the Holy Spirit for comfort and guidance, so it is a good thing what God does. Some Business Servants are stubborn as a mule, and they need to get hit hard in their minds and emotions to wake up to wrong thinking, wrong emoting, and wrong beliefs. Most immature Business Servants make bad decisions through wrong associations and making unwise decisions, and are enticed by greed, avarice, and covetousness.

Business Servants are captains of their ship. They have no power to change the direction of the wind; but with experience, they can learn to adjust their sails to capture the power of the wind to get them to their ultimate destination where God is sending them. There will always be storms to battle, but a good experienced captain can see the business through the storms that come to try to destroy the business ministry.

Business Servants must realize that although, as Believers, they are not under the Hebrew law but under Christ's grace, there are God's laws that will be written on their hearts that will operate in their lives. For example, Galatians 6:7 says, "Do not be deceived, God is not mocked, for whatever a man sows, that he will also reap." Thus, for the most part, until Business Servants become wise unto their salvation, they normally engage in causing their own problems by reaping what they personally have sown in their business.

Business Servants should lead in setting the standard of being godly obedient with good morals and caring motives instead of being popular by being politically correct, which changes as the seasons change in every generation in the world. The Lord's moral code, righteousness, and covenants do not change, as they are eternal and should give Business Servants confidence and the best security. Malachi 3:6 says, "For I am the LORD, I change not; therefore, the sons of Jacob are not consumed."

As Believers, Business Servants are in Christ Jesus of the Tribe of Judah, a son of Jacob. The Lord's Business Servants serve the King, which is the Lord Jesus Christ and should not adopt as a new philosophy the cultural changes that occur in the society. Proverbs 24:21 warns, "My son, fear thou the LORD and the king: and meddle not with them that are given to change." God is the ultimate Judge in our world, culture, family, and for everyone. The Lord's justice and principles for every area of Business Servants' lives produce righteousness. Isaiah 26:9 says, "...For when Your judgments are in the earth, the inhabitants of the world will learn righteousness." The Lord's Kingdom principles produce righteousness in a nation. God is about the business of making His Business Servants Biblitarians. Thus, the issue is what and who are Business Servants going to trust? Proverbs 3:5-7 says, "Trust in the Lord with all your heart, and lean not on your own understanding. In all your ways acknowledge Him, and He shall direct your paths. Do not be wise in your own eyes. Fear the Lord and depart from evil." Psalms 20:7 says, "Some trust in chariots, and some in horses: but we will remember the name of the LORD our God."

Through daily work and some suffering, the Lord's Business Servants will learn to obey the Lord and the leading of the Holy Spirit. Even Jesus learned obedience by the things He suffered here on earth (Hebrews 5:8) through discipline by arduous work in His stepfather's carpenter business as God's assignment for maturation and good character through the daily business transactions with customers and solving other business economic problems incrementally on a daily basis.

FALSEHOODS EXISTING IN THE FALLEN HUMANISTIC WORLD

It is a falsehood that the Socialist and Humanistic Civil Government Politicians and Bureaucrats are responsible to minimize the risks of personal failure for its citizens.

It is a falsehood that the Socialist and Humanistic Civil Government Politicians and Bureaucrats can use the fiscal monetary strength to avoid the principles of God which exist to govern individuals, families, businesses, and governments.

It is a falsehood that the Socialist and Humanistic Civil Government Politicians and Bureaucrats can solve problems and handle power better than any other segment of society to create a buffer zone between sin and God's consequences for sin.

GOD'S TRUTHS IN HIS KINGDOM

Risks and possibility of failure teach Business Servants that decisions have consequences.

God matures His Business Servants by engaging them in the world which is like walking through a mine field. The fallen world is riddled with many risks and more potential for failure than success, so Business Servants must be disciplined and learn to come to God with their problems. In so doing, God will teach them to pray, seek justice, learn wisdom, knowledge, and understanding by meditating on His Word and will learn not to do anything until they are led by the Holy Spirit. If Business Servants feel uncomfortable about a business decision or transaction, that is normally a sign that more research is needed, thoroughly checking out the reputation of those involved, and making sure the business is strong enough to handle the losses that may result if the transaction fails.

The truth is that the Socialist and Humanist Civil Government Politicians and Bureaucrats are not biblically empowered to solve problems that are personal in nature to the residents of the nation. Solving personal problems must be done through godly self-government, the interaction with others in the family, the fellowship with brothers and sisters in the Church, the transactions and relationships encountered by people working in the same business, and printing godly principles into schools' educational textbooks.

Socialist and Humanist Civil Government Politicians and Bureaucrats cannot spend their way out of the consequences of the sins of its people and leaders. The false belief of the Socialist and Humanist Civil Government Politicians and Bureaucrats is that money solves all problems. However, throwing money on a problem often is positive reinforcement to continue the problem, so the recipient can receive more money, which in the end becomes self-perpetuating bondage. It is like when the Hebrews sold themselves into Egyptian slavery. They exchanged their freedom for food and shelter.

DEPENDENCY ON GOVERNMENT IS LESS LIKELY TO CHANGE BELIEVERS' BEHAVIOR THAN BELIEVERS' OWN MATURE SELF GOVERNMENT

2 Corinthians 4:4 describes the people in the fallen world who are perishing "whose minds the god of this age has blinded, who do not believe, lest the light of the gospel of the glory of Christ, who is the image of God, should shine upon them."

Some immature people foster the belief that the Civil Government owes them a living. The Socialist and Humanist Civil Government Politicians and Bureaucrats cannot regulate your personal life, cannot follow you around and keep you out of trouble, and do not have the money to support you from cradle to grave, or from womb to tomb, without the government and people going into debilitating debt.

For example, if you are a young teenage girl from a middle-class family, and you get pregnant at age 16, chances are you will be impoverished for most of your adult life. The reason is that you will have to care for the child, will not be able to receive the best education, will not be flexible in traveling on your job for higher pay, may not be able to marry a professional spouse, or will not have the freedom or money to obtain a degree from an institution of higher education. In fact, you may find yourself on welfare, living a substandard life, economically. Conversely, with the help of the Lord, many have overcome these difficulties, but it will certainly be a much tougher life. However, these negative facts do not justify God's laws by murdering an unborn child through abortion.

The Socialist and Humanist Civil Government Politicians and Bureaucrats pass laws and promote policies that reward sin. Instead, the Politicians and Bureaucrats have the charge and duty to promote God's will here on earth and discourage sin (Romans 13: 3-4). Government workers are supposed to be ministers of what God considers good and not be ministers of what God considers evil.

The Socialist and Humanist Civil Government Politicians and Bureaucrats reward disobedience to God and His word by attempting to provide income and support through the subsidies from the Civil Government, muffling, outlawing and postponing the consequences of disobedience.

In truth, the Socialist and Humanist Civil Government Politicians and Bureaucrats minimize the risk of failure to the people, and people never are given reality training to learn that decisions have spiritual and natural consequences.

"Safe sin" is the goal of the disobedient Socialist and Humanist Civil Government Politicians and Bureaucrats, and they ridicule through political correctness and do not espouse any rewards for living a righteous life in God's Kingdom.

AMERICA'S HISTORY SINCE 1900 FROM GOD'S PERSPECTIVE

Let's look at modern history of the United States from God's perspective instead of man's perspective. In the early 1900's, America had zeal to embrace modernism that was being promoted in Europe. World War I came, and millions of American Soldiers went to war in Europe and were exposed to new ideas, and they brought back with them Modernism with its Socialist and Humanist thoughts. American theologians teaching God's principles to operate within society came under great criticism like what is happening today. These Soldiers and so-called Modernist Intellectuals started embracing Freudianism from Austria. Politicians and Bureaucrats in Civil Government, along with product marketing companies, started listening to these Soldiers and family members as voters and consumers; and these new beliefs eventually became the mainstream popular thoughts in America. Once something is widely accepted in the marketplace, people believe that it is the truth or an enlightened fact.

Also, evolution from Darwinism was being taught in Europe and now was being accepted in America and eventually taught in the schools as scientific truth, when there was no scientific natural evidence to support

Darwin's conclusions. Darwinism was part of Eugenics, and the complete title to his racist book is: <u>On the Origin of Species by Means of Natural Selection, Or The Preservation of Favoured Races in the Struggle for Life</u>. The last part of the title was removed in the new editions, and people did not catch on to the fact that Darwin was a racist.

The study and implementation of Eugenics became popular. Planned Parenthood founder, Margaret Sanger was a racist who advocated sterilization of "unfit" African American women. She also favored the practice of Eugenics for the preservation of what she felt was the more favored races. Margaret Sanger founded "The Birth Control Review" in 1917. She wrote articles such as, "Some Moral Aspects of Eugenics" (June 1920), "The Eugenics Conscience" (February 1921), "The Purpose of Eugenics" (December 1924), "Birth Control and Positive Eugenics" (July 1925), "Birth Control: The True Eugenics" (August 1928), and many others of the same topic.

Margaret Sanger had the personnel in her organization specifically solicit black ministers to help overcome objections based upon religious issues in the use of birth control, with the real intent to decrease the black population in the U.S. Planned Parenthood targeted the black population in inner cities to encourage them to use birth control, as the blacks had a greater percentage per capita of single parent pregnancies. Alan Guttmacher, president of Planned Parenthood, advocated population control of blacks through involuntary abortions and sterilization. Then Planned Parenthood received tax subsidies to pay for low income (with a greater percentage of blacks) receiving abortions. The false issue of "over population" motivated Planned Parenthood to push birth control and abortion on demand as an acceptable policy amongst the black Pastors and eventually to become the law of the land.

As of the writing of this book, since the 1973 <u>Roe v. Wade</u> Supreme Court decision of making abortion on demand a Constitutional right, Planned Parenthood has killed over eight million black babies which is more than the six million Jews killed in the German holocaust during WWII. George Grant in his book, <u>Killer Angel</u> revealed the true motive of Margaret Sanger as being a blatant racist, a revolutionary Socialist, and a promoter of Eugenics through birth control, voluntary abortion, eventually forced involuntary abortion, and forced sterilization of what she believed were the "inferior races." In 2015, Planned Parenthood received over 500 million dollars in government funding. However, in 2015 it was revealed that Planned Parenthood had been involved in supplying fetal tissue and baby body parts to medical facilities or research laboratories, with abortion doctors specifically avoiding the crushing of the organ areas of the fetus to preserve brains, kidneys, hearts, lungs, and liver; so they can be used for "research" with the aborting mother's consent. Title IV of the Public Health Services Act says abortion providers cannot alter the "timing, method, or procedures" used to terminate a pregnancy solely for the purpose of obtaining fetal tissue. Although it is illegal to sell the fetal tissue, Planned Parenthood receives money for "preparing and transporting" the fetal tissue, which is allowed under existing law.

Since there are God's Business Servants, there are also very wealthy business men and women who do not promote God's sanctity of life. In "The Gates Operating System," Time, Jan. 13, 1997, the billionaire Bill Gates, co-founder of Microsoft said, "church represents an inefficient use of his time."

Bill Gates' father, William Gates, Sr., a successful corporate lawyer, was a member of the Board of Planned Parenthood in the Pacific Northwest. William Gates Sr. contributed to Planned Parenthood that promoted abortion on demand, and he did not condition his donations that the money given was not to be used for abortion.

In 2006, when Bill Gates Jr. gave an interview with Bill Moyers, Bill Gates said the following: "When I was growing up, my parents were always involved in various volunteer things. My dad was head of Planned Parenthood. And it was very controversial to be involved with that. And so it's fascinating. At the dinner table, my parents are very good at sharing the things that they were doing. And almost treating us like adults, talking about that."

William Gates Sr. told Salon.com regarding Bill Gates Jr.'s interest in overpopulation that "It's an interest he's had since he was a kid." Like his father, Bill Gates Jr. along with his then wife, Melinda Gates, supported Planned Parenthood, especially regarding abortion rights for women.

However, Bill Gates Jr. believes that contraceptive use and abortion are both tools for population reduction. During a talk on population reduction and climate change, at "Ted Talk" in 2010, Bill Gates Jr. said, "The world today has 6.8 billion people. That's heading up to about nine billion. Now, if we do a really great job on new vaccines, health care, reproductive health services, we could lower that by perhaps ten or fifteen percent." How does "vaccines" which are designed to save people from pandemics help reduce the population?

Similarly, in an interview in 2011 when asked by CNN's Sanjay Gupta about Bill Gates Jr.'s "Decade of Vaccines Initiative," he said: "The benefits [of vaccines] are there in terms of reducing sickness, reducing population growth."

Lowering the population with abortion and vaccines does not seem like saving lives. However, when confronted with the comments, Bill Gates' then wife, Melinda Gates, explained that vaccines improve health; and when parents see healthier children who will live into adulthood, the parents usually decide to have fewer children. Thus, vaccines help reduce the population. This explanation seems to be weak at best and sounds more like Eugenics taught by Margaret Sanger.

Bill Gates and his then wife were not furthering biblical principles of sanctify of life of the unborn in their charitable giving, as they wanted to reduce the population by killing the unborn as a right in other countries as well as the U.S. For example the International Planned Parenthood Federation, Western Hemisphere Region, Inc. received $1,730,000 as a donation from the Bill & Melinda Gates Foundation. International Planned Parenthood Federation, Western Hemisphere Region, Inc. (IPPF/WHR) used the gift to implement family planning programs and education against gender violence in Latin America and the Caribbean. The gift from

Bill & Melinda Gates Foundation was being used to support three programs: the South-North Adolescent Partnership; the Project to Combat Gender-Based Violence in Latin America; and Brothers for Change. The South-North Partnership on Adolescent Reproductive Health was touted as an innovative approach to educating youth on the sensitive issue of sexual and reproductive health. The priorities of the Bill & Melinda Gates Foundation were to improve the health of women in the developing countries through providing available contraception and abortion, along with combating gender-based violence in Latin America and the Caribbean Islands. The major recipient of the charitable gift from the Bill & Melinda Gates Foundation was IPPF/WHR who advocates strongly for the sexual and reproductive rights (including abortions on demand) of the underserved in the Western Hemisphere region and believes that having access to family planning information and sexual and reproductive health services is a basic human right that contributes to the wellbeing of women, children, and men throughout the world.

NOW BACK TO THE HISTORY OF THE U.S. FROM GOD'S POINT OF VIEW

Historically in America, because of the sins of the Roaring Twenties, God allowed the consequences of disobedience on the people living in America, and others, and allowed the Great Depression of the 1930's to awaken the people that there are consequences to sins of the flesh's indulgence and for a Christian nation to turn its back on God and His biblitarian principles. God wanted the people in America to repent and turn back to Him, but He was thwarted in the short run by President Franklin Roosevelt and his idea of economic recovery, called the New Deal and eventually WWII.

The New Deal came along with the philosophy called the "Keynesian Modern Socialist State" invented and fueled by John Maynard Keynes. Keynes' economic program said the following falsehood: that the solution is not the repentance of sins and turning back to God by people and the leaders of the nation, but the solution is strong Socialist and Humanist Civil Government Politicians and Bureaucrats which have the power to shield people from the consequences of their sins or disobedience to God. The Lord's plan to bring the U.S. and the world out of the Great Depression was "Repent for the Kingdom of heaven is at hand" (Matthew 4;17), which should have sparked a spiritual revival in America, but did not. Keynes' Socialist and Humanist disobedient and rebellious plan was to engineer a buffer zone between God's penalties of disobedience and sin by using monetary and fiscal Socialist, bigger government spending policies, to kick start the economy again. Keynes fueled the economy through the bankers' creditor/debtor system putting the United States government into billions of dollars in debt. In other words, Keynes' idea was to make the U.S. a debtor nation to be slaves to the Federal Reserve.

A nation cannot borrow and spend money to save a nation which violates God's laws of economics. The economic principle is that you cannot spend more than you earn. The U.S. Government earns money through income taxes, fuel taxes, royalty income from mining of precious metals, and from the extraction of oil and gas from government owned lands. If the government spends more than it receives in income, then they have to borrow the rest that the government wants to spend. When the U.S. government raised the capital gains taxes upon the sale of capital assets, those who hold these investments simply sit back and do not sell their capital assets and refuse to invest in business, which causes a decrease in taxes paid and a decrease in economic growth. Also, raising income taxes on businesses causes businesses to simply pass on the additional taxes by raising the retail prices to the consumers, so the consumers suffer from increase of income taxes on businesses. When business income taxes are too high, employment figures fall and unemployment figures rise. Yet, normal employees do not understand these basic principles of business and economics that result in increase of business income taxes.

The problems of the Great Depression were never solved. Americans simply went to war, and the people as a culture and society never repented and did not come back to faithful obedience to God's biblitarian principles. It was WWII that stimulated all the economic changes, not the biblical economic principles of God being applied, and certainly not the principles of Roosevelt's New Deal programs.

The United States continues to stimulate the economy through war which allows the Politicians to issue more U.S. Treasury Bonds to go into further monstrous debt to finance wars. War does stimulate the economy in the short run for those companies that have to hire more employees to supply the weapons, transportation, and supply line to make war successful against an enemy. In the meantime, after the war is over, the country's national debt increases while the "war corporations" become wealthier. Thus, Americans fought every war on credit since WWII, and the Bankers printed money without proper gold or silver backing the money and started the economic monster indebtedness of the United States, who currently is the largest debtor nation of the world.

THE PROBLEM WITH MODERNISM

In WWII, the American soldiers went overseas again, and became indoctrinated even further with Modernism. After WWII, the young soldiers returning from war had pent up energy and emotions from undiagnosed PTSD. Having experienced facing death, they wanted to live life back home to its fullness. The soldier's desire was to just get back home where there was peace, get married, grow a large family, have a house, car, and a good job. They ignored biblical economic wisdom not to go into debt enslavement. Yet, a new kind of consumer financing came into the marketplace which was called consumer credit without security. The post WWII soldier families started using credit to purchase what they wanted now instead of later, as no one knew how long they were going to live, so why wait for what they wanted. Besides, they thought that the real issue is whether they could afford the monthly payments, and if they could, why not supply their families with what the middle class had in "things" instead of saving and investing a percentage of income for the future.

These post WWII young soldier parents gave birth to the "baby boomers" generation. These post WWII young soldier families had all that pent up energy that went into the economy that resulted in buying and selling because the parents of the baby boomers did not want their children to suffer as they had suffered in the Great Depression. These post WWII young soldiers felt they deserved a better life since they were the victors of war against Germany and Japan. Since they opted to avoid the lessons that should have been learned during the economic hardship of the Great Depression, themselves, they certainly did not want their children experiencing any economic hardships growing up. By raising their children in a new middle class, and having their children get a good education, the post WWII young soldier parents believed they were giving their children opportunities for advancement they did not have.

Often, allowing children to go through hardships is a better teacher than creating an artificial environment that takes away the risk of failure when bad decisions are made. Overindulgences by parents teach children that wrong decisions have no consequences. God allows His children the freedom to make choices, but His children do not have the freedom to choose the consequences of those choices that have turned to unwise and sinful actions.

God's economic principles, and the principles of sowing and reaping apply indiscriminately to all people. The rich, famous, and wealthy are not immune from severe depression and mental illness. Christine Onassis, after her father Aristotle Onassis died, became the wealthiest woman in the world, but she died of a legalized anti depressant drug over dose. The treating physician reported that death was caused by heart failure. The physician was right because had she turned her life over to Jesus, she would not have had to suffer an early death. Unfortunately, there was a time when the wise King Solomon was not so wise. He said in Ecclesiastes 10:19 that money was the answer for all things. Money often simply rewards the faithful for his actions in a safe way, but also rewards the irresponsible in a bad way.

God allowed all this energy to be released, in the U.S., which was expressed in the rebellious music of the 1950's and 1960's. In the 1960's, the citizens of the U.S. had another opportunity to make a choice about whether they were going to repent or once again vote for Socialist and Humanist Civil Government Politicians who promised to use monetary and fiscal policies to shield people from their sins. The Socialist and Humanist Politicians and Bureaucrats running the U.S. chose instead to further distance themselves from a disciplining Father God.

For the U.S. to not be bothered with Father God in the future, the Socialist and Humanist Civil Government Politicians and Bureaucrats took prayer out of school. It took only one atheist, Madeline O'Hara, to file a lawsuit in the early 1960's to have prayer taken out of our schools by the Supreme Court deciding that prayer was a violation of the rule of separation of Church and State. The children's prayer that was outlawed was for God to bless the Parents, the Teachers, the Country, the State and Federal Legislators, Judges and the Governor and President. The very next year after prayer was taken out of the public schools, President Kennedy was assassinated. The more the Supreme Court expands the separation of Church and State rules, the more that God is taken out of the Socialist and Humanist Civil Government laws and policies. Socialism does not want God as a disciplining Father in government rulership. Socialist and Humanist Civil Government Politicians and Bureaucrats do not want to be accountable to God, be disciplined by God, or follow God's biblitarian principles of wise economics.

Vietnam was divided in the Geneva Conference of 1954, which ended France's colonial presence in Vietnam and partitioned the country in two states and when the north tried to force reunification the U.S. went to war. The Vietnam War was a consequence of the failure of the leaders and citizens of the U.S. to repent and come to obedience to God and His Word. The War in Vietnam was the reaping of the harvest caused by sowing the seeds of disobedience and the consequences of sins of the nation for some time. American governmental leaders thought another war would cause economic betterment for the nation. However, they did see many young people refusing to rally around the cause of freedom through war as they had not done in WWII. Even in the Korean War, there was not an outcry by the youth, questioning the moral purpose behind their leaders' decisions to go to war. Yet, the leaders in government during the Vietnam War were faced with an enemy without and a resistance within amongst the youth being drafted to fight in that war.

The consequences of disobedience caused social disorder at home in the U.S. during the Vietnam War. The "student rebellion" shook the U.S. nation and caused a major distrust towards the government leaders. This nation saw soldiers shoot and kill unarmed students at the Kent state anti-war protest in the 1960's. Eventually, the parents became tired of their own young men coming home in body bags and caused the politicians to put an end to the Vietnam War or be voted out of office. Stopping the war became a political issue and the subject of campaign speeches of presidential candidates like Eugene McCarthy, Robert Kennedy, and Richard Nixon. Stopping the war was not based upon the recognition that we, as a people, need to repent, nor did anyone in politics say that the Vietnam War was just the consequences of disobedience of God's biblitarian principles by the older generation, for which there was still no repentance.

In addition, because of the biblitarian economic disobedience, Americans had to face up to the sins of racism and all these problems all at once. One of God's answers for racism was the Azusa Street Revival in the early 1900's, where all nationalities were joined together to experience the unifying power and love of God under the guidance of a one blind-eyed black man, named Pastor William J. Seymour, who dropped religious traditions and took up the sincere intimate relationship with the Lord and invited the Holy Spirit in the meetings where all races came together to worship and experience spiritual revival. The Holy Spirit was moving in other denominations as well, but eventually the Believers did not remain in the spirit but started living again in the flesh and had offshoot denominations from the Azusa Street Revival.

Many American people, and their leaders, adopted *mammon* as their new god, and Socialism as its guiding philosophy, while at the same time most U.S. residents professed they were still believing Christians. People would rather look toward money as the answer to their problems rather than obeying the disciplining Father God, who was interested in changing their hearts and character by them seeking first the Kingdom of God. People would rather have the security of a big Socialist and Humanist Civil Government ran by Politicians and

Bureaucrats than Father's God's Kingdom perfect economic principles.

However, instead of repenting, America became secular and more concerned about matters of the needs of the flesh and providing the comforts afforded by a rich U.S. society. The people wanted to revamp the world and take away the authority of the predominant Christian base of our society. Throughout the 1900's the Civil Socialist and Humanist Government Politicians and Bureaucrats wrongfully used fiscal social policies to try and stop the consequences of the nation's sins.

To try to escape God's discipline, in the U.S. the "Brenton Woods Agreement" was signed. This agreement moved America off the gold standard backing our currency, and the federal government, through the Federal Reserve, and decided to print more money that was not backed by gold or silver. The Civil Government went deeper and deeper into debt by selling Treasury Bonds to try to economically buffer the people from the consequences of their disobedience of God's principles of economics. Since the U.S. was off the gold standard, and since the printing of money was granted to the Federal Reserve, the printing of money was not limited to the availability and deposit of a scarce commodity such as gold or silver which had God's limitations built in due to the lack of supply.

In exchange for the Federal Reserve receiving Treasury Bonds, the Federal Reserve printed "fiat" money, so the Socialist and Humanist Civil Government Politicians and Bureaucrats had worthless money to pay for its social welfare entitlements and military engaging in continuous wars without restrictions from God.

To understand how this works: the Federal government issues Treasury Bonds and the U.S. Treasury prints fiat money not backed by assets of gold or silver. The Federal Reserve Board agrees to purchase all the Federal Civil Government's Treasury Bonds and Notes, but it always purchases these Treasury Bonds and Notes by newly printed money, not money already in circulation. This means the Federal Reserve really pays nothing for these Treasury Bonds and Notes, but the banking families who own the Federal Reserve make 100% profit when they sell these Treasury Bonds to qualified institutions, such as broker dealers, which are licensed to purchase and re-sell these Treasury Bonds to the public at large. The money printed is backed by the Treasury Bonds and the good faith and credit standing of the U.S. Government. The Federal Reserve also sells Treasury Bonds at different discount rates to foreign governments based upon whether they are supportive of the Federal Reserve's banking policies. Thus, who is it that really controls America's foreign policy? Money causes countries to have allegiance to the Federal Reserve not the U.S. government.

Inflation immediately springs forth because of the new influx of money into the economy. Riches are created right out of the printing presses and not based upon wealth as defined by God. This fiat money in exchange for government debt through issuance of Treasury Bonds and Notes has been going on for many decades. Since 1996, the Federal Civil Government does not collect enough taxes to pay the dividends promised on the Treasury Bonds it has issued. Every year the Federal Civil Government is required to sell new Treasury Bonds and Notes to the Federal Reserve to have enough fiat money to pay the dividends or interest on its debt. Each year, the Federal Civil Government increases its national debt. The U.S. National debt as of January 2023 was 31.4 trillion (Source: Department of Treasury) The U.S. is by far the largest debtor nation in the world. The U.S. National debt is robbing the economic freedom of future generations in America. This activity is forcing the onslaught of a one-world economic system headed up by the Antichrist. The Federal Civil Government is trying to offset this horrible financial disaster for the U.S. by using confiscatory laws to go out and forcibly take property primarily from small family businesses, which is the devil attacking the very institution God has been using to mature His children.

Nobody in leadership amongst the Socialist and Humanist Civil Government Politicians and Bureaucrats talks about the fact that the economic problems of this nation are caused by sin because those in power are absolutely convinced that the Civil Government's job is to try and safeguard the people from the consequence of sin by its monetary fiscal and wealth distribution policies.

In the 1970's, the U.S. deficit and the national debt grew larger and larger, and at a faster pace, and at the same time the government started passing laws that legalized all kinds of activities God called sin.

The Church has lived under anti-biblical judicial tyranny for decades. The Justices of the U.S. Supreme Court made prayer and reading scriptures in schools illegal (Engel vs. Vitale, 1962 against school sponsored prayer, and Abington School District vs. Schempp, 1963 against school sponsored reading of Scriptures), but prayer and reading scriptures by children is lawful with God (Ephesians 6:18; Jude 1:20). The U.S. Supreme Court Justices declared abortion on demand legal (Roe vs. Wade, 1973), but it is unlawful to kill the innocent under God's law (Psalms 94:21; 106:38) (Roe v. Wade has now been overturned by Dobbs in 2022: see decision in chapter 7). The U.S. Supreme Court Justices decided that same sex marriages were legal and a Constitutional right (Obergefell v. Hodges, 2015), but same sex marriages are unlawful under God's law (Leviticus 18: 22; 20:13; Romans 1:27). Unrighteous Supreme Court Jurists took prayer and the reading of Scriptures out of school and thereby threw out the greatest Teacher, the Holy Spirit. Unrighteous Supreme Court Jurists legalized abortion on demand and in so doing caused mass murder for hire of millions of unborn babies as a form of Eugenics. This constitutes infanticide and genocide. In this last case, unrighteous Supreme Court Jurists have rejected scriptural truth and legalized what God considers to be an abomination that demands God's judgment for breaking His law. Abortion has been banned only in a few states after Dobbs made abortion not a constitutional right for the unborn but still allow states to continue the murder of the unborn.

2 Chronicles 7:19-20 says, "But if you turn away and forsake My Statutes and commandments which I have set before you, and go and serve other gods (such as Socialism, Humanism, and mammonism?), and worship them, then I will uproot them from My land which I have given them; and this house which I have sanctified for My name I will cast out of My sight, and will make it a proverb and a byword among all peoples."

The Law of God is simple. It says, "abortion is killing the innocent and is the worst kind of murder as it is 'murder for hire,' because the mother hires a medical doctor to do the killing of her baby." The Law of God says, "Thou shalt not murder..." (Deuteronomy 5:17). Psalms 10:8 says, "He sitteth in the lurking places of the villagers in the secret places doth he murder the innocent; his eyes are privily set against the poor." Similarly, Psalms 94:6 says, "They slay the widow and the stranger, and murder the fatherless." Psalm 24:1 says that people that dwell in the world belong to the Lord. Acts 17:25 says, "...He gives to all life, breath and all things." Acts 17:28 says, "For in Him we live and move and have our being." God owns the pre-born babies and all of us who have been born.

People cannot murder innocent lives for convenience, even if it sounds reasonable because the woman "has a right over her own body." A woman does not have a right over her own body, as the body is to be the temple of God, and a baby in the womb has its own body and has a right to life. It is a crime for a woman to attempt to kill herself, so a woman does not have a right to her own body. A woman cannot take drugs and use as a defense that a woman has a right to her own body. A woman who takes illegal drugs during her pregnancy, and the baby is born addicted to the illegal drugs, the mother can be prosecuted for parental abuse and neglect. In most states, it is illegal for a woman to sell her body for sex. Yet, the drug-addicted mother can kill the baby through abortion, and she exonerates herself from parental abuse and neglect. Thus, the mother cannot addict the baby in the womb with drugs, but she can kill the baby in the womb. Therefore, a woman's right to her body is limited.

Under California law, when a hunter shoots a cow by mistake in the womb and kills both the cow and calf inside, the judge orders the hunter to pay for two cows, not one, as a cow is a cow at conception, not viability or at birth. The law is that a baby is a human at conception if a pregnant woman is intentionally killed so, the defendant is charged with two murders, such as in the criminal case against Scott Peterson in 2002, who was found guilty of double murder of his wife, Laci and their unborn child, Conner. On the other hand, if a pregnant woman is in an automobile accident, having been hit by a drunk driver and the woman and baby are killed, the law is that there is only one homicide, which is that of the mother, not the baby. Thus, the baby is a baby at conception in some cases, but not in other cases. Who does that make sense to? Certainly not God!

The National Debt is now increasing so rapidly that it is like a rocket blasting off to outer space leaving the limitations of the earth's gravitational pull, which will wipe out the financial security of several upcoming generations, even if the Socialist and Humanist Civil Government Politicians and Bureaucrats try to stop some governmental spending. Unfortunately, the Socialist and Humanist Civil Government Politicians and Bureaucrats have placed themselves in a major trap by voting to approve automatic increases in governmental entitlements to keep up with cost of living.

People in a debate on CNN on October 13, 1992, said the U.S. had over four trillion dollars in debt, growing at the pace of 400 billion a year. In 1996, the National Debt was close to five trillion dollars. In 2014, the National

Debt was over seventeen trillion U.S. dollars. In 2015, the National Debt rose to over nineteen trillion. Obamacare was to be instituted in 2016, and the National Debt was destined to increase at a faster rate unless Obamacare was amended or replaced with a better health care system. Because of the Covid-19 pandemic expenditures in 2020 and 2021, along with the continuous wars the U.S. is engaged in, the National Debt is headed to over thirty trillion dollars. As of January 2023, the National Debt is $31.4 trillion and increasing everyday. In January 2024 the National Debt increased to $34 trillion and increasing even faster.

The public National Debt of the United States was around $26.73 Trillion U.S. dollars, around $1.7 Trillion more than a year earlier in 2020 when the first Covid-19 payments were made, but in 2021, there was a $1 Trillion Infrastructure Bill passed by the Senate. The National Debt was raised to $31.23 Trillion Dollars and still rising. Why is this fearful to our nation? This debt is secured through the issuance of U.S. Treasury Bonds, and the income taxes collected from Americans by the IRS will not even pay the dividends or interest owed each quarter which are required to be paid on the U.S. Treasury Bonds purchasers. The Federal Reserve sells the U.S. Treasury Bonds to other Countries and investors here in the U.S. The Federal Government must borrow more money from the Federal Reserve each quarter to pay the Treasury Bonds Dividends and Interest, as the income taxes collected are not enough, so the U.S. National Debt continues to rise. It's like a family that borrows from Master Charge to pay Visa, which means eventually you will go bankrupt. If the government cancels the agreement with the Federal Reserve and allows the U.S. Treasury to print the money there would be no more National debt.

Let's look at just the National Debt. How much is a trillion dollars? Well, let's compare the U.S. national debt (over 30 trillion) to the passage of seconds in time, with each second equal to one dollar! Let's look at how many years are in one trillion seconds? Do the math with your calculator or Google the question. Then think about how many years would go by for thirty trillion seconds.

It would take almost 12 days for a million seconds to elapse. It would take 31.7 Years for one billion seconds (thousand million) to elapse. Finally, it would take 31,709.8 years for one trillion seconds (thousand billion) to elapse. It would take an unimaginable number of years for thirty trillion seconds to elapse.

Think about this. A trillion seconds ago, there was no written history. A trillion seconds ago, the pyramids had not yet been built. A trillion seconds ago, neither the Garden of Eden nor Adam and Eve had been created. How long will it take America to pay off its National Debt?

At the time you read this book, the national debt will have increased in monumental proportions if something is not done. This country is headed for an economic collapse. However, as individual Business Servants, we do not have to participate in this crash because we know the truth, and the truth can set us free from this mammon monster. We can change our national thought through public discourse, avoid the creditor-debtor system, live debt free, and follow all the other principles of long run thinking; but it has to be a grass roots renewal of thought and action to return the people's thinking back to God's business biblitarian principles of long run planning, long run budgeting, investing for R&D to stay up to date with the latest products and services, spending to capture a market share, projected savings for needed future expenditures, and changing the philosophy of the fundamental principles of starting and operating a business to be for the spiritual maturation of the workers through their daily encounters in solving problems and performing services.

When God stops trying to deal with the sins committed by the people of any nation, this becomes the ultimate punishment because God lifts His hedge of protection; and His desire to disciple children through His love to make them better Kingdom servants and ministers is put on hold.

Ephraim was one of the two sons of Joseph who had been elevated as a tribe along with his brother, Manasseh through adoption by Jacob, and Joseph's two sons had been given the tribal spiritual and financial blessing by Jacob that was intended for Joseph (Genesis 48:12-20). However, Ephraim's descendants became disobedient, and the spiritual blessing passed from the family of Joseph to the family of Judah, of which King David, and the Lord Jesus Christ's humanity nature through His mother, Mary, was descendent. "Ephraim is joined to idols, let him alone" (Hosea 4:17).

God has an interesting discipline. If His people continue to rebel and not seek first the Kingdom of God and His righteousness, the first thing is His people will lose hope in God delivering them. God says, "I will take my hands off and let My people's own disobedience bring forth their own judgment." This is where America and many other Socialist countries are today, as they have not learned the devastating lessons of the Iron Curtain Countries and other Socialist countries.

Instead of searching for the root causes of our problems, which is habitual sin, a lukewarm gospel of salvation instead of preaching the authoritative gospel of the Kingdom (Matthew 24:14) along with repentance and remission of sins (Luke 24:47), here on earth, along with a few Church leaders disparaging Believers who see their business as their venue of ministry, a disintegration of the family unit, and trying to solve spiritual and moral problems with money, much of the Church has been given over to tradition and religion that looks to the Civil Government to "buy even the Church's way out of the consequences of sin and disobedience." As did Ephraim, many religious leaders have joined with secular big businesses, Socialist Politicians and Bureaucrats, sports figures, the music industry, and entertainment actors and producers and have joined themselves to idols, especially the god of mammon. Believers must pray that God does not lose interest in His children in America or the Believers of the nation in which you live, as He did with Ephraim.

God says to the Socialist and Humanist Civil Government Politicians and Bureaucrats, "All right, you think you can collect enough taxes and borrow enough money by selling your Treasury Bonds and Municipal Bonds to buy the people's way out of the consequences of their sins? You will overtax your people and will become enslaved as a debtor nation because you pay for government entitlements and wars through debt financing, but you ignore God's biblical economic principles and the need for repentance. You think your money printing presses can outrun the consequences and results of violating My biblical economic principles? Then I will let you spend yourself to death and unto annihilation."

Our nation needs Believers praying and gathering for a revival, a renewal, a repentance, and a restoration by going back to God, preaching repentance and remission of sins along with the gospel of 'the Kingdom is at hand', a resistance against the devil, and a rejection of the god of mammon as their idol and their source to fulfill their needs and dreams. This country can only be great financially again when the people proclaim, "For the Lord is great, and greatly to be praised: He is to be feared above all gods" (Psalms 96:4).

RISK AND POSSIBILITY OF FAILURE NECESSITATE
LEARNING CONSEQUENCES OF ACTIONS

The current situation in our Socialist and Humanist Civil Government Politicians and Bureaucrats in trying to shield the consequences of the people's sins by supplying money to them has caused them to depend on Civil Government Entitlements instead of taking responsibility over their own problems and becoming mature through godly self-government. This has come about as the Civil Government regulates away the rights and responsibilities of discipleship by parents. There must be a re-emphasis on the parents' authority over their children and honor of parents in the families.

The world system over which Satan rules (2 Corinthians 4:4) encourages disobedience to God and His laws by attempting to provide cradle to grave security through Socialist and Humanist Civil Government Politicians and Bureaucrats muffling, outlawing, and promoting as legal those activities called sin by God, and thereby fighting against God by postponing the consequences of sins and disobedience of the secular people, business operators, and Politicians.

The avoidance of the consequences of sins and disobedience of the principles of God is the spirit of this age and is the world system in which we live. For example, teenager Suzie is told not to speed when she is driving the family car. She is disobedient and gets her license suspended. Mothers often say, "Do not worry, I'll drive you to school." On the other hand, fathers are more inclined to say, "You've been disobedient, you can walk to school, and I hope you have learned your lesson."

A harmful spiritual principle operating in the Civil Government is a maternal "misplaced sense of mercy" which tries to keep the disobedient child or citizen from the disciplining father, both the natural father and the Father in heaven.

There is an evil prince of darkness ruling over every Socialist and Humanist nation. This evil prince of darkness is trying to keep the people away from the disciplining Father Creator by substituting Father God with

Socialist Mother Government. Russian people refer to their country as "Mother Russia." The real fight between the Jews and the Arabs are in defense of their great, great, great, great, grandmothers, Sarah and Hagar.

Because Father God loves us, He will not allow the maternal Civil Government to keep Him away from disciplining His children since believers are His adopted children in Christ Jesus. God looks at His children through His eyes as living in eternity instead of the limited time whereby life begins and ends here on earth.

Since the United States has mostly Christian Believers living here, God is strict on His children; otherwise, He would not be a good Father. God is strict on Believers because He is the best Father, and He wants to present to His only begotten Son a chaste Bride, "...a glorious church, not having spot, or wrinkle, or any such thing; but that it should be holy and without blemish" (Ephesians 5:27). God is going to discipline His children to make us His mature disciples in Christ. It is not a question of "if" but rather "when." God is not mocked, for whatever a man or a collection of people called a nation, sows, so shall he or the nation reap (Galatians 6:7-8). God's principles do not need man's permission or government's permission to make them work. God is King, and His Kingdom laws work throughout His Kingdom universe. When man is, or a collective people are, disobedient, he or they bring God's principles to work against him or them. God's principles of life, and especially His economic principles, either work for you or against you.

An absolutely free society encourages obedience to God. A truly obedient Civil Servant encourages people to obey God and His biblitarian principles and moral laws. Yet, the opposite is what is being done today in the Socialist and Humanist Civil Government with the espousing of its maternal Socialist philosophy and laws and the enforcement in a reverse way of the Doctrine of Separation of Church and State. The Constitution was written to keep government from setting up a government-sponsored state church, but it was not designed to keep God out of Civil Government. Debt and sin have put our entire nation into various degrees of slavery. Sins committed over a prolonged period of time, which sins God considers abomination, invite foreign powers to attack the nation. The reaction of the unrepentant Socialist Civil Government Politicians is to increase their police powers; so America has become a police state.

To keep Father God away from interfering with secular Civil Government ruling this nation with Socialist and Humanist Civil Government Politicians and Bureaucrats they enforce the Doctrine of Separation of Church and State, or do they? Both the House of Representatives and the Senate have full time government paid Chaplains. Chaplains are official members of both Houses of Congress. Chaplains are appointed as individuals by members of both Houses of Congress but not as representatives of any religious community, body, or organization. In addition to opening sessions of Congress with prayer, the Chaplain provides pastoral counseling to the Congressional Community, and their staff, coordinates the scheduling of guest chaplains, arranges memorial services for the Representatives and Senators, and their staff, and performs marriages and funeral ceremonies for the Members. To date, all House Chaplains have been Christian but can be members of any religion or faith group, such as Muslim. Guest Chaplains, recommended by congressional members to deliver the session's opening prayer in place of the regular Chaplain, have represented many different religious groups, including Judaism and Islam.

With the Kingly ministry being activated, then these are areas that Believers can start campaigns to maintain the Christian traditions in our government. How is having a full time, paid Chaplain practicing separation of Church and State lawful?

Here is another example. Throughout the Capitol in the U.S. are scriptures or references to God chiseled on government buildings. The Supreme Court building was finished in 1935, long before the Doctrine of Separation of Church and State was a prominent theme in Supreme Court decisions. The Supreme Court has decided that the Ten Commandments cannot be posted in a school as that would violate the requirement of total sectarianism of government. The Supreme Court in Stone vs. Graham, 1980, struck down a Kentucky law that posted on school walls the Ten Commandments. Also, Moses and the Ten Commandments are contained in the artistic embellishment of the U.S. Supreme Court building.

Additionally, on the oak door that leads from the hallway to the Courtroom where the U.S. Supreme Court Justices sit and hear cases contains a representation of Moses' tablets bearing the Roman Numerals I through X. If it is not unconstitutional to display the Ten Commandments on the Supreme Court building, why is it unconstitutional to display the Ten Commandments on State Court buildings and schools with the proviso that the common law was partly based upon the Ten Commandments to maintain its inclusion as having sectarian, historical relevance?

The Supreme Court Justices declared these practices of reverencing God in government as not in violation of the Doctrine of Separation of Church and State, but ceremonial and traditional. It cannot be denied that the foundation of our primary Christian society is from the beginning of the United States and is part of the ceremonial and practical traditions of our nation. Before U.S. history is rewritten, Believers need the wisdom and the tenacity to fight a good intellectual and spiritual battle for the body of Christ and the continued presence of the Kingdom of God with our King, Jesus Christ, and the Holy Spirit as the providential Overseer of believers who espouse freedom of religion for all.

Thus, godly civil servants should try to promote biblical principles of economics, which would make them compassionate to the needy, while they permit citizens and people living in their country to be freely blessed or freely penalized by the consequences of their own choices. 2 Corinthians 3:17 says, "Now the Lord is that Spirit: and where the Spirit of the Lord is, there is liberty."

TAKING CALCULATED RISKS AND EXPERIENCING THE POSSIBILITY OF
FAILURE WHEN CONDUCTING BUSINESS IS NECESSARY FOR MATURITY
AND THE GROWTH OF GOD'S BUSINESS IN MINISTRY

There is a healthy fear that leads to respect and the taking of precautions while a Business Servant conducts business, and an unhealthy fear that leads to paralysis of the business. Proverbs 1:7 says, "The fear of the Lord is the beginning of wisdom." A wise Business Servant will obey the principles of the Creator. The Creator created Believers for the purpose of fulfilling His purpose, not their own purposes; and He has made the rules for Believers to follow to best accomplish each of their God chosen purposes in a timely manner.

The more problems Business Servants and their employees successfully handle, the more responsibility God grants to them to handle bigger problems. Those problems Business Servants and their employees once thought were unsolvable will be solved easier and are no longer a threat to the business ministry. Once solved, managing similar problems will become routine, but Business Servants and employees still must maintain watchfulness in handling the daily business problems and not think that problems will automatically resolve themselves. God's Business Servant and managers still must keep a watchful eye if the problem is delegated to immature or inexperienced employees in the business.

Having a healthy fear of the Lord is not the terror toward a Tyrant, but the kind of awe and respect which leads to obedience to the Lord Who is the wisest of all.

The fear of the Lord leads to spiritual security and abundance through the acquisition and application of God's wisdom, knowledge, and understanding, not just earthly prosperity or acquisition of physical things.

Without taking risk and accepting the consequences for bad choices, Believers would never learn to resist the temptation of touching the "hot stove" of sin, activating the law of sin and death, which robs them of the benefits in God's Kingdom.

Sometimes, the good father and mother will allow the child to touch the hot stove, under supervision, so the child will learn to avoid danger. This is not cruelty, but merely the parent who knows when the child is not obeying, and that the child must experience the consequences of choices to learn to avoid the risks of harm in the future. A non-harming burn, although temporarily traumatic to the child, is better than a major, scaring burn later when supervision is not present. This rule applies also to business when the Business Servant insists on taking too great of a risk in business or breaching a contract. When a businessperson breaches a contract and is sued for damages, the next time he wants to enter a contract, he will take great pains to try and write protective conditions in the contract that protect him or her when something goes wrong in the business. The Business Servant will have to acquire the knowledge of "risk management."

When God's Business Servant seeks approval of the Lord to do a business transaction with someone, and God says, "No!", the scary thing is when you persist and keep praying for permission. Often, God finally says, "Okay, go ahead and touch the hot stove because the burn from touching the stove will teach in a certain way what My verbal admonitions and written biblical principles will never teach because of your stubbornness."

God is a good Father who loves the Believers in America and all Believers in other countries, and He has allowed us to touch the hot stove of the Socialist and Humanist Civil Government Politicians and Bureaucrats who try to spend our way out of problems. We are going to come off of this hot stove screaming very soon as the heat burns through our cover up disguises and outer garments to reach the raw flesh. It will be at that time that revival will break out because the people are going to repent. Upon repentance, God will start binding up the wounds of the people through His Church. The Church has a big job ahead of it, but don't be shocked if the Church venue for revival may be business offices.

In the 1930's during the Great Depression when the banks failed, and the economy came unglued in America, we still had a Judeo-Christian principled base in the society who were praying, reading God's Word, and acting as a remnant holding back to a degree the severe discipline of the Father. When the economic crash hits this time in America, will there be a Judeo-Christian base to fall back on? This economic upheaval may be a warning or a major discipline by the Father, but the Father wants to bring spiritual renewal to America because His heart is here with His children. We still are the strongest nation militarily and where mostly Christians live. God promises times of refreshing in the presence of the Lord (Acts 3:19), and people will realize that the Socialist Civil Government has not been their "father" or "mother" but has been used as an instrument of the devil to attempt to steal, kill, and destroy the Judeo-Christian base of American culture. The once Soviet Union has already suffered a demise of their union, and the previous nations making up this old Socialist state have emerged with independent ideas and self-expressions. The problem is that these smaller countries have nuclear weapons which may have been sold to extremist or even terrorist groups in exchange for needed economic benefits. This has brought greater instability in the world.

The weakening of the influence of the Judeo-Christian values in American society is going to create a set of problems beyond human control by the Socialist Engineers. When the Socialist and Humanist Civil Government Politicians and Bureaucrats lose their control, then the economic laws will automatically cause divestitures from the government, adjustments, and a heading back to economic sanity by the biblical economic principles of accountability and stewardship under Almighty God. We will truly have an economic system where the heart cry will be, "IN GOD WE TRUST!"

"STRUGGLE" AND THE "POSSIBILITY OF FAILURE" DEVELOP
MORAL STRENGTH AND CHARACTER IN BELIEVERS

"Rewards and penalties" teach Believers God's principles, thoughts, purposes, and, eventually, His ways.

Silkworms are caterpillars that spin silk cocoons. They live inside the silk cocoons and transform into moths. The silk that we use for clothing comes from the cocoons of the silkworms. If a little child sees a silk cocoon and sees the silk moth fighting its way trying to get out of the silk cocoon, often the little child, out of a compassionate nature, cuts open the cocoon to help the silk moth get out to fly away. The silk moth comes out and dies. What the little child did not understand was the way God built the silk moth in the cocoon. The silk moth gets its respiratory strength by expending energy as it fights its way out of the silk cocoon to survive once it is out. If you cut the silk cocoon, the silk moth comes out premature and dies.

How many human beings are on the blood stained hands of the Socialist and Humanist Civil Government Bureaucrats and Politicians today, who cut the people's silk cocoons and often contribute to the immaturity of their souls and to their economic struggles?

When you become an employer, one thing God must have in you is the knowledge that sparing employee Believers the consequence of their disobedience helps keep them in a state of immaturity. The reason is that a Believer's failure, along with chastisement of God, teaches people to fear the Lord as a loving and discipling Father, Who has boundaries, patterns, principles, and conditions that are designed to mature the souls of His children. Why does God discipline His children? He wants maturity of souls, so He can prosper them and keep them healthy (3 John 2).

Thus, if your employment policies keep employees from experiencing the consequences of their disobedience, you are keeping them from the fear of their disciplining Father and thus contributing to their spiritual immaturity.

American culture, and its leaders, still espouse the philosophies of the post Great Depression Dr. Benjamin Spock, baby boomer generation.

Dr. Spock, a rather famous pediatrician came along to the post WWII mothers and fathers of this nation and said, "Do not spank your children when they disobey as it will cause them to lose their creativity." Dr. Spock wrote the book, entitled, The Commonsense Book of Baby and Child Care, published in 1946. It sold over fifty million copies, and became the second best-selling book, next to the Bible in the Twentieth Century in America. By 2011, Dr. Spock's book had been translated into thirty-nine languages.

Dr. Spock said the Bible was an archaic book, so the absolutes in the Bible were replaced with the rules of relativism and the Humanist rules of psychology which primarily direct the attention to the preservation of self, which in the Bible you enter the crucifixion of Christ to resurrect into the life and character of Christ. The pursuit of self just creates selfishness and countermands the maturation of discipleship training by God to make His children spiritually mature as servant leaders who obey His commands.

Dr. Spock taught that any physical discipline causes little Jack and Jill to grow up as social cripples. Biblically, a physical swat that leaves no marks should be accepted as discipline of children. Yet, there are a host of other disciplines that can cause the child to learn godly self-discipline, especially as they get older.

While raising my children, we required our children to write "lines." A line was a verse from the Bible that directed their attention to their bad behavior. For example, if one of the boys stole the other's toy, the scripture he may have to write 50 times; "Thou shall not steal."

Dr. Spock's teachings were accepted as truth by Americans because the parents who went through the Great Depression vowed in their hearts not to let their children ever to go hungry and overcompensated by showering their children with cars, clothes, toys, etc. Many parents stopped spanking their children altogether. Since Dr. Spock was an expert, the general belief was that he must be right. However, Dr. Spock's grandson, Peter Spock, the son of Dr. Spock's son, Michael Spock, on December 25, 1983, committed suicide by jumping off the Boston's Children's Museum, where Michael Spock was the director of the museum. The place where, and the date when Peter Spock committed suicide must have had some significance to him.

Children need a disciplining father to establish borders to feel safe. One can see the failure to discipline as we see a generation in power today who were the rebels of the 1960's who regularly go against the mandates of Father God. Father God does not abuse, but He does lovingly discipline His children to promote maturation, not fractures in personalities from abuse. Discipline must be with the motive of love. The Humanist government Bureaucrats would have people believe that Christians are abusers of children, which is not true. In fact, Christian families have the true agape love in their homes, which is designed to maximize mental health, maturity, education, and success of the children. Show me an adult who was not disciplined as a child, and I will show you someone who often is lazy, with no godly self-government.

Everybody looked at the long haired hippie kids that came out of the 1960's and said, "How can this rebellious generation be?" when they should have asked, "How can it not be?" The youths were singing, "Let it be!"

The rebellious children of the 1960's were produced by how the Humanist, secular parents failed to discipline that generation. These 1960's rebellious children are governing America with Humanist and Socialist philosophies today and reject God's principles of economics. They think of themselves as intellectual elites.

RISK TEACHES PEOPLE PROPER DEPENDENCY AND
OBEDIENCE TO GOD'S LAWS, WHEREAS
DEPENDENCY ON CIVIL GOVERNMENT ENTITLEMENTS SHIELD
PEOPLE FROM CONSEQUENCES OF SIN AND DISOBEDIENCE

God prefers that His children depend on godly relationships rather than Socialist and Humanist Civil Government Politicians and Bureaucrats handouts when they have a need. Fellowship with other Believers manifests love, faith, and true life. Yet, there cannot be free loaders in the body of Christ who prey on the giving nature of other Believers. You cannot take risks unless you are working. Lazy people take no risks, and they do not learn there are consequences to risks taken. Thus, Believers who do not work avoid God's maturation discipline designed for His children.

God's order is for every Believer to contribute to their families and the household of God. God's order and design is for Believers primarily to depend upon their families and fellow Believers, and their family businesses, not civil mother government.

A RISK-FREE PHILOSOPHY CAUSES A DESTRUCTION OF THE
FAMILY UNIT THROUGH DIVORCE AND SINGLE PARENT LIFESTYLES

We see the Socialist and Humanist Civil Government Politicians and Bureaucrats stepping in and keeping a man and a woman from having to deal with sin and immaturity when they want to get a divorce. The Socialist and Humanist Civil Government Politician and Bureaucrat law makers created "no fault divorce." "No fault divorce" means a husband and wife do not have to legally work it out in covenant, and they do not have to go through the hassle of reconciliation. They do not have to admit they are at fault, and they are not required to confess their faults to each other and seek reconciliation. The family is God's basic institution in society, which He wants to maintain strong, "easy divorce" is a scourge of a society that is predominately decadent, narcissistic, and has sinful individuals.

The Socialist and Humanist Civil Government Politicians and Bureaucrats say to the mother, "If you get a divorce and you and your children start having financial trouble, the government will help you out financially." Therefore, the incentive to change and mature, so the husband and wife can live peaceably together, is no longer there.

The Socialist and Humanist Civil Government Politicians and Bureaucrats represent themselves as being the ultimate safety net for the people residing in America. They explicitly or impliedly tell the welfare mothers, "We will give you money to live on, food stamps to buy groceries, government medical help to take care of your family's medical needs, and Section 8 housing to ensure that you and your children have a place to live. All we ask you to do is get rid of the 'head of the family,' your husband or the father of your children. So, little mother, why do you need a husband and a father for your children? The state will be your husband and your children's father to support you and take care of you. Why do you need God to take care of you? The state can supply all of your needs according to its riches in government and do everything God has promised to do for you. However, unlike God, we are 'user friendly' as your 'sinful ways' do not bother us so long as it involves sexual 'sins.' In fact, we are interested in making sexual freedom (sins) 'safe' for you, and we will even supply your teenage children with free condoms to allow them to engage in 'sexual freedom' and free abortions' if they make a mistake. We will redefine when a human becomes a person and take away any guilt for killing the unborn. The government wants you and your teenage children to have 'sexual freedom' and will not cause you or your teenage children to experience any negative consequences to exercise your right to engage in sexual freedom. Children out of wedlock justify the need for, and existence of, the state to be a 'husband' and 'father' in society to those of you in disintegrated families. It is okay to fornicate and have an affair with another man, so long as you do not allow him to move in and be a husband and father because that takes away from the 'authority' the government Bureaucrats desire. It is okay that you are a homosexual, as a person's 'sexual preference' is guaranteed by law in our 'user friendly Socialist and Humanist Civil Governmental run society.' Even if you get AIDS while exercising your sexual freedom, we will pay all your medical bills. Come to the government for help. We have offices in every county in the state to make it easy for you to sign up for our assistance. Remember, when it comes time to vote in elections, vote for us instead of God's servants. We give you freedom to engage in what God calls sins, but we take away the consequences and call it the exercise of freedom instead of rebellion. Who do you want to rule over you? Do you want a disciplining Father Creator or a loving Mother Government?"

The Socialist and Humanist Civil Government Politicians and Bureaucrats do not want any competition, and they really reward mothers if they divorce their husbands and go out and get pregnant with another man. The state just wants to be a "parent to the children." Therefore, the state has set up a "reward system" to encourage "unwanted" pregnancies. The Socialist and Humanist Civil Government Politicians and Bureaucrats want to be the parent of the children to train them through Socialist and Humanist Civil Government Politicians and Bureaucrats so they can vote for them.

The Socialist and Humanist Civil Government Politicians and Bureaucrats have increased the national debt to pay for these entitlement programs. The reward of money encourages sinful behavior in a society, breaks up the family units, and makes the children belong to the state.

HOMELESSNESS IS A FAMILY PROBLEM, AND GOVERNMENT AND SOCIETY SHOULD LOOK TO THE FAMILY TO SOLVE THIS PROBLEM

Homelessness is caused by the destruction of the home because of the disintegration of the family unit as the foundational base of society.

The Socialist and Humanist Civil Government Politicians and Bureaucrats say, "The government will build shelters for homes, feed the homeless, and fulfill the responsibilities that really belong to the families because the families and churches are not fulfilling the needs of the indigent."

What we should do for the homeless is give them a one-way ticket to their nearest relative, and grant tax breaks to the relative for the time he or she takes care of, and the financial support rendered to, the homeless person that helps the homeless get back on the road of living a normal life.

Thus, send the homeless home! Do not make them more dependent on government handouts. Do not build hotels for the homeless. Make the family provide for the homeless and provide tax incentives for doing so. The

brother-in-law who will not be his brother's keeper will cause the man to clean up, put on some better clothes, to go out and get a job a whole lot better than any government Bureaucrat can do. God likes working people because God matures His children while at work as stewards of His creation.

 This is the true compassion of God. God wants to re-establish His order in a person's life by having the correct institution called family take care of the homeless problem, because all these problems were caused by the re-focus away from the importance in society of the family unit and the Socialist and Humanist Civil Government Politicians and Bureaucrats trying to take on the responsibilities of the family.

Historically the Socialist and Humanist Civil Government Politicians and Bureaucrats have done everything possible to destroy or marginalize the family unit by saying, "Regardless of what immorality you commit, Mother Government will financially support you." They say, "Mother government will take care of you from cradle to grave, from womb to tomb. Why do you need parents? Why do you need a husband? Why do you need God? You have Mother Government as your financial source." This is the spirit of antichrist. The Socialist and Humanist Civil Government Politicians and Bureaucrats try to be a never-ending source of money and power to those in "need" to justify Socialist and Humanist philosophy and existence. The truth is that since 1963 the United States has been crippled by continuous wars, buyouts of failed big businesses, and runaway expenditures for social entitlement programs by those social engineers in government trying to promote the religion of Humanism and Socialism without any restraints from God. If America gets back to biblical economics, we will see the trend change from annihilation to salvation.

TEN

PRIVATE PROPERTY PROMOTES FREEDOM AND MATURITY

THE SOCIALIST/COMMUNIST MOVEMENT HAS FOUR
STRATEGIC GOALS IN ITS REVOLUTION.

THE FIRST GOAL IS TO TAKE THE CHILDREN AWAY FROM THE PARENTS AND GIVE THEM TO THE STATE. The Socialist Civil Government's policy is to break the family bond between parents and children through a state-run educational system, a strict child protection system that forbids most negative reinforcement discipline of children, and no-fault divorce to make it easy to destroy the family unit.

This happened, for example, in the Socialist revolutions of Cuba, Ethiopia, Nicaragua, Soviet Union, China, and North Korea.

In ancient Rome the "proletariat" consisted of the poor landless freemen, who were not landowners and had little or no capital to contribute financially in taxes to the Roman government. Yet, they were a needed labor force. They were the lowest class of society. The proletariats only resource was the bearing of children that continued to replace the citizens in ancient Rome with a new generation. Ancient Roman government considered the children as their property. The members of the proletariat were used to plant citizens of Rome in new conquered territories to bring the Roman law and culture in the foreign lands.

In the theory of Karl Marx, he used this ancient term "proletariat" to designate a class of wage workers who were engaged in industrial production and whose chief source of income was derived from the sale of their labor to survive. The Socialist state claims "ownership" of the children as the proletariat's contribution to the government.

The state's "ownership" of the children is set in motion by a strong compulsory educational system ran by the U.S. local and State Civil Government that teaches that Socialism is better than Capitalism or free enterprise. Yet, free enterprise with a moral base with God's Business Servants running them is a suitable place of ministry where employees learn about true economics in their daily incremental problem-solving work and are matured spiritually being about the Father's business. Every state in the U.S. adopts the law called *parens patriae*, which is a doctrine that has its roots in English Common Law. In feudal times, various obligations, and powers, collectively referred to as the "Royal Prerogative," were reserved to the King. The King exercised this authority and function in his role as the Father of the country. In the United States, the doctrine of *parens patriae* has its greatest use in the states inherent power to protect children. The state is the ultimate supreme guardian of all children within its borders and jurisdictional authority. State courts have the inherent power to intervene to protect the best interests of the children whose welfare may be jeopardized by controversies of the parents or if one or both parents have an alcoholic or illegal drug addiction or other dangerous activity is done by the parents. This common law *parens patriae* is often defined by Legislative Acts or Code Sections that define the scope of the child protection in the State.

Thus, in every state in America there is a division of Child Protective Services or a division with a similar name. They make rules as to how the government wants children to be disciplined, including the total abolition of spanking a child, even when there is no mark left on the child. Child Protective Services in the State of California is trying to call abuse if parents insist on their teenage children attending church or insist on a certain religious belief on the children. The State's focus is what is supposedly in the best interest of the children and not what is in the best interest in maintaining the family unit. There has been a continuous erosion of parental rights.

Ephesians 6:4 says, "And, ye fathers, provoke not your children to wrath: but bring them up in the nurture and admonition of the Lord." Similarly, Proverbs 22: 6 says, "Train up a child in the way he should go: and when he is old, he will not depart from it." The rights of the children, independent of their parents, are increasing in every state.

In California guardianship proceedings there is no policy favoring reunification of the children with their biological parents.

No fault divorce laws in California make it easier to destroy the family unit. There is always a strain between the children and stepparents. Children suffer a degree of abandonment because of the divorce of their parents. There is always a strain between parents and teenage children. Should the child's immature wish always reign?

Psalms 127:3 says that children are a gift to parents from God and it is a reward from God to have children. Since children are a gift from God, the courts should be very cautious of the exercise of the law of *parens patriae* to take children away from the parents.

Children are also called the children of God. Is the State also trying to replace God as the parent as well, especially in cases where parents have insisted that the children be raised as Christian? Is there an insidious plan of the devil to remove children from Christian homes?

THE SECOND GOAL IS TO ABOLISH REAL PROPERTY TITLE HELD BY PRIVATE INDIVIDUALS. The Socialist government's policy is to gradually abolish private property title and its use, so future generations have no wealth or power from real estate stewardship.

The Socialist and Humanist Civil Government Bureaucrats and Politicians desire to nationalize the means of production, such as steel mills, car manufacturing, public utilities, textile mills, food production, etc.

The Socialist and Humanist Civil Government Bureaucrats and Politicians want more businesses nationalized to give them more power, especially the production of energy, whether oil and gas wells, coal mining or solar energy.

The Socialist and Humanist Civil Government Bureaucrats and Politicians confiscated lands and buildings are purchased or confiscated from the private sector through imminent domain, zoning laws, use restrictions, and taxation just because they have more real property tax revenues when the land is forced to be sold to another.

The Socialist and Humanist Civil Government Bureaucrats and Politicians pass laws that all land is owned by the state. Residential dwellings are restricted by acreage size, use, and designed to restrict the family size to a single-family dwelling, usually not allowing room for grandparents to live. In the Kingdom of God, the biblical principles mandate that the elderly parents are brought into the homes of the children with honor to be a source of wisdom and teaching for grandchildren. In God's Kingdom real businesses and real property are owned by God and entrusted to His children for stewardship that works in them maturity and godly self-government.

THE THIRD GOAL IS TO TAKE CONTROL OF ORGANIZED RELIGION. The Socialist and Humanist Civil Government Bureaucrats and Politicians want to take control of religion by criticizing and regulating organized religion. They restrict people from fellowship regarding their faith to times and places that are regulated by the state or local government. They make it difficult by zoning and parking restrictions for a church to establish a building where people of faith meet to worship. They restrict home fellowships meetings because of parking restrictions. The State and local government officials proclaim authority when there is a pandemic to close church buildings as we have seen in the Covid-19 pandemic.

The Socialist and Humanist Civil Government Bureaucrats and Politicians want to replace traditional religion with state run, state managed, state-ruled religious institutions as it was at the time of the Roman Emperor, Constantine. In America, the doctrine of the religion of Humanism dictates most of the principles and policies underlying the laws of the Civil Government and educational centers, even though the Civil Government is constitutionally forbidden to espouse any official state religion under the First Amendment of the U.S. Constitution. Humanism is a religion paid for by the state, and it has captured the thoughts of the Socialist Politicians and Humanist Bureaucrats in Civil Government and educational institutions.

Since the state-run schools teach Humanism and evolution as fact, then secular schools are a state-run religion. John Dewy, the father of education in the U.S. wrote in an article that secular education was a religion ("Education As A Religion", The New Republic August 1922, p64f). In 1961, the U.S. Supreme Court in a case entitled *Torcaso v. Watkins* (1961) 367 U.S. 488 held that Humanism was a religion. The ethical cultural movement is one division of secular Humanism which teaches moral and cultural relativism, situation ethics, and attacks beliefs in Almighty God in the Old and New Testaments of the Bible. Humanism is a religion even though it does not have as a doctrine, that God exists. Thus, under the Doctrine of Separation of Church and State why is Humanism taught in secular schools as truth? Teaching Humanism is teaching a particular religion in public schools.

Parents should have strong family Bible study and worship in their homes. Parents should consider home schooling with an emphasis that the best Teacher in the universe is the Holy Spirit, so the children of Believers should be taught the Christian foundation of our great nation. Children need to be inculcated with biblical knowledge concerning Christian history, Christian economics, Christian families, Christian marriage, Christians in business ministries, Christian movies, Christian books, etc. etc.

Before my natural father came back to the Lord, he said to me, "You know, you are brain washing your children with this religion of yours." I responded, "Yes, you are right. I am washing out their brains from all knowledge and sin in the world. We all need to be brain washed."

THE FOURTH GOAL IS TO TAKE AWAY THE GUNS FROM PRIVATE PEOPLE. Sarah Brady (President of Handgun Control, Inc.) wrote to Senator Howard Metzenbaum -- The National Educator, January 1994, Page 3 that "Our main agenda is to have ALL guns banned. We must use whatever means possible. It doesn't matter if you have to distort facts or even lie. Our task of creating a Socialist America can only succeed when those who would resist us have been totally disarmed."

"The most foolish mistake we could possibly make would be to allow the subjected people to carry arms. History shows that all conquerors who have allowed their subjected peoples to carry arms have prepared their own downfall by so doing. Indeed, I would go so far as to say that the underdog is a sine qua non for the overthrow of any sovereignty. So let's not have any native militia or police." -- Adolph Hitler, Edict of March 18, 1938.

"All military type firearms are to be handed in immediately...The SS, SA and Stahlhelm give every respectable German man the opportunity of campaigning with them. Therefore anyone who does not belong to one of the above named organizations and who unjustifiably nevertheless keeps his weapon...must be regarded as an enemy of the national government." – (Director, SA Oberfuhrer Bad Tolz, March 1933.)

Much of the 1968 "American Gun Control Act" was copied, virtually word-for-word, from Hitler's 1938 Nazi Weapons Law? "The 1938 Nazi Weapons Law" that disarmed, enslaved & murdered ... is alive and well in the United States, and is called, "The Gun Control act of 1968," and is enforced by the modern-day Gestapo, known as the "Bureau of Alcohol, Tobacco, & Firearms (BATF)." (*"Death By Gun Control: Gateway To Tyranny"*, http://www.jpfo.org/GCA 68.htm)

"In the 20th Century, governments murdered four times as many civilians as were killed in all the international and domestic wars combined. Further, governments murdered millions more people than were killed by common criminals." (*"Death by Gun Control"* by Aaron Zelman and Richard W. Stevens, http://www.jpfo.org/deathgc.htm).

Once the guns were taken away from its citizens and residents, the Socialist, Fascist, and all dictators killed their own citizens and innocent people. "This does not even count the numbers from World Wars and secondary deaths or deaths we do not know about, not to mention the crime deaths from people not being able to protect themselves. The historical truth: evil governments did wipe out 170,000,000 innocent non-military lives in the 20th Century alone. Almost 1/5 of a BILLION people have died last century when guns were rounded up." (*"Death By Gun Control"*, by Aaron Zelman and Richard W. Stevens) These evil governments included the Soviet Union Marxism under Stalin who killed more than 20 million, including the Ukraine famine genocide created by Stalin, German Fascism under Hitler killed over 20 million, Red China Marxism under Mao Tse-tung killed from 40 to 70 million, and Cambodian Marxism under Pol Pot killed about 2 million people, which represented about 25% of the people. The past few decades have seen terrifying examples of genocide in other places such as Rwanda, Darfur, and Bosnia. The people had no guns to defend themselves against their own tyrannical government. History is full of examples where the government turned against their own citizens to maintain law and order after they first confiscated their guns and took away the people's rights to have guns or weapons in the country.

To avoid political tyranny, the Founders of the United States passed the Second Amendment which says, "A well regulated Militia, being necessary to the security of a free State, the right of the people to keep and bear Arms, shall not be infringed." In *District of Columbia v. Heller* (2008) 128 S. Ct. 2783, 554 US 570, 171 L. Ed. 2d 637, the U.S. Supreme Court handed down a landmark decision that held the Second Amendment protects the rights of individuals to possess and carry firearms. In *McDonald v. Chicago* (2010) 130 S. Ct. 3020, 561 US 742, 177 L. Ed. 2d 894, the U.S. Supreme Court held that the Fourteenth Amendment applies the rights to bear arms in the Second Amendment to state and local governments to the same extent that the Second Amendment applies to the federal government.

The Second Amendment is to arm residents of this country against tyranny and for self-defense, primarily in the home. Those Politicians who promote gun control by gun confiscation, most have bodyguards themselves. Those citizens and residents who cannot afford bodyguards have to defend themselves. These Politicians and wealthy people insist that their bodyguards have the right to carry guns, so every citizen and resident should have the same rights.

If the Socialists take away the citizens and residents' right to own a gun, then only the criminals will have guns.

What kills people with guns are deranged people and criminals. Law abiding citizens and residents have a right to own a gun for self-defense and have the right to defend themselves against tyranny of the government. Saying a gun has killed someone is like saying a spoon has made a person overweight. It was neither the gun, nor the spoon that hurt someone; it was the external manifestation of someone's will to do the wrong.

Police are not military. What has happened to our police? The military is equipped and trained to fight an enemy who has no Constitutional rights. The military has armored vehicles, automatic weapons, planes, helicopters, and other fire power to kill an enemy. The police are not supposed to have or use military weapons against citizens because citizens are not the police's enemy. Police are to follow the Constitution and ensure the protective freedoms delineated in the Bill of Rights which are afforded to every person. Instead, the military has been sending war equipment and weapons to the local law enforcement departments in the cities of the United States, and the result is that the local police start acting like military personnel who treat common citizens as their enemy. If the police have these military weapons, there will be a time when they will use them against citizens and residents in their community. Military soldiers are trained to kill the enemy. The police are supposed to be trained to protect people's rights and arrest the offenders of the law, not kill them, unless the officer is personally threatened with deadly force from the alleged criminal. We have recently seen several black men who are mere citizens being killed by police. Most of them participated in a petty crime, so they should not have been killed during the arrest. We should be supporters of the police, but more so, we should be supporters of the freedoms and liberties afforded people under the U.S. Constitution.

The *"Posse Comitatus Act"* was passed to limit the powers of the federal government in using its military personnel to act as domestic law enforcement personnel. The Act does not apply to the National Guard or the Coast Guard. On September 26, 2006, President George W. Bush urged Congress to consider revising federal laws so that U.S. armed forces could restore public order and enforce laws in the aftermath of a natural disaster, terrorist attack or incident, or other condition. These changes were included in the John Warner National Defense Authorization Act for Fiscal Year 2007. One has to wonder whether there are forces behind the scenes doing things to escalate domestic protests or cause weather changes to authorize the federal government to station military soldiers as domestic law enforcement personnel in cities throughout the land. We have seen military personnel brought in at Ferguson, Baltimore, and Jade Helm 15; and it is difficult to believe these events do not have ulterior motives involved by the powers that are behind the current government.

The "enemy" of the Socialist state now is seen by the government as those who protest, those who resist authority, those who own guns, those who follow a "religion" that disagrees with the Socialist laws of the government, and those who speak out to demand the free exercise of their Constitutional rights to assemble together to protest, to exercise their freedom of speech and religion, and to have the right to bear arms to protect themselves. God requires us to be disobedient and protest a tyrannical government but do it peaceably like the Reverend Martin Luther King Jr. did back in the 1960's. Yet, when the government's tyrannical laws and oppression are so great, the Second Amendment gives rights to citizens to own guns to protect themselves against tyranny.

Citizens and residents of the U.S. must wake up to the fact that taking away their guns is the first step towards tyranny, persecution, FEMA camps, and executions for mere sedition by the Socialist state.

GOD'S PRINCIPLE: LASTING WEALTH IS BUILT GENERATIONALLY
THROUGH FAMILIES USING WISE STEWARDSHIP OF PRIVATE
PROPERTY, NOT THROUGH GOVERNMENT OWNERSHIP

In Acts 3:25 Peter said, "You are sons of the prophets, and of the covenant which God made with our fathers, saying to Abraham, 'And in your Seed all the families of the earth shall be blessed.'" (The reference to "Seed" in this verse is Jesus Christ).

The family unit is the "pipe" through which the blessings of Jesus Christ, the "Living Water," is to flow. God sends forth His blessings through the family.

God is building a family business (Luke 2: 49), and the family unit is the institution in society in which the Abrahamic Covenant is to flow, the business is to run, and wealth is to be accumulated and transferred to the next generation. God is interested in His children establishing a family dynasty of wealth to be used to spread the gospel of God's Kingdom.

There are two institutions that will go on throughout eternity, nations and families; although we really do not know what those will look like entirely throughout eternity.

FAMILIES: Ephesians 3:14-15 says, "For this reason I bow my knees to the Father of our Lord Jesus Christ, from whom the whole family in heaven and earth is named."

NATIONS: Revelation 22:1-2 says, "And he showed me a pure river of water of life clear as crystal, proceeding from the throne of God and of the Lamb. In the middle of its street, and on either side of the river, was the tree of life, which bore twelve fruits, each tree yielding its fruit every month. The leaves of the tree were for the healing of the nation."

POINT: God is committed to **families and nations** eternally as a community lifestyle pattern for all cultures and societies who become citizens of the Kingdom of Heaven. Believers belong to the nation and family of God. Philippians 3:20 says, "For our citizenship is in heaven; from whence also we look for the Saviour, the Lord Jesus Christ." Ephesians 2:19 says, "Now therefore you are no longer strangers and foreigners, but fellow citizens (God's new extended holy nation) with the saints and members of the household of God (God's new extended family)." 1 Peter 2:9 says, "But ye are a chosen generation, a royal priesthood, an holy nation, a peculiar people; that ye should shew forth the praises of him who hath called you out of darkness into his marvellous light."

GOD'S DIVINE PURPOSE: Ephesians 3:10 says, "... (It is God's) intent that now the manifold wisdom of God might be made known by the Church to the (good and evil) principalities and (good and evil) powers in heavenly places." God's intent is to show the good angels and heavenly beings His manifold wisdom that He has made known to the Church, which is not the perfection of wisdom, nor Jesus as wisdom or Sophia of God, nor the Scriptures, themselves, but the gospel of the Kingdom (Matthew 24:14) and repentance and remission of sins (Luke 24:47) that is to be preached to the whole world, where fallen, but now forgiven mankind is brought into the family and nation and Kingdom of God. God's wisdom in choosing fallen mankind through redemption by and through Christ's sacrifice on the Roman Cross to secure their forgiveness of sin and eternal life, was a witness to even the angels in heaven that they are also secure, not in their works but in the grace of Father God. God the Father proved His love by sending His only begotten Son, Jesus Christ, as Redeemer of fallen mankind who believe in Him as Savior and Lord, who is both God the Word with an infinite divine nature and the Son of God as finite humanity nature in one person, totally disguisable, inseparable, immutable, but holy and without sin, upholding God's honor, holiness, and justice.

On the other hand, Satan and the Kingdom of darkness are mortified by God's display of this manifold wisdom, where sin is condemned by putting the sin on Jesus to satisfy justice, while the repentant sinner is saved and becomes justified through Christ Jesus as a display of grace and mercy by Father God. This manifold wisdom is where Jesus, without sin, laid down His own life to save those who were born into sin, but God through the gospel of the Kingdom (Matthew 24:14) and repentance and remission of sins (Luke 24:47) has brought these children by adoption into the family of God and the nation as citizens of the Kingdom of heaven. This manifold wisdom was foretold by God in Genesis 3:15 when the Seed of the Woman would crush the head of the seed of the serpent. This manifold wisdom is displayed before the heavenly hosts and the evil kingdom of darkness as to how God manifested grace, wisdom, mercy, redemption, and adoption of fallen mankind into the family and nation of God by making them new creatures in Christ (2 Corinthians 5:17).

POINT: God's intent is to display the Church before all powers, both good and evil, in the spiritual realm as His instruments to manifest the Kingdom of God throughout the earth which was the mission of our Priestly King, Lord, Savior, Jesus Christ (Matthew 4:17), and for which the Church is also commissioned to accomplish as Believers who receive redemption and allow Christ to live His spirit and life in them and through them (Galatians 2:20).

Ephesians 3:14-21 says, "For this reason I bend my knees to the Father of our Lord Jesus Christ from **whom the whole family in heaven and earth is named**, that He would grant you, according to the riches of His glory, to be strengthened with might through His (Holy) Spirit in the inner man, that Christ may dwell in your hearts through faith; that you, being rooted and grounded in love, may be able to comprehend with all the saints what is the width and length and depth and height **to know the love of Christ which passes knowledge; that you may be filled with all the fullness of God.** Now to Him who is able to do exceedingly, abundantly above all that we ask or think, according to the power that works in us, to Him be glory in the Church by Christ Jesus to all generations, forever and ever. Amen."

Ephesians 3:14-21 says that God's intent is for the Holy Spirit's power to fill every Believer to accomplish His divine purpose of manifesting His Kingdom filled with Christ's *agape* love here on earth through obedient children in the family here on earth, patterned after the family in heaven, who are obeying Christ's Commandment to *agape* love one another (John 13:34-35).

Ephesians 3:14-15 says that it is through those who are in the family of God, as His children by adoption (Romans 8:15) that God's eternal purpose will be accomplished.

The word "family" is a spiritual word rooted in God: God the Father, the Father of the Humanity Nature of our Lord Jesus, (God's only begotten Son) indivisibly connected with, but distinguishable from, God the Word, Christ's divine nature, as the Incarnate Christ and the Holy Spirit, as One Godhead. In the One Godhead, Himself, is the First Family as the pattern for all saved families here on earth.

The godly family here on earth is designed after God's pattern of the Divine Family in Heaven and is mandated to be caring, loving, compassionate, willing to sacrifice for others, giving, holy, follows God's principles, furthers God's purposes, filled with God's power and authority, and is the living Temple of God (John 14:17, 23; 1 Corinthians 6:19-individually; 1 Corinthians 3:16- collectively in local church; and Ephesians 2:21-collectively in the universal church)

Also, God relates to people in terms of family: God is our Father (Ephesians 4:6); God was Husband to His people Israel in the wilderness (Jeremiah 31:32); God is like a nurturing mother (Isaiah 66:13), and Christ is the Bridegroom of the Church (Ephesians 5:22,33; Revelation 21:9).

When a man and woman come together in marriage, God extends to them this name that in essence belongs to God – "family." We as father, mother, and children must reflect the nature and life of the divine family in Heaven.

Malachi 4:5-6 says, "Behold, I will send Elijah the prophet before the coming of the great and dreadful day of the Lord, and he (Elijah) will turn the hearts of the fathers to the children, and the hearts of the children to their fathers. Lest I come and strike the earth with a curse."

The consequential tribulation that is on every nation is because the fathers and the children have lost their relationship of love, honor, and respect. A larger percentage of the children are born to unwed mothers in the U.S. People have brought this consequential tribulation upon themselves because they have been disobedient to God's law.

This short run thinking of disobedience to God's principles has full negative economic consequences for the families within the nations.

The economic dire consequences come when the family unit is divided because it is through the family unit that the blessing of the Abrahamic covenant is to be transferred. The Abrahamic blessing is to pass generationally in Christ through the family of God, who has invited in the family the manifest presence of the Holy Spirit (Galatians 3:14) and Jesus' divine nature of God the Word (Matthew 18:20).

FALSEHOODS IN THE HUMANISTIC (MAN-CENTERED) SOCIETY

FALSEHOOD NO. 1: Private property is a limited right by the possessor or private owner and is subject to the discretion of the Socialist Bureaucrat in the Civil Government.

FALSEHOOD NO. 2: Because life is short, people should have as a goal profit and pleasure.

TRUTHS IN GOD'S KINGDOM

TRUTH NO. 1: Privately owned real property is essential (not optional) to both societal and personal maturity. The management by people of God's property is the vehicle designed by God to carry His discipleship training to mature His children.

The foundation of the United States was the opposite – real property rights rested absolutely with God's steward of the real property. Trespass of land even without specific intent was an actionable cause for damages. Zoning was virtually unheard of in the early years of the colonies. A man's home was his castle, where he reigned as lord and king under the rulership of the King of kings and the Lord of lords.

Under the law of God, title to real property should not belong to the Civil Government, but to those who lawfully steward it under God's law (i.e. to families ultimately who have been given the right to steward real property by God since God is the true Owner of the land). Presently all property in America where private residents hold title shall escheat back to the state if claim is not made by the heirs in a reasonable time after the death of the one who has fee simple title.

TRUTH NO. 2: Psalm 24:1. Who owns the earth? God! Since God owns the earth, then imminent domain by the Civil Government should have only a limited conceptual definition and use in man's law. Private property rights should be superior to public rights to the use of land in a republic, where individual rights are supreme over governmental authority.

Land tax by the government is forbidden under God's law, as the government cannot lawfully tax what does not belong to the government. There was no land tax in America until the 1700's because it was viewed as government theft to tax the land since Psalm 24:1 says the earth is the Lord's.

TRUTH NO. 3: First Amendment guarantees freedom of religion. *Internal Revenue Code*, section 501(c)(3) or section, 508(c)(1)(A) pertains to non-profit organizations, but the exemption provided by 508(c)(1)(A) maintains the freedoms of speech and religion afforded to the Church. The whole concept of not taxing the Church was to avoid a theological violation by the Civil Government. The early colonial government did not believe it had the right to tax the Church since it was God's institution. In fact, under *Internal Revenue Code*, section 508(c)(1)(A), churches and affiliate ministries today are exempt from filing for a determination letter from the IRS that the organization is exempt under *Internal Revenue Code*, section 501(c)(3). [See www.irs.gov/pub/irs-pdf/i1023.pdf]

Tax free churches: Therefore, the law in the U.S. making all churches and ministries tax exempt was passed as a theological recognition of a Sovereign God.

TRUTH NO. 4: There is a problem with single generation consumption. Wise stewardship over God's property requires long term planning and use by multi-generation investing, which is long run thinking rather than by single generation consumption, which is short run thinking. Long run thinking is God's pattern for business and for God's obedient families and nations. Family Christian dynasties planning for families from one generation to another can build a snowball of wealth to be used for the purpose of building God's Kingdom. God is the God of Abraham, Isaac, and Jacob, so God expects family dynasty wealth to flow forward to at least three generations (Proverbs 13:22).

The Socialist Civil Government is trying to keep the long run family generational dynasty wealth from transferring to the next generation through high income taxes, estate taxes, generation-skipping taxes, inheritance taxes, and probate fees because their Humanist Civil Government is in competition with the family. Instead of passing to your heirs the wealth that you as parent have earned after paying income taxes to acquire that wealth, the Civil Government demands that you as parent pass a portion to the Civil Government. The better thing to do is to take out a life insurance policy or annuity to cover the estate tax burden upon the parents' deaths, so the parents' heirs receive all of the parents' wealth in the estate to fulfill God's desire.

Business leaders are teaching other Business Servants and Executives about stimulating the Christian business community to understand the dangers in the implementation by the societal and governmental institutions of non-theological practices and tax policies in opposition to the freedom envisaged by the Founding Fathers of this nation and the biblical principles in the Bible.

GOD'S PRINCIPLE: PRIVATE PROPERTY, MATURITY,
AND FAMILY GENERATIONAL TRANSFER OF WEALTH
ARE TO BE WITHIN FAMILIES NOT CIVIL GOVERNMENTS

The stewardship and care of privately-owned real property is essential to a family within an ethnic group for their maturity. People take better care of what they hold title to than when they rent from another. Again, Psalm 24:1 says God owns all the land, which is why property tax is a usurpation of God's ownership rights and the rights of those whom God entrusts with His property. Property income, in the form of rent, should only be collected by someone who rightfully has control of the land. God has given land on the earth for control to and for families, so they can be matured through stewardship responsibilities. There are family groups that make up ethnic groups, and without real property trusteeship from God, then ethnic groups are impoverished.

LAND WAS CHOSEN BY GOD FOR EACH NATION: Acts 17: 26 says, "And He has made from one blood (Adam) every nation of men to dwell on all the face of the earth and has determined their pre-appointed times and the boundaries of their dwellings." Every nation of people has been given stewardship of land on the planet by God, but its possession of the land is not forever. The history is full of the rise and fall of governments, but the ethnic group citizens still possess the land. America no longer has a focus of unity because the enemy is not outside the country but inside the hearts of the people within the ethnic groups that make up inside the U.S. Hoards of people of America and people of many other nations have turned away from God and have started worshiping idols. The biggest idol in the U.S. is the god of mammon. Money is not designed to solve problems that God considers to be sin in a nation.

ABOMINATIONS THAT CAUSE THE LAND TO BE DEFILED: The following is not my opinion but God's law. As an ambassador of Christ, I can only repeat what my King authorizes me to say. If you have a problem with this section, then you have to argue with my God and King, not me.

Leviticus 18:21-28 says, "And thou shalt not let any of thy seed pass through the fire to Molech, neither shalt thou profane the name of thy God: I am the LORD. (22) Thou shalt not lie with mankind, as with womankind: it is abomination. (23) Neither shalt thou lie with any beast to defile thyself therewith: neither shall any woman stand before a beast to lie down thereto: it is confusion. Defile not ye yourselves in any of these things: for in all these the nations are defiled which I cast out before you: (25) And the land is defiled: therefore I do visit the iniquity thereof upon it, and the land itself vomiteth out her inhabitants. (26) Ye shall therefore keep my statutes and my judgments, and shall not commit any of these abominations; neither any of your own nation, nor any stranger that sojourneth among you: (27) (For all these abominations have the men of the land done, which were before you, and the land is defiled;) (28) That the land spue not you out also, when ye defile it, as it spued out the nations that were before you."

Sacrificing children to Molech was considered an abomination. The Bible contains many warnings against an abhorrent abomination practiced by the Canaanites, who were dispossessed of their land by God, who then gave the land to Israel. One such admonition was throwing children into the fire of the false god, Molech

(Leviticus 18:21) to seek Molech's favor by the Canaanites sacrificing their own children by fire. A *Channel 4 Dispatches* episode in the United Kingdom— "Exposing Hospital Heartache," first aired Monday, March 24, 2014, revealing that many British hospitals for years were not only incinerating the remains of aborted and miscarried babies as "clinical waste" but were also burning some of those bodies as a means of heating their buildings in "waste-to-energy" programs. Was this like sacrificing children to Molech by the Canaanites? Did this practice defile the land of the United Kingdom?

There is redemption to heal the land. 2 Chronicles 7:14 says, "If My people, which are called by My name, shall humble themselves, and pray, and seek My face, and turn from their wicked ways; then will I hear from heaven, and will forgive their sin, and will heal their land."

FALSE IDOL OF MAMMON: There are people in America and other nations who have received the revelation that God wants to make the businesses a place of ministry to change the hearts of the people with whom they are interacting. Since the idol of mammon is so strong, God has decided to attack this idol where the transactions are being conducted by changing the hearts of the people doing the business to become His servants.

NATION SALVATION: Matthew 28:18-19 says, "All authority has been given to me in heaven and on earth. Go therefore and make disciples of all nations (ethnic groups) ...baptizing them in the name of the Father, Son and Holy Spirit teaching them to observe all things that I have commanded..." What are the motivating biblical principles involved in nation salvation? Primarily, the motivation must be love for others, but with discipline to make Believers involved in godly self-government. Since Believers of the same race often congregate, fellowship together, and often live in the same community, racial characteristic behavior became common through group psychology and a desire to conform to the norms of the group.

FAMILIES: The biblical mandated possessors of land in geopolitical habitations in the Promise Land were given to Hebrew families (Leviticus 25) as a pattern for all nations, not the government. Leviticus. 27:24 says, "In the year of Jubilee the field shall return to him from whom it was bought to the one who owned the land as a possession."

LAND OWNERSHIP BY GOVERNMENT NOT BIBLICAL: The Civil Government was not given land in Israel when the children of Israel came into the promise land. All the land of promise was given to families of the children of Israel by God's command. The land was divided up by families and given to the nation of Israel, even the Levite priesthood. Samuel warned the people that if God granted the people's request for a king, a king would take the land from the families. 1 Samuel 8:14 says, "And he (king) will take the best of your fields, your vineyards and give them to his servants." Eminent domain by government was not considered to be God's best for the people. Another better system would be that private stewards of land would donate without compulsion and for the public use, such as for schools, libraries, parks, and roads. This would be the preference to eminent domain.

INCOME TAX: The prophet Samuel warned the people of Israel that the Civil Government (king) would tax also a tenth of all their increase like God. 1 Samuel 8:15 says, "He (king) will take a tenth of your grain and your vintage and give it to his officers and servants." 1 Samuel 8:17 says, "He (king) will take a tenth of your sheep. And you will be his servants."

The prophet Samuel could not comprehend a people tolerating a king taxing as much as, or more than, God's flat tax of ten percent. Therefore, the Civil Government does not have biblical authority to tax the people on income more than 9.9999 percent. If the Civil Government taxes income 10% or more, then it is holding itself out as equal to God. When the Civil Government Politicians pass laws to tax people more than 9.9999 percent of their net income, then Civil Government Politicians act as capricious "gods," arbitrarily burdening the people. God is a jealous God, and He will not tolerate any other god before Him. Thus, the Civil Government rulers have sowed disobedience upon the land and nation and have brought the violation of God's principles to have their consequential negative effect in the economy and the families of the nation.

Under Hebrew law (Leviticus 25: 8-13), the 50th year of Jubilee, was a year of restoration. The biblical requirement is that the Jubilee year was to be treated like a Sabbatical year, with the land lying fallow, but also required the compulsory return of all property to its original family owners or their heirs, except the houses of laymen within walled cities, in addition to the manumission of all Israelite indentured servants. Israelite families owned the land as a gift from God when they originally crossed the Jordan River from Egypt into the Promise Land, and title to their Family's property was restored to them. The 50th year of Jubilee caused the original families not to lose their heritage of land through mortgage foreclosure. Under the Hebrew law debts were canceled every seven years, and the U.S. allows bankruptcy every seven years from that pattern. The land always was designed to remain in the ownership, possession, and stewardship of chosen families, descendants from the sons of Israel as it is God's tool for maturing and blessing His children.

A lot of Believers are excited about the Israelites returning to the land of Israel; however, a real sign of the end times is when the Israeli Civil Government returns the land back to the original family descendants of the twelve sons of Israel, as they should during the Year of Jubilee. It will be best to see land held in trust by families, not by Socialist government.

Eminent domain should not be a rule or an overriding right of Civil Government, but a very rare exception to the rule. Eminent domain should be restricted for use to acquire public parks, military bases, public roads, public waterways, and construction of public governmental buildings to legislate, execute, and adjudicate the laws of the land. However, governmental buildings should be kept at a minimum, favoring private property rental to accommodate the governmental officials. The large amount of land under the authority of the Bureau of Land Management in the U. S. presently is not biblical. Also, the government should only monopolize the absolute essential utilities, such as electricity, gas, water, and sewage; however, if private industry can truly compete with the utility monopolies, then they should be allowed to do so.

We have seen this in the installation of solar panels in homes that produce electricity. Transportation should be conducted by private industry for a fare based upon usage. Medicine should be left to the private sector and all other matters related to social welfare should be overseen by the families with tax incentives. The family should be given special tax incentives instead of as it is today where the families are penalized under the current tax system. Likewise, the right to educate your children belongs to the parents and pre-dates the Constitution as an inalienable right from the Creator. Children are gifts from God, not gifts from the Civil Government. The private business sector, families, and the Church in the local community should be taking responsibilities over most of the areas now considered "sacred cows" of the Socialist and Humanist Civil Government Politicians and Bureaucrats.

ELEVEN

GOD'S ORDER OF STEWARDSHIP PROMOTES LASTING WEALTH

GOD'S BUSINESS SERVANTS WILL BE JUDGED
AT THE JUDGMENT SEAT OF CHRIST FOR THEIR
STEWARDSHIP OF GOD'S POSSESSIONS

First order of stewardship-OUR BODIES:

We have been given authority over our bodies which belong to God. 1 Corinthians. 3:17 says, "If anyone defiles the temple of God, God will destroy him. For the temple of God is holy, which temple you are." 1 Corinthians 6:19 asks, "Or do you not know that your body is the temple of the Holy Spirit who is in you, whom you have from God, and you are not your own?"

Do the Socialist and Humanist Civil Government Politicians and Bureaucrats believe that life is precious? Do they believe in the freedom to kill an innocent life by a mother and her doctor? Do they believe that life begins at conception or at birth? Do they believe that as part of the stewardship over her body, a woman has a right to kill the unborn child growing in her womb? Is this good stewardship over her body? Is the first order of stewardship over our own bodies the protection of the rights of others to have the right to live in their bodies here on earth? Is the right to life of all humans a fundamental principle of God Almighty? Is life promulgated and guaranteed by the U. S. Declaration of Independence and the U.S. Constitution? Was the fundamental right to life a principle of the Bible? Did Jesus come to give us life and life abundantly? Life, liberty, and pursuit of happiness are the foundational rights of people in the U.S., and the first fundamental right is life.

Second order of stewardship-OUR CHILDREN:

Our children: Children are an inheritance from the Lord. Parents have been given authority and responsibility to lovingly educate and raise their children. All authority is balanced with responsibility. Parents have authority over their children but must raise them in the admonitions of the Lord.

The Socialists' Proletariat: Again, the "Proletariat" is the lowest workforce of a nation who have no capital or assets, except for their children. The Socialist State mandates that children are taught by the state school system to be educated with Socialism and Humanism as the norm but not taught religion, especially not Christianity. Yet, institutions do not love. Parents love their children. Teachers are forbidden to be too close to their students.

THE EDUCATED ELITE: The Socialist and Humanists believe that those who are educated know better about every aspect of life than those who are not educated.

However, the parents should be questioning educators: "Mr. Socialist, Mr. Humanist, you do have a lot of knowledge from your education, but what is the source of your knowledge? Does your knowledge come from eating from the Tree of the Knowledge of Good and Evil, embodied in the public educational system, or the Tree of Life embodied in the Bible and an intimate relationship with Christ? Have you been educated concerning the foundational beliefs of the modern Socialist ideas and definitions of what is good or secular, and what is freedom? Or, have you been educated from the Bible, where God's principles and ideas are written? Do you use the Bible as the foundation of your belief system? If you do not, then the solidity of your beliefs is in question, especially since you are trying to teach the falsehood of Humanism as truth to my children."

SOCIALIST REVOLUTION: One of the primary principles of the Socialist revolution was to take away the stewardship of the children from the parents, who have been given the authority by God, and grant that authority into the hands of the Socialist and Humanist Bureaucrats. The Socialist civil state wants to be the formulator of values concerning the children in the state, rather than the parents. The reason is that these children are the future voters, and the Socialists want these children to vote them back into office when they become adults.

EDUCATION FALSEHOOD: One of the main falsehoods in school is the study of history based strictly on materialism, or a perception that the people historically were only concerned about material inventions and economic advancements. Karl Marx's concept of evolution that he postulated leads to a better world through Socialism and Communism and is based upon this perception of history from only an economic class struggle between the haves and the have nots. He saw the main thought of history was economics. He saw life pursuits strictly as to who is in control of the material world of means of production of: food, transportation, housing, education, medical services, legal services, and sale of consumer products. The people's search for a spiritual experience and relationship with God was thought to be simply a religious drug that had little importance. This influence is why the Socialists in the U.S. took prayer out of school and promoted separation of church and state, but really the separation of God and state. Children are taught history in school from the focal point of what class controlled the means of production. The teachers are mandated to leave God out of the course of study. In truth, teaching history in school should be taught as His story.

LIFE REDEFINED: The Socialists redefine "life" to mean having equal opportunity to education, adequate health insurance, equal employment rights, equal housing rights, and non-discriminatory practices throughout society. This is one way of looking at "life," but what they really mean is that they do not want you to think they are killers of innocent babies, but the promoters of "Pro Choice," even though the choice is to take away another human being's right to be born and thereby to live.

Third order of stewardship-PRIVATE PROPERTY:

Stewardship over real or personal property, business, or ministry entrusted to you by others brings maturity.

This stewardship forms an essential part under God's plan of incremental problem-solving leading to maturation and greater responsibility, along with rewards. First, God gives us possession over the natural things, then the spiritual things. Second, God gives us possession of another man's property, business, or ministry; and based upon our faithfulness to those assignments, He gives us our own property, business, or ministry. God promotes and assigns future responsibility based upon faithful stewardship of our prior assignments.

GOD IS LOOKING FOR FRUIT THAT REMAINS
(WHICH IS INCREASE FOR THE LONG RUN
FROM THE PRACTICE OF LONG RUN THINKING)

John 15:16 says, "You did not choose me, but I chose you and appointed you that you should go and bear fruit and that your fruit should remain (God's long run thinking), that whatever you ask the Father in My Name He may give you." Whatever the Father gives you in Jesus' Name, God expects you to use it based upon long run planning and thinking and bear fruit that will remain for the enhancement of His Kingdom, will, and purpose.

Fruit is produced by loving, caring and demanding work of cultivating, watering, and pruning with patience to wait for everything to become beautiful in its time of maturity. Ecclesiastes 3:11 says, "He has made everything beautiful in its time."

Parable of the ten *minas*. Luke 19:11–26.

Luke 19:12 says, "Therefore He said, 'A certain nobleman went into a far country to receive for himself a Kingdom and to return. So he called ten of his servants delivered to them ten *minas* (a mina is about three months' pay) and said to them, "do business until I return."'"

In Luke 19:13, the Master gave *minas* to each of his bondservants or *doulos* in the Greek to properly steward in his absence and bring multiplied increase. Bondservants were those who had the right to be set free but chose to remain with their master. The master, under the law, would take an awe and jam it into and through the ear lobe of the bondservant and put an earring there as a symbol of the peculiar office. He became known as a love servant." Also, the master would give the bondservant possession or stewardship of his goods but not ownership. This bondservant would be like a trustee today. They were called A peculiar people" back then. In 1 Peter 2:9, Christians are referred to as "peculiar people" because we have stewardship or trustee possessory rights over things on the earth, but the ownership rests with our King of kings. Those who deal with granting possessory rights are called lords, such as a landlord.

Luke 19:16 says, "Then came the first, saying 'Master, your *mina* has earned ten *minas*.'"

Luke 19:17 says, "And he said to him, 'Well done, good servant; because you were faithful in a very little, have authority over ten cities.'" The Lord refers to money as a "little thing," of which He uses its faithful stewardship to mature His people, so that they can then be promoted to stewardship over people, which is an important thing with God. In Luke 19:17, the Master rewarded the diligent, faithful bondservant with authority to rule over ten cities. God judges the way you handle money, considered to be a little thing, as a measuring stick on how you will handle weightier problems which involve the supervision of people.

Jesus then spoke to the unjust steward. Luke 19:22 says, "...You knew that I was an austere master, collecting what I did not deposit and reaping what I did not sow."

Luke 19:24 Jesus continued, "And he said to those who stood by, 'Take the *mina* from him and give it to him who has ten minas.'"

A major principle was pronounced in the parable of the ten *minas* for stewardship and wealth distribution. Here is Jesus' principle which He uses in His Kingdom for Business Servants to follow: Luke 19:26 says, "For I say to you, that to everyone who has more will be given; and from him who does not have, even what he has will be taken away from him."

The truth for the Business Servant to teach the employees is that he who has multiplied what he has, he will be given more because he has exercised good stewardship with that which he has been entrusted with which has resulted in increase. Therefore, as a reward for faithfulness, more will be given. He who has not been a good steward with what was entrusted to him, he has nothing to show from his efforts. Consequently, those little things like money with which he has been entrusted will be taken away from him because he has nothing to show as increases during his entrustment with stewardship responsibility.

REMAINING FRUIT: In a day of short run dividends, returns seen from long run planning is almost an unthinkable concept in the United States' Socialist and Humanist society and economy. However, God mandates His Business Servants to seek "fruit remaining" as a biblitarian principle. To achieve this goal, Business Servants must involve long run thinking and wealth accumulation, as opposed to the accumulation of riches of this world and single generation consumption.

Because people in the U.S. have lost the application of Christian principles in society and the business world, the United States' economic power brokers no longer think about wealth in the long run but rather riches in the short run. Some immature Business Servants and investors who have money usually think only to maximize returns on their money in the short run. Few investors hold on to long term bonds or other securities, and few invest in long-term wealth projects to do R&D or capture a market share. This is primarily why those who used to be in industry have lost their creativity, outside of the computer industry and the creation of new weapons for the promulgation of war.

One of the major reasons it is hard for Americans to compete with the Japanese, Germans, South Koreans, and Chinese, or any other nation which has a family concept of economics, is because American business owners, ignorant of God's biblitarian principles, are short run thinkers. The family concept of economics always involves long run thinking, planning, and spending to pass on wealth to children and children's children (Proverbs 13:22), and do not involve short run thinking for the following reasons:

Short run thinking is anti-family, anti-Kingdom, because unsaved and immature business owners in the U. S. continue distributing dividends and short run profits, instead of investing the profits on market share, R & D, savings for future expenditures instead of debt financing, and long term economic return. The business people following the world's system of economics, spend profits on short run economic consumption in the form of dividends to attract investors who want short term investments and returns. Investors and even some immature Business Servants have adopted the anti-biblical Humanist philosophy that spending money to satisfy selfish desires for bigger houses, newer cars, boats, etc. is the reason to make money in the first place.

Our industries in the U.S. get farther and farther behind all the other industries in the first world countries that are "long run" thinking in business and investment spending. We no longer save or invest for the future in America.

If we do not have a Christian economic renewal, this country (U.S.) will be irreparably injured because of its disobedience to the biblical law of economics. Although America as a people has the greatest percentage of Christian Believers, the American citizens vote to put Socialists and Humanists as Politicians in Civil Government. Christians in America are disobedient to Father God's principle, and they will reap what they sow.

The other family based nations will out do the U.S. as our economic competitors. Although they are not strong Christians, they are family oriented with long run thinking to a higher degree than Americans are, and this pro family philosophy has affected their economic policies to their wealth accumulation.

SAVINGS RATE: The U.S. has the lowest savings rate per capita than all the other major industrial nations because of short run thinking. People in the U.S. do not see the worth in saving money for future expenditures or for the next two generations.

R & D: The U.S. has one of the lowest R & D funding ratios of any of the major industrialized nations, whereas the U.S. was once number one in this category. People think it wise to invest in business opportunities which promise short run returns.

GOD'S TRUTH: The above mindsets of short term as opposed to long term thinking are spiritual choices, not just economic choices. These short run mindsets are a hatred for future generations and the children and grandchildren of this nation.

GOD'S WARNING: When God's biblical principles of government, family, business, education, and life are removed from our American culture, this culture will go down the tubes, economically. Again, economics is the direct result of the spiritual policies of the society, businesses, Civil Government, and culture.

ABSENT FATHER DISCIPLINARIANS: What is the reason for this consequential economic disaster? Malachi 4: 4-6 gives the answer. Because negative consequences come upon the people when the disciplinary hearts of the fathers are separated from the children and replaced with a false maternalistic desire to protect the citizens from the consequences of their sins or bad decisions. Also, the fathers of our nation are no longer thinking long term wealth accumulation for the benefit of their posterity and instead are thinking "short term, single generation consumption," then economic failure is certain for the nation and culture. The economic devastation caused by the violation of biblical principles that disdain "short term" thinking is already flowing in the U.S.

GOD ENTRUSTS BUSINESS SERVANTS WITH CARING FOR NATURAL THINGS THE SAME AS SPIRITUAL MATTERS

In Luke 16:10-12, Jesus says, "He who is faithful with what is least is faithful also in much; and he who is unjust in what is least is unjust also in much. Therefore, if you have not been faithful with unrighteous mammon who will commit to your trust the true riches? And if you have not been faithful in what is another man's, who will give you what is your own?"

GOD'S PRINCIPLE: God gives Business Servants care over bigger things based on their care firstly of little things well done and based upon the care of another person's things before He gives them care of their own things.

Matthew 25:14-29 gives the account of "The parable of the talents." In the Bible, money is referred to as a little thing."

In the long run nobody is going to steward abundant wealth who has not been a good steward over small things first in the short run.

GOD'S PATTERN: Jesus gives us a superb pattern of His concern for proper stewardship in John 17.

John 17 is really a stewardship accounting by Jesus to the Father. "I have manifested your name to the men whom you have given Me out of the world. They were Yours. You gave them to Me, and they have kept Your word. For I have given them the words which you have given to Me; and they have received them. And all Mine are Yours and Yours are Mine, and I am glorified in them."

Jesus' report to the Father was:

Not a report on miracles
Not a report on ministry
Not a report on meetings

Jesus' communication with the Father was a report on preaching the gospel of the Kingdom (Matthew 24:14) and repentance and remission of sins (Luke 24:47), being faithful to steward, train and care to disciple them that have been entrusted to Him by His Father in His Father's family business. Jesus learned obedience by the things He suffered (Hebrews 5:8) or had stewardship over, as He was growing up and working as a Carpenter, first for His step-father, Joseph, and then having been trained as a Journeyman Carpenter, He then trained His half-brothers, as He was required to do under the Law as head of the carpentry business after Joseph's death to support His widow mother and sisters. This journeyman training of His brothers as to how to conduct business as Carpenters, Jesus used these same principles of daily training in training His disciples in ministry to preach the gospel of the Kingdom and repentance and remission of sins, healing the sick, and casting out demons.

> A MAJOR PROBLEM IS THE ANEMIC GOSPEL OF INDIVIDUAL SALVATION, INSTEAD OF WHAT JESUS' MANDATED, WHICH WAS BOTH THE GOSPEL OF THE KINGDOM (MATTHEW 24:14) AND REPENTANCE AND REMISSION OF SINS (LUKE 24:47), HAS BEEN PREACHED BY THE CHURCH LEADERS FOR OVER 1,800 YEARS, WHICH HAS BECOME CHRISTIAN RELIGIOUS RITUALS INSTEAD OF GOD'S KINGDOM 24/7 LIFESTYLE, ALONG WITH RELATIONSHIPS BASED UPON AGAPE LOVE, OBEDIENCE, AND SUBMISSION TO THE LEADING OF THE GODHEAD

The church leaders by and large have made the initial salvation experience with God the most important beneficial message to Believers. They have left out Jesus' gospel of the Kingdom (Matthew 24:14), and only preached just a gospel of salvation for the remission of sins (Luke 24:47), when Jesus mandated both messages to be preached. In so doing, they have rejected the gospel of the Kingdom which embraces the dominion mandate of God and the primary mission of Jesus from Father God's perspective, Who wanted possession of the earth and the people returned to Him. God's priority is to give the dominion to the earth, here and now, to Christ, and through Him to the Believers (Daniel 7:13-14, 22,27). After Jesus' overcoming the temptation in the wilderness by Satan, Jesus returned and stated His mission that Father God gave Him in Matthew 4:17, "Repent: for the kingdom of heaven is at hand."

The word "repent" here in this context means to get back up to the "penthouse" with God, in God's kingdom: 1). As God's children by adoption (Romans 8:15), 2). As citizens of heaven (Philippians 3:20); 3). As members of the spiritual assembly of Kingdom Ambassadors of God's *Ekklesia* (2 Corinthians 5:20), and 4). As members of the spiritual assembly of Kingdom Soldiers of God's *Ekklesia* (2 Timothy 2:3-4).

The Greek word *Ekklesia* has been incorrectly translated as "church," and the English word "church" is a Scottish word from the word "kirk." Yet, the Greek word for Church in the Bible is *"Kuriakos"* (Strongs reference G2960), which is derived from the Greek word *"kurios"* (Strongs G2962). For example, in Acts 19:37 the word translated as "churches" is the Greek word *"hierosulos"* not *"ekklesia."* The Greek word *ekklesia* (Strongs G1577) means either a government assembly or a military assembly, not Church. For example, in Acts 19:34-41 the word *ekklesia* three times was translated as government "assembly." Here the secular council meeting, called an *ekklesia*, was formed to determine what to do with Paul and his co-ministers for preaching the gospel of the Kingdom (Matthew 24:14) and repentance and remission of sins (Luke 24:47) in their city. The secular rulers in the city were threatened because Paul and his co-ministers were introducing a new Kingdom rule in their city. Also, the Roman Senate was called an *ekklesia*, and Jesus took this Greek word and applied it to His body of Believers. In fact, in the Roman Empire any group of citizens who were "called out" to do a work for the government was called an *ekklesia*.

In Acts 19, what caused the uproar in Ephesus is revealed in Acts 19:8 which says, "And he (Paul) went into the synagogue, and spake boldly for the space of three months, disputing and persuading the things concerning the kingdom of God...And this (teaching about the Kingdom of God) continued by the space of two years; so that all they which dwelt in Asia heard the word of the Lord Jesus, both Jews and Greeks." The Gentiles in the city of Ephesus did not want to get in trouble with Rome because Paul was spreading that God's Kingdom was greater than the Kingdom and government in the city. The ruler and citizens of Ephesus dreaded and feared- Paul's teaching about another Kingdom all over the city, other than the Kingdom of Rome, which potentially could cause a Centurion with his soldiers to bring the strongarm of the Roman government and military into the city. They wanted to stop Paul preaching this Kingdom of God.

What did Jesus tell His disciples how to pray? Jesus said in Matthew 6:10 to pray, "Thy kingdom come. Thy will be done in earth, as it is in heaven." Jesus said in Matthew 6:33, "But seek ye first the kingdom of God, and His righteousness [to be in right standing with God in His Kingdom and to be spiritually righteous and holy (Ephesians 4:24)]; and all these things shall be added unto you." The only time Jesus spoke about being born again is in John 3, where He told Nicodemus in verse 3, "Verily, verily, I say unto thee, 'Except a man be born again, he cannot see the Kingdom of God.'" Then in verse 5, Jesus said, "...Verily, verily, I say unto thee, 'Except a man be born of water and of the Spirit, he cannot enter into the kingdom of God." Here the emphasis is not getting born again to go to heaven, but to be born again to see and enter the Kingdom of God. Jesus' mission was that the Kingdom of heaven is here on earth since His arrival.

It is especially important for disciples to follow Jesus' example and commandments. Jesus only preached the good news as the gospel of the Kingdom and repentance and remission of sins (Luke 4:43; 8; 9:11; 16:16-17;

24:47), and Jesus instructed His disciples to preach both the gospel of the Kingdom (Matthew 24:14) and preach repentance and remission of sins (Luke 24:47). Jesus told His disciples, "And as ye go, preach, saying, 'The kingdom of heaven is at hand'" (Matthew 10:7). Why are the current Pastors and Ministers preaching only a gospel of initial salvation to receive eternal life as the "good news" and not along with that the gospel of the Kingdom that Jesus and His disciples' preached as the good news? Initial salvation and eternal life are indeed benefits, along with teaching on provision, healing, and importance of giving tithes and offerings to the Church. Is the failure to preach the correct gospel of the Kingdom (Matthew 24:14) and repentance and remission of sins (Luke 24:47) holding back the end of the Church Age? Jesus said in Matthew 24:14, "And this gospel of the Kingdom shall be preached in all the world for a witness unto all nations; and then shall the end come."

God is concerned about Believers maturing spiritually to transform their carnal nature in their souls (Romans 12:2) and to make mature submitted Kingdom Ambassadors and Kingdom Soldiers that will continue the mission of the Lord Jesus Christ. The message of the initial salvation experience is an easy sell because it is a gift, which is true; but afterwards there is a requirement of maturation and transformation of the soul and the doing of faithful works ordained by the Father (Ephesians 2:10) requiring Believers to be led by the Holy Spirit as the sons of God (Romans 8:14). God is also genuinely concerned about Believers' soul sanctification and development as mature ministers of the gospel of the Kingdom in the marketplace, home place, government place, school place, and all places in our society and culture.

The real issue with God after initial salvation is for all Believers, especially Business Servants, to have excellent and trustworthy stewardship in the Kingdom of God over the things, people, businesses, words, and purposes He has given them.

We have a whole church that has mobbed the door to see the Kingdom of God to be born again but have not entered the Kingdom of God to partake of fellowship with the divine nature of the Lord's presence (John 3: 5) and to be His Kingdom Kings, Lords, and Priests of the order of Melchizedek (1 Timothy 6:15; Hebrews 7:21; 1 Peter 2:9; Revelation 1:6).

Similarly, only a few Business Servants are pressing into what is important to God, which is stewardship and servanthood with love to people, especially other Believers (John 13:34-35), and stewardship over property, business, and spiritual engiftments that the Holy Spirit imparts to you, leading to soul spiritual transformation and maturity. God wants to make mature leaders, not just burping, diaper-changing, baby Christians. This requires ongoing fellowship with God and brothers and sisters of like mind over their work and ministry assignments. Yet, unfortunately what the Church is teaching is mostly carnal "followship" instead of spiritual fellowship.

God is interested in His Business Servants and the training of God's sons and daughters to:

Steward His entrusted gifts.

Steward His entrusted property.

Steward His entrusted business.

Steward His entrusted people.

Steward His entrusted ministries.

With proper stewardship training increased responsibility can come to those mature spiritual sons and daughters who have faithfully managed God's gifts, properties, businesses, people, and ministries well.

Why is the above management analysis important? Because the more Father God gets His children involved in the management of His gifts, properties, businesses, people, and ministries, the more maturity and God's point of view in their thinking in first seeking the Kingdom of God, that comes to reside in them the better Kingdom Ambassadors and Kingdom Soldiers they become.

To God's Business Servants, this is a simple and sound concept which must become a guiding, motivating factor in their decision making.

God's Business Servants must recognize that when they promote someone in business, that person comes into a higher level of fellowship with his or her superiors; and these superiors must be more mature spiritually about the things of the Kingdom of God. Because the more responsibility an employee begins to handle and share with his godly supervisors, the greater fellowship required, because the employee begins to adopt the supervisor's godly point of view. Therefore, the stewardship of God's entrusted gifts, properties, businesses, people, and ministries is an essential training procedure by God.

It is when the Believers' experience of acquiring more responsibility and managing it well occurs that God begins to speak to them on a more spiritually mature level. The more problems a Business Servant assigns to an employee that through the assignment he or she becomes mature to oversee in God's physical world over His creation, the more responsibility the employee will receive to handle God's more important spiritual assignments to promote His spiritual Kingdom.

Business Servants have the task and duty to mature their employees to the point of seeing God's things, activities, and people the way He sees them. This is being about God's business.

If a Business Servant wants to build a "relationship-based business," the Business Servant needs to stimulate each employee to take on more responsibility, which will lead to each employee having an increase in maturity in areas of dealing with people, skills for job performance, and strong character as Biblitarians. Increased spiritual maturity of employees will cause the Business Servant to prosper relationally, financially, and in building up each member of the family business.

VALUES THAT UNDERCUT PRIVATE PROPERTY
RIGHTS PRODUCE IMMATURITY AND DEBT

Since personal stewardship presupposes the personal management of property entrusted to your responsibility, values that undercut private property will produce immaturity and debt.

EXPLANATION: Since the management of private property, business, or ministry, or the stewardship thereof, presupposes that we must be accountable to somebody for the way we manage something that is genuinely for our own personal use, or people with whom we have covenant, any laws or values that take private property or business away from us or are going to tend to lead us into debt and immaturity. This would make us unrestrained. Proverbs 29:18 says, "Where there is no revelation, the people cast off restraint; but happy is the man who keeps the law." Private property management trains us to be lords of the Lord.

Why does short run thinking produce debt? Because wealth and prosperity are the result of wise stewardship of property and people with long run thinking, and indebtedness is the opposite of wealth and prosperity and is the unwise stewardship of property and people with short run thinking.

WHAT WEALTHY PEOPLE DO TO STAY WEALTHY: If all the wealth were taken away from the wealthy, they would have it back in 20 years, because the wealthy people have learned the skills of stewarding things over the long run. They have learned to invest only in wealth assets like real property, precious metals, and business, and have learned how to manage people with ongoing accountability, cash flow management, and cash flow security.

The reason is that money gravitates in the long run (not the short run, such as with illegal exploitative gain, drug runners, etc.) to move toward those who are good stewards of private property and people with mature responsibility. Planning for future expenditures, so they can be paid with savings instead of debt creates wealth in the long run.

The problem is that when the Socialist and Humanist Civil Government Politicians and Bureaucrats remove the stimulus of private property stewardship, business, and private responsibility of things personally owned in a culture, debt is produced because debt is the result of people who do not know how to steward things or motivate or manage people properly. Accountability requires training, and assigning small problems until they are well done before more complex problems are assigned. Complex things are built on small things well done.

Immaturity is the fruit produced of business employees who are not held accountable to bring increase to what they touch or with whom they come into contact.

Conversely, if Business Servants increase the value of the private property which is entrusted to them by good management, as Jesus has commanded us to do (parables of *talents* and *minas*), Business Servants are going to be maturing and prospering because God is going to give Business Servants more and more property, wealth, and responsibility over assets and people to train and manage. The reason is that God rewards the faithful, and following this principle of faithfulness; Business Servants should reward their employees as they develop managerial skills with people and the knowledge of God's principles of long run thinking and furthering God's Kingdom biblitarian principles of discipleship training of other employees unto servanthood. Jesus said in Matthew 23:11, "But he that is greatest among you shall be your servant."

It is no accident that the demonic principalities and powers which are operating in the U.S. have for the last one hundred years systematically worked into the economic fabric and the taxation policy fabric of this nation. There is a plan to devalue the concept of private property and business, so private property and privately-owned businesses will be removed as having value in the minds of people. The devil does not want mature or prosperous Christians, as God uses the stewardship over private property to mature His children. Early American history, regarding franchise (voting) rights, shows a recognition of the maturity as a citizen connected with private property stewardship and management.

In America, franchise rights were originally only extended to real property stewards. If you had a personal stake in the land, it was believed that what you vote for or against will affect you and your family personally. It is easy to vote for something when it will not cost you anything. The same is true in business. But if you have a vested interest in the company, you will be very careful how you vote in the Board Room. I am not advocating that you must own real property to qualify to vote in a political election. I am advocating those voters take the time to learn biblical principles of economics, business, and government and apply these principles when they go into the voting booth.

God requires that you be responsible before you exercise authority. The right to vote and the right to hold office were connected with stewardship of property in the early years of America. If legislators could be sued for malpractice for the bad economic laws they pass, we would start seeing legislators exercising much greater fiscal responsibility. The men who signed the Declaration of Independence put their entire estates subject to confiscation by the British government at that time.

THE ORIGINAL FRANCHISE RIGHTS LAW WAS
BUILT ON THE CONCEPT OF PROPRIETORSHIP

GREEKS: Greece was known as the "cradle of democracy." Yet, the development of democracy in the Greek City states was done by permitting only the male landowners to vote. This was considered very democratic and responsible.

IN THE U.S.: Our Republic today allows voters who do not have a proprietor stake in the execution of those choices to vote. This is one of the reasons why our Civil Government has made too many unwise economic decisions which have hurt our posterity. Our Politicians buy votes by extending entitlements to large groups of people from cradle to grave.

SOCIAL CLUBS: Why aren't the Kiwanis, Chamber of Commerce, Lions Club, and Christian Associations teaching these biblical truths? We need to have an economic revival to apply God's word, instead of the Humanist user friendly concepts of modern-day Christian thought. Many Christians congregate together with other business men and women of God, but they do not have a source to learn God's biblical principles. This becomes the blind leading the blind in business.

THE LESSON OF THE END RESULT OF SOCIALISM: The example of the end results of taking away private property from the families is seen with the countries which use to be behind the iron curtain where the Civil Government had virtually nationalized all industries and retail markets, save a few agri-markets and black markets. This Marxist, so-called "great Socialist experiment" left the people depressed, downcast, impoverished, and confused; and eventually they caused the fall of the Iron Curtain.

SOCIALISTIC OWNERSHIP OF REAL PROPERTY
AND BUSINESSES BRINGS BAD RESULTS IN FAMILIES

Socialist ownership of property and business promotes irresponsibility of people, income disassociated with work, disrespect for God's institutions, debilitating national debt for the country and individuals, unproductive actions of residents, and regulations against free enterprise in the economy, except for those with special interests who had given into Politicians' political campaign.

PRINCIPLE: That which is owned by everybody is owned by nobody.

EXAMPLE: Collectivized agriculture. Pilgrims landed at Plymouth Rock in 1620 and started with collectivized agriculture the first winter. They nearly starved the whole community and almost half died. The next year, people found some land and grew their own gardens on their own land, and the families had enough to give away and sell to others. Thus, in the first Thanksgiving celebration, the food provided was plentiful because the Pilgrims abandoned Socialism.

To a degree you can gauge freedom in a country by its food production. Every time the Socialist revolution comes to a country, the people lose their abilities in food production and famine occurs.

The continent of Africa was once a net exporter of food, but many people are starving today because of Socialism.

Ethiopia was once a net exporter of food, but the people are seeking food from other countries. Again, the Humanist philosophers sound reasonable, but promote a work free life.

SOCIALIST FREE HOUSING: Appropriation by Civil Government of land for socialized housing causes people to go without because there is no initiative, no individual effort, and no creativity which are all needed for human production of goods and services, for maturity, and for transfer of generational wealth.

Socialism or collective ownership destroys initiative, individual effort, creativity and diminution of goods and services; and therefore, collective "ownership" by the Civil Government hinders increase in gross national profit and wealth.

There is no biblical mandate or biblical authorization for Civil Government to own land or business. Taking land or nationalizing businesses through eminent domain by Civil Government is a restricted biblical mandate and privilege and should have limited use. Taxing land (property taxes), regulating strict zoning laws, and restricting occupancy permits lead to civil tyranny of all land use in the country, just as it did with Israel when they wanted a king (1 Samuel 8:14). The bigger the government, the more additional employees have to be employed by the federal, state, and local governments. When a society changes its Humanist and Socialist philosophies and exchanges them for biblical principles, then the government will decrease in size and cost.

The Supreme Court held in *Kelo v. City of New London*, Conn (2005) 545 U.S. 469 that a local government could use its eminent domain power under the 5th and 14th Amendments of the U.S. Constitution to transfer land from one private owner to another private owner to further economic development, not just because the community wanted a general public purpose such as building a library, school, or park, but to sell the property to a more substantial business who will be a higher real property tax payer. Small business stewards who have spent a lifetime building up a business to transfer the business to the next generation are now subject to forfeiture of the business without cause. This forfeiture of future generations' right to a family business attacks righteousness in the nation since a righteous man is biblically mandated to leave an inheritance to his children's children (Proverbs 13:22).

Why are there so many employee complaints in the utility companies and the U.S. Post Office? The reason is that these companies represent a limited monopoly, highly regulated by the government, where profit margins are restricted, and operations that tend toward making profit are discouraged. In other words, these businesses are not run by principles of free enterprise, but by false principles of Socialism and state-authorized monopolies.

TWELVE

HANDLING BEING RIPPED OFF IN BUSINESS AND SPIRITUAL PRINCIPLES OF WISDOM

DECEPTION IS STANDARD BUSINESS PRACTICE IN GODLESS BUSINESSES

Jeremiah 9:1-9 says, "'Oh that my head were waters, and my eyes a fountain of tears, that I might weep day and night for the slain of the daughter of my people! For they are all adulterers, an assembly of treacherous men. And like their bow they have bent their tongues for lies. They are not valiant for the truth on the earth. For they proceed from evil to evil, and they do not know Me,' says the Lord. 'Everyone take heed to his neighbor, and do not trust any brother; for every brother will utterly supplant, and every neighbor will walk with slanderers. Everyone will deceive his neighbor, and will not speak the truth; they have taught their tongue to speak lies; they weary themselves to commit iniquity. Your dwelling place is in the midst of deceit; through deceit they refuse to know Me,' says the Lord. Therefore thus says the Lord of hosts: 'Behold, I will refine them and try them, for how shall I deal with the daughter of My people? Their tongue is an arrow shot out; it speaks deceit; one speaks peaceably to his neighbor with his mouth, but in his heart he lies in wait. Shall I not punish them for these things?' says the Lord. 'Shall I not avenge Myself on such a nation as this?'"

The application of the above passage of Scripture to the business world is that God's word speaks specifically the way the world operates, i.e., by deception, deceit, and general lack of integrity. These evil practices in the world are methods of doing business which must be curtailed by the Christian businesses, families, and churches in order to receive God's blessings.

God's Business Servants must be valiant warriors for truth here on the earth.

God is beginning to do a new thing in the realm of business. God is beginning to anoint people who will walk in integrity and go forth and recapture the wealth of the wicked and bring it into the Kingdom of God.

God is specifically anointing and choosing Business Servants to walk in the purpose of taking the wealth of the wicked and bringing it into the Kingdom of God.

Yet, God's unlimited power in His anointing will not work the way the world operates a business.

It is no wonder that God's Business Servants are being ripped off by the world business owners and charlatans, for the world is full of deceit and wickedness. The world and Satan are laying traps and snares for the righteous to fall.

HOW MUST ONE ACT WHEN ONE IS RIPPED OFF?

As a Business Servant, how does the influence of your flesh cause your soul to react when you have just been ripped off?

A Business Servant's carnal soul often first wants to go and physically harm the person. However, Matthew 5:38-42 says, "You have heard that it was said, 'An eye for an eye and a tooth for a tooth.' But I tell you not to resist an evil person. But whoever slaps you on your right cheek, turn the other to him also. If anyone wants to sue you and take away your tunic, let him have your cloak also. And whoever compels you to go one mile, go with him two. Give to him who asks you, and from him who wants to borrow from you do not turn away."

After the Business Servant overcomes this urge, many immature Business Servants next want to go over and slap a lawsuit on the person. However, Matthew 5:38-42 says otherwise. Also, Proverbs 25:8-10 says, "Do not go hastily to court; for what will you do in the end, when your neighbor has put you to shame? Debate your case with your neighbor, and do not disclose the secret to another; lest he who hears it expose your shame, and your reputation be ruined."

Think how it looks to the Lord for two of God's Business Servants to have a lawsuit over a relationship that started out with a commitment to abide by covenant agreement. What a bad testimony to the Body of Christ. Both Believers should try mediation with a neutral person first before you file an action in court. Go the extra mile to seek settlement and reconciliation instead of seeking the ruling of a secular judge.

When God's Business Servants are ripped off and they have discerned it is of Satanic origin, they can get a "greater return" if they walk in faith and righteousness, trusting the Lord to protect business and household, and doing spiritual battle with the full armor of God, especially the Sword of the Spirit which is the word (*rhema*) of God (Ephesians 6:10-17).

A Business Servant can have the opportunity to walk in integrity and truth of God's word or walk in the sins of the deeds of the flesh in the soul or under the influence of a demonic spirit. If the Business Servant walks in the Holy Spirit when resolving disputes, then the Business Servant will not lose peace of mind or joy of heart. If the Business Servant walks in the carnality, or succumbs to the influence of a demonic spirit, the Business Servant will not walk in the love of God and forgiveness. Then, a Business Servant's "pipeline" to heaven may be temporarily cut off, as far as receiving God's blessings here on earth. The Business Servant will not lose eternal salvation, but the Business Servant may lose his sense of righteousness, peace, and joy in the Holy Spirit. The Business Servant must trust in the Lord's unlimited power, knowledge, and presence to take care of the problems and replace that which has been stolen. The Business Servant must trust in and act according to God's Word.

Romans 12:19 says, "Dearly beloved, avenge not yourselves, but rather give place unto wrath: for it is written, 'Vengeance is mine; I will repay,' saith the Lord."

Proverbs 12:7 says, "The wicked are overthrown and are no more, but the house of the righteous will stand." Proverbs 19:14 says, "Houses and riches are an inheritance from fathers, but a prudent wife is from the Lord." Proverbs 22:4 says, "By humility and the fear of the Lord are riches and honor and life." Proverbs 28:1 says, "The wicked flee when no one pursues, but the righteous are bold as a lion."

Isaiah 26:3 says, "You will keep him in perfect peace whose mind is stayed on You, because he trusts in You." Isaiah 35:4 says, "Say to those who are fearful hearted, be strong, do not fear! Behold, your God will come with vengeance, with the recompense of God; He will come and save you." Isaiah 49:25 says, "But thus says the Lord: Even the captives of the mighty shall be taken away, and the prey of the terrible be delivered; for I will contend with him who contends with you, and I will save your children."

Isaiah 54:17 says, "No weapon formed against you shall prosper, and every tongue which rises against you in judgment you shall condemn. This is the heritage of the servants of the Lord, and their righteousness is from Me, says the Lord." Isaiah 59:19 says, "So shall they fear the name of the Lord from the west and His glory from the rising of the sun; when the enemy comes in like a flood, the Spirit of the Lord will lift up a standard against him."

Proverbs 6:30-31 says, "People do not despise a thief if he steals to satisfy himself when he is starving. Yet when he is found, he must restore sevenfold; he may have to give up all the substance of his house." John 10:10 says, "The thief does not come except to steal, and to kill, and to destroy. I have come that they may have life, and that they may have it more abundantly."

YOU MUST FORGIVE OTHERS OF THE DEBTS THEY OWE YOU
IF THEY TRULY CANNOT AFFORD TO PAY YOU

This is where you have loaned money to a business partner or to a brother in the Lord and he did not repay you. If you take self-help revenge, you will lose your peace of mind, joy of heart, and righteous consciousness with the Lord, who has said, "Love your enemies."

Matthew 5:44 says, "But I say to you, love your enemies, bless those who curse you, do good to those who hate you, and pray for those who spitefully use you and persecute you."

Luke 6:27-31 says, "Which of you by worrying can add one cubit to his stature? So why do you worry about clothing? Consider the lilies of the field, how they grow: they neither toil nor spin; and yet I say to you that even Solomon in all his glory was not arrayed like one of these. Now if God so clothes the grass of the field, which today is, and tomorrow is thrown into the oven, will He not much more clothe you, O you of little faith? Therefore, do not worry, saying, 'What shall we eat?' or 'What shall we drink?' or 'What shall we wear?'"

Luke 6:35-36 says, "But love your enemies, do good, and lend, hoping for nothing in return; and your reward will be great, and you will be sons of the Most High. For He is kind to the unthankful and evil. Therefore, be merciful, just as your Father also is merciful."

Matthew 5:40-42 says, "If anyone wants to sue you and take away your tunic, let him have your cloak also. And whoever compels you to go one mile, go with him two."

Truth has long run rewards, but practicing truth sometimes hurts in the short run.

We have to walk in forgiveness because oftentimes we suffered loss because we were immature with bad stewardship and were not sharp as a serpent in our business or investment decisions.

Matthew 6:12-15 says, "And forgive us our debts, as we forgive our debtors. And do not lead us into temptation, but deliver us from the evil one. For Yours is the Kingdom and the power and the glory forever. Amen. For if you forgive men their trespasses, your heavenly Father will also forgive you. But if you do not forgive men their trespasses, neither will your Father forgive your trespasses."

Mark 11:25 says, "And whenever you stand praying, if you have anything against anyone, forgive him, that your Father in heaven may also forgive you your trespasses."

Luke 23:34 says, "Then Jesus said, 'Father, forgive them, for they do not know what they do.'" We are to have this mindset of Christ and be willing to forgive.

Matthew 10:16 says, "Behold, I send you out as sheep in the midst of wolves. Therefore be wise as serpents and harmless as doves."

You must especially forgive your brother or sister in the Lord who has trespassed against you. If you do not forgive them, you put yourself in bondage.

Matthew 18:21-22 says, "Then Peter came to Him and said, 'Lord, how often shall my brother sin against me, and I forgive him? Up to seven times?' Jesus said to him, 'I do not say to you, up to seven times, but up to seventy times seven.'" Forgiveness releases God's grace and special blessings back to you.

The parable of the servant's failure to forgive his fellow servant after he had been forgiven of a much larger debt by the master is a good teaching for a Business Servant to practice forgiveness, since the Lord has forgiven us of so much.

Matthew 18:32-35 says, "Then his master, after he had called him, said to him, 'You wicked servant! I forgave you all that debt because you begged me. Should you not also have had compassion on your fellow servant, just as I had pity on you?' And his master was angry, and delivered him to the torturers until he should pay all that was due to him. So my heavenly Father also will do to you if each of you, from his heart, does not forgive his brother his trespasses."

Luke 17:3-4 says, "Take heed to yourselves. If your brother sins against you, rebuke him; and if he repents, forgive him. And if he sins against you seven times in a day, and seven times in a day returns to you, saying, 'I repent,' you shall forgive him." Forgiving trespasses causes you to have Christ-like character. Live a life of forgiving others who trespass you and you will not be preoccupied with failure.

If we take on the yoke of the Lord and conduct business His way, business will become a restful place, even during times of persecutions. Matthew 11:28-30 says, "Come to Me, all you who labor and are heavy laden, and I will give you rest. Take My yoke upon you and learn from Me, for I am gentle and lowly in heart, and you will find rest for your souls."

If you seek the hundredfold blessing from God, you will be persecuted. Mark 10:29- 30 says, "So Jesus answered and said, 'Assuredly, I say to you, there is no one who has left house or brothers or sisters or father or mother or wife or children or lands, for My sake and the gospel's who shall not receive a hundred fold now in this time   houses and brothers and sisters and mothers and children and lands, with persecutions and in the age to come, eternal life.'"

Especially be careful not to touch God's prophets or God's anointed but allow God to deal with them.

1 Chronicles 16:22 says, "Do not touch My anointed ones, and do my prophets no harm."

God has a purpose He wants His anointed Business Servants to fulfill and will come to their aid until the purpose is completed. So be especially cautious doing business with these people.

God will deal harshly with prophets who prophesy out of their souls instead of their spirits under the direction of the Holy Spirit. These are soulish people. Ezekiel 13:1-3 says, "And the word of the Lord came to me, saying, 'son of man, prophesy against the prophets of Israel who prophesy, and say to those who prophesy out of their own heart, "Hear the word of the Lord!"' Thus says the Lord God: 'Woe to the foolish prophets, who follow their own spirit and have seen nothing!'" Soulish prophecies are not of the Lord.

David said no one was to touch Saul, God's anointed, as God would deal with Saul in God's own way and in God's own timing. 1 Samuel 26:9-10 says, "But David said to Abishai, 'Do not destroy him; for who can stretch out his hand against the Lord's anointed, and be guiltless?' David said furthermore, 'As the Lord lives, the Lord shall strike him, or his day shall come to die, or he shall go out to battle and perish.'"

God will personally deal with any person who offended you with His justice, love, and patience, desiring that the offender repents and restores to you what he ripped off. The story of Zacchaeus (Luke 19:1-10) is a good example.

Luke 17:1-2 says, "Then He said to the disciples, 'It is impossible that no offenses should come, but woe to him through whom they do come! It would be better for him if a millstone was hung around his neck, and he was thrown into the sea, than that he should offend one of these little ones.'"

1 Thessalonians 4:6 says, "That no one should take advantage of and defraud his brother in this matter, because the Lord is the avenger of all such, as we also forewarned you and testified." It is the Lord who will avenge against the brother in the Lord who defrauds another brother.

Proverbs 24:15-20 says, "Do not lie in wait, O wicked man, against the dwelling of the righteous; do not plunder his resting place; for a righteous man may fall seven times and rise again, but the wicked shall fall by calamity. Do not rejoice when your enemy falls, and do not let your heart be glad when he stumbles; lest the Lord see it, and it displease Him, and He turn away His wrath from him. Do not fret because of evildoers, nor be envious of the wicked; for there will be no prospect for the evil man; the lamp of the wicked will be put out."

BUSINESS SERVANTS MUST BE TRUSTWORTHY, BUT BE SHREWD IN BUSINESS

Business Servants must learn how to apply all of God's economic principles and how to counter those principles in the fallen world used by the competition.

Proverbs 28:20(a) and 28:25(b) says, "A faithful man will abound with blessings..." "He who trusts in the Lord will be prospered."

Zephaniah 3:7 says, "I said, 'surely you will fear Me, you will receive instruction so that her dwelling would not be cut off, despite everything for which I punished her, but they rose early and corrupted all their deeds.'"

Read this strange account of Jesus telling the parable of the unjust servant who was rewarded by his master. Luke 16:1-8 says, "He also said to His disciples: 'There was a certain rich man who had a steward, and an accusation was brought to him that this man was wasting his goods. So he called him and said to him, "What is this I hear about you? Give an account of your stewardship, for you can no longer be steward." Then the steward said within himself, "What shall I do? For my master is taking the stewardship away from me, I cannot dig; I am ashamed to beg. I have resolved what to do, that when I am put out of the stewardship, they may receive me into their houses." So he called every one of his master's debtors to him, and said to the first, "How much do you owe my master?" And he said, "A hundred measures of oil." So he said to him, "Take your bill, and sit down quickly and write fifty." Then he said to another, "And how much do you owe?" So he said, "A hundred measures of wheat." And he said to him, "Take your bill, and write eighty." So the master commended the unjust steward because he had dealt shrewdly. For the sons of this world are more shrewd in their generation than the sons of light.'"

The lesson was that you must learn one hundred percent of the rules and apply the principles of the Kingdom you are operating in. The worldly man used worldly principles and his employer benefited from his servant's actions. Luke 16:9-13 says, "And I say to you, make friends for yourselves by unrighteous mammon, that when you fail, they may receive you into an everlasting home. He who is faithful in what is least is faithful also in much; and he who is unjust in what is least is unjust also in much. Therefore if you have not been faithful in the unrighteous mammon, who will commit to your trust the true riches? And if you have not been faithful in what is another man's, who will give you what is your own? No servant can serve two masters; for either he will hate the one and love the other, or else he will be loyal to the one and despise the other. You cannot serve God and mammon."

God's Business Servant cannot apply the rules in two different Kingdoms and expect to be profitable. You cannot serve God and mammon (Luke 16:13).

Making "friends" with unrighteous mammon in Luke 16:9 means to get your heathen business friends saved so when you die you have laid up treasures in the "everlasting habitations" because you cannot take the unrighteous mammon with you. This is the call and duty of the Christian Business Servants in ministry.

He who is faithful in least is also faithful in much. God is not only interested in your faithfulness in tithing ten percent of your income. As a Believer, all your income belongs to the Lord. When the Holy Spirit says to the Business Servant to give a certain amount, then obey Him as it usually is a test of whether you can handle a larger income. Luke 6:38 says, "Give, and it will be given to you; good measure, pressed down, shaken together, and running over will be put into your bosom. For with the same measure that you use, it will be measured back to you."

The next principle taught by Jesus was that you first must be faithful with the unrighteous mammon (stewardship over that which makes the natural world operate) before God will trust you with and allow you to have stewardship over His true riches (God's spiritual gifts, shepherding over His flock, and His anointing- Luke 16:11).

The next point made by Jesus was that you first must prove you are faithful toward another person's business before you are trusted and given stewardship over your own business (Luke 16:12).

You must know the ways of the world to avoid being trapped, but do not practice the sinful ways of the businesspeople in the world. Matthew 10:16 says, "Behold, I send you out as sheep in the midst of wolves. Therefore, be wise as serpents and harmless as doves."

You must have and apply wisdom from above in business to overcome and defeat the wisdom of this world. Proverbs 23:4-5 says, "Do not overwork to be rich; because of your own understanding, cease! Will you set your eyes on that which is not? For riches certainly make themselves wings; they fly away like an eagle toward heaven." Riches are those profits from the investment of money into such things as stocks, mutual funds, treasury notes, annuities, and other equity or debt instruments. Riches of this world are deceitful (Mark 4:19). Riches are here today and gone tomorrow.

THE KNOWLEDGE, WISDOM, AND WAYS OF GOD, IF
APPLIED BY BUSINESS SERVANTS, WILL BRING
PROSPERITY AND STOP THEM FROM BEING RIPPED OFF

For Business Servants, acquiring wisdom and knowledge of God's ways is more precious than money or success in the natural. Proverbs 24:3-4 says, "Through wisdom a house is built, and by understanding it is established; by knowledge the rooms are filled with all precious and pleasant riches."

If a Business Servant catches an employee stealing, then you have to decide to dismiss the employee, and do not do any further business with that employee. Since the employee stole, the employee is a thief, and as a Business Servant, you may decide not do business with a thief. You can forgive the employee, but you owe a duty as the Shepherd of the business to protect investors, customers, and other employees from thieves. Thus, the thief has to be under strict oversight and he or she must confess his or her sins and be given scriptures to memorize. He or she cannot handle any money or checks.

Learn the ways of the Lord, as they will lead you to prosperity. Psalm 25:4-5 says, "Show me Your ways, O Lord; teach me Your paths. Lead me in Your truth and teach me, for You are the God of my salvation; on You I wait all the day."

God is all powerful. Fearfully respect Him and give Him honor in all that you do. Psalm 25:12-15 says, "Who is the man that fears the Lord? Him shall He teach in the way He chooses. He himself shall dwell in prosperity, and his descendants shall inherit the earth. The secret of the Lord is with those who fear Him, and He will show them His covenant. My eyes are ever toward the Lord, for He shall pluck my feet out of the net."

Business Servant, you have the duty to daily pray for God's protection and deliverance when you encounter being ripped off in business. Be upright in all things and continue dealing with integrity, even though you are in dire need and attacked financially. Do not allow your need to dictate your actions but be guided by the Scriptures as illuminated by the Holy Spirit in all things. Psalm 25:19-22 says, "Consider my enemies, for they are many; and they hate me with cruel hatred. Keep my soul, and deliver me; let me not be ashamed, for I put my trust in You. Let integrity and uprightness preserve me, for I wait for You. Redeem Israel, O God, out of all their troubles."

Wisdom is how to apply knowledge to live a healthy and prosperous life in all areas of the Business Servant's life. James 3:13-18 says, "Who is wise and understanding among you? Let him show by good conduct that his works are done in the meekness of wisdom. But if you have bitter envy and self-seeking in your hearts, do not boast and lie against the truth. This wisdom does not descend from above, but is earthly, sensual, demonic. For where envy and self-seeking exist, confusion and every evil thing are there. But the wisdom that is from above is first pure, then peaceable, gentle, willing to yield, full of mercy and good fruits, without partiality and without hypocrisy. Now the fruit of righteousness is sown in peace by those who make peace."

Wisdom and understanding of how God wants His Business Servant to conduct the business will have as rewards prosperity and will protect the Business Servant from being ripped off. Proverbs 4:7-9, 11, 12, 18, 20 says, "Wisdom is the principal thing; therefore get wisdom. And in all your getting, get understanding. Exalt her, and she will promote you; she will bring you honor, when you embrace her. She will place on your head an ornament of grace; a crown of glory she will deliver to you....I have taught you in the way of wisdom; I have led you in right paths. When you walk, your steps will not be hindered, and when you run, you will not stumble....But the path of the just is like a shining sun, that gives ever brighter under the perfect day....My son, give attention to my words; incline your ear to my sayings."

The Business Servant must be rid of all anger, all uncleanness, and all wickedness out of his or her soul. Then the soul transformation of the Business Servant will bring prosperity and health (3 John 2) in his or her life and business.

The Business Servant must live a genteel life, which means being a Biblitarian. Allow the fruits of the Spirit to grow in your soul, so that character in your personality matures as you are transformed into the likeness of Christ with His character, who also was in the natural a businessman when He walked here on earth. James 1:19-21 says, "So then, my beloved brethren, let every man be swift to hear, slow to speak, slow to wrath; for the wrath of man does not produce the righteousness of God. Therefore lay aside all filthiness and overflow of wickedness, and receive with meekness the implanted word, which is able to save your soul."

If you are around angry people while doing business, understand that they can cause an interruption in your quest to live a prosperous life in God's Kingdom. Angry people, with unrestrained emotions, can rub off on you, and you will find yourself acting as they do. Anger turns people away, as this is the way of the predators. Proverbs 22:24-25 says, "Make no friendship with an angry man, and with a furious man do not go, lest you learn his ways and set a snare for your soul."

Proverbs 19:19 says, "A man of great wrath will suffer punishment; for if you rescue him, you will have to do it again."

A BUSINESS SERVANT MUST BE A DOER OF GOD'S WORD IN BUSINESS TO RECEIVE PROSPERITY

The biblical work ethic is to be a doer of God's word. The blessings of God come through your faithful performance of His word. God will give you a harvest of what you sow as a Business Servant (Galatians 6:6-8). James 1:22-25 says, "But be doers of the word, and not hearers only, deceiving yourselves. For if anyone is a hearer of the word and not a doer, he is like a man observing his natural face in a mirror; for he observes himself, goes away, and immediately forgets what kind of man he was. But he who looks into the perfect law of liberty and continues in it, and is not a forgetful hearer but a doer of the word, this one will be blessed in what he does."

God is not a man that He should lie (Numbers 23:9). If He promises you something, He is ready to perform it and fulfill His promise when you meet His conditions. Isaiah 55:11 says, "So shall My word be that goes forth from My mouth; it shall not return to Me void, but it shall accomplish what I please, and it shall prosper in the thing for which I sent it."

As God's Business Servant, live a life of faith that your covenant making and covenant keeping God will cause all things to work together for your good because you love God and are called unto His purpose (Romans 8:28). God wants to prosper you in business. He wants you to have a testimony of His goodness to those that diligently seek Him. Jeremiah 1:12 says, "Then the Lord said to me, 'You have seen well, for I am ready to perform My word.'"

The only things that will last beyond the grave is the work, character traits, and talents you acquire by doing the Lord's will as a Business Servant. Let the business be an outreach center, a healing center, a hospitality center, and a training center on the practical application of biblical principles and God's grace and love. Be a principled person. Proverbs 16:3 says, "Commit your works to the Lord, and your thoughts will be established."

The biblical lifestyle as a Business Servant will bring you contentment and purpose. It will bring you joy and prosperity. It will promote and mature others in the business. 1 Thessalonians 4:1,9-12 says, "Finally then, brethren, we urge and exhort in the Lord Jesus that you should abound more and more, just as you received from us how you ought to walk and to please God. But concerning brotherly love you have no need that I should write to you, for you yourselves are taught by God to love one another; and indeed you do so toward all the brethren who are in all Macedonia. But we urge you, brethren, that you increase more and more; that you also aspire to lead a quiet life, to mind your own business, and to work with your own hands, as we commanded you, that you may walk properly toward those who are outside, and that you may lack nothing."

GOD'S BUSINESS SERVANT MUST SPEAK FORTH AND APPLY GOD'S BIBLICAL PRINCIPLES IN EVERY BUSINESS DECISION

God has a pattern for business, and God has a word for all situations that you may encounter as a Business Servant. Your tongue has to be trained to speak God's scriptural truths. Your tongue can encourage, build up, edify, and construct, or it can discourage, tear down, and destroy. James 3:6 and 3:8-11 says, "And the tongue is a fire, a world of iniquity. The tongue is so set among our members that it defies the whole body, and sets on fire the course of nature; and it is set on fire by hell....But no man can tame the tongue. It is an unruly evil, full of deadly poison. With it we bless our God and Father, and with it we curse men, who have been made in the similitude of God. Out of the same mouth proceed blessing and cursing, My brethren, these things ought not to be so. Does a spring send forth fresh water and bitter from the same opening?"

As a Business Servant, if you practice always walking in the spirit, promoting service, love, grace, and truth, God will make you prosperous without adding sorrow to it (Proverbs 10:22). Truth and prosperity begin by you speaking and applying biblical principles from God's word. Proverbs 8:6-8 says, "Listen, for I will speak of excellent things, and from the opening of my lips will come right things; for my mouth will speak truth; wickedness is an abomination to my lips. All the words of my mouth are with righteousness; nothing crooked or perverse in them."

Proverbs 18:21 says, "Death and life are in the power of the tongue, and those who love it will eat its fruit." Having a positive attitude is important. However, being positive cannot replace truth. Wisdom is better than a cheerful outlook. Sometimes, truth is negative, not positive. Yet, those who come to God must worship Him in spirit and truth (John 4:24).

To obtain God's wisdom regarding business principles, Business Servants need to be supervising their own business, and then share this godly wisdom with others who inquire of your advice. Do not be afraid to correct someone who is doing something wrong. Yet, be loving, graceful, and gentle in your communication, as the person may be doing things out of ignorance. Proverbs 25:11-13 says, "A word fitly spoken is like apples of gold in settings of silver. Like an earring of gold and an ornament of fine gold is a wise rebuker to an obedient ear. Like the cold of snow in time of harvest is a faithful messenger to those who send him, for he refreshes the soul of his masters."

Proverbs 29:20 says, "Do you see a man hasty in his words? There is more hope for a fool than for him." There are a lot of fast talkers out there in the business world who spend a lot of time coming up with methods to close a transaction to get you to buy into their business or idea.

A Business Servant must not become a predator in business. Maintain and follow biblical principles of morality and good stewardship. Be honest in the business dealings. Keep your mind on the eternal instead of the temporary things of this world. Do not adopt the mores or actions of the world. Colossians 3:2, 8-10 says, "Set your mind on things above, not on things on the earth.... But now you yourselves are to put off all these: anger, wrath, malice, blasphemy, filthy language out of your mouth. Do not lie to another, since you have put off the old man with his deeds, and have put on the new man who is renewed in knowledge according to the image of Him who created him."

Business Servant, every day pray that you, your business, and your employees will prosper and be protected by the Holy Spirit and that all be about the Father's business. Stand strong against the enemy of your soul. The abundance of spoils is taken by the Business Servants from defeating the enemy in spiritual warfare.

When doing warfare, the Business Servant must put on daily the full armor of God, and the Business Servant must stay faithful, even though the Business Servant becomes tired of the spiritual battles and the continuous resistance against the business and him personally.

Ephesians 6:10-17 says, "Finally, my brethren, be strong in the Lord and in the power of His might. Put on the whole armor of God, that you may be able to stand against the wiles of the devil. For we do not wrestle against flesh and blood, but against principalities, against powers, against the rulers of the darkness of this age, against the spiritual hosts of wickedness in the heavenly places. Therefore take up the whole armor of God, that you may be able to withstand in the evil day, having done all, to stand. Stand therefore, having girded your waist with truth, having put on the breastplate of righteousness, and having shod your feet with the preparation of the gospel of peace; above all, taking the shield of faith with which you will be able to quench all the fiery darts of the wicked one. And take the helmet of salvation, and the sword of the Spirit, which is the word of God."

THIRTEEN

CONCLUSION

In writing this book, I have spent much effort teaching you to think as a Biblitarian Business Servant, instead of a worldly business man or woman who is only after profit from the business. God has called you into ministry, but the venue of that ministry is in your business or profession that He led you to operate or practice. God will mature you in handling money, assets, employees, and finances. He will prosper you as you become spiritually transformed, matured, and sanctified in your soul [mind, emotions, and heart (where your beliefs are and where your will operates)]. As God's chosen Business Servant, allow each day to be a new opportunity to serve the Lord in your business. Seek first God's Kingdom and His righteousness in your business, and He will provide for your every need. Come to the resolve that your business is God's chosen venue for ongoing soul transformation, maturation, and sanctification of you and your employees as to their God ordained potential in Christ Jesus. Encourage your employees to share their faith, not in a forceful, religious, or self-righteous way, but in a gentle, loving way. Teach your employees God's biblical principles of economics and servanthood. As a Business Servant of God, be loving, tolerant, and forgiving, but do not allow blatant sin to come into the business. Be a Pastor of the employees in your business, and see yourself as a biblitarian apostle, prophet, evangelist, pastor and teacher, equipping your employees by your example of applying God's biblical principles of sound business, with long run thinking, capturing a market share, setting aside money for research and development, establishing a savings account for future needed expenditures, avoiding debt, and contributing back to your community what God has given to you. Be about God the Father's business with love, humility, and faith; and God will exalt you in due season as He rewards those that diligently seek Him.

As a fellow Business Servant of God, I pray that God blesses you with wisdom, knowledge, and understanding as His Business Servant. I pray that He blesses your family and blesses you in your future business plans that the Holy Spirit leads you in. Be led by the Holy Spirit in all that you do. I pray that He blesses you with health, prosperity, and long life even as your soul prospers. I pray that you discover the fullness of the truths written in this book and enjoy biblical freedom, the liberty to take dominion in the sphere of influence that the Holy Spirit grants you.

Finally, go apply in your business the biblical principles you have learned from this book and enter the righteousness, peace, and joy of the Holy Spirit, which is the Kingdom of God. Bring the business into God's Kingdom and be about the Father's
business.

Amen

BIO

Dr. Nova Dean Pack

Dr. Nova Dean Pack's father left the family when he was 3 years old, and at age 10 his mother died at age 32, leaving six children behind. Dr. Pack and his brothers and sisters were raised on his grandparents' farm where there was continuous hard work as chores - taking care of 120 acres, along with feeding many cows, pigs, chickens, duck, geese, and other animals and milking two to three cows morning and night, along with yearly soil preparation, seed planting, cultivating, the harvesting of hay and crops. For solace, on the farm, was a beautiful wooded area where Dr. Pack spent many hours alone praying and seeking God. The farm life was very tough, but the work ethic was engrained in Dr. Pack's foundation of beliefs. Southern Illinois was part of the Bible Belt; so, most everyone went to Church as a lifestyle, although it was mostly a religious experience.

After his mother died, Dr. Pack, at age 11 was born again and had a very intimate relationship with Jesus and the Holy Spirit. He taught Sunday School from the Bible to other students near his age and baptized several people his age and younger in the creeks of Illinois at age 13 and onward.

Dr. Pack moved to California at age 15. He worked his way through college and graduated from Cal State University Long Beach in 1971. He graduated from Pepperdine University School of Law, a fundamental Christian based top rated law school, in 1974. He passed the State Bar exam on the first sitting also in 1974. He immediately started practicing law with other partners, but he left the partnership and started his sole practice of law in 1981.

Dr. Pack personally was ordained by two known prophets in California in 1992; namely Dr. Chuck Flynn and Dr. Richard Maiden. Dr. Pack received ordination papers with the Independent Assemblies of God International (IAOGI), Santa Ana, CA in 1993 and has been the corporate attorney for IAOGI since that year. Dr. Pack was the Senior Pastor of a Church fellowship from 1994 through 1999 in Redlands, CA. Dr. Pack was overseer of two ministries from 1993 through 2020 and ministered monthly at those ministries, along with other churches. In 2004, the Holy Spirit inspired Dr. Pack to use the name "Biblitarian," so Dr. Pack formed the ministry called "Biblitarian Ministries." Dr. Pack broadcasted a radio talk show entitled "Business in Ministry" in San Bernardino, CA., for two years from 1992 through 1994 where he taught business men and women how to make their businesses a place of ministry. In 1994 through 1996, Dr. Pack taught a daily radio teaching that aired in Riverside and San Bernardino Counties, California, where his ongoing sermons in Church became the subjects of radio broadcasts.

During this period, Dr. Pack conducted monthly teachings for 50 straight weeks at several churches, teaching men and women that their businesses were their venue of ministry. Dr. Pack sees his law practice as a place and opportunity for ministry to those in need, where he witnesses to the unsaved, prays for the sick, takes care of those in need, and educates his clients and employees on the Biblical principles of business and economics. Dr. Pack is one of the very few attorneys at law that actually brings the wisdom and principles in the Bible into his law practice for the benefit of his Christian clients and all those seeking his advice.

Dr. Pack is a prolific writer, having written over 30 Christian books on various spiritual topics, some directly for the believer in business. Also, he is an accomplished public minister who teaches under a strong anointing. Dr. Pack has learned how to bring the dynamic of intellectual endeavor under the authority and anointing of the Holy Spirit. He has preached and taught more than a thousand messages over the years.

Dr. Pack's ministry focus is preaching the gospel of the Kingdom (Matthew 24:14) and the message of repentance and remission of sins (Luke 24:27), which Jesus commanded to be the dual priority of preaching and teaching.

Dr. Pack sends his regular teachings to Believers in over 65 different countries. Dr. Pack currently broadcasts his podcasts under the name "Biblitarian Ministries" on the priority of seeking first the Kingdom of God and His righteousness, God's grace extended for repentance and remission of sins, and the receiving of benefits of living in the Kingdom of God. Biblitarian Ministries can be viewed on The Marketplace Network, a Christian media network broadcasting on Amazon Fire TV, Facebook, YouTube and Twitter platforms. Dr. Pack may be contacted at ***packnovapack@aol.com.***